W9-BIT-187

The New Local Government Series
No 12

DEMOCRATIC THEORY AND
LOCAL GOVERNMENT

The New Local Government Series

GENERAL EDITOR

PROFESSOR PETER G. RICHARDS

DEMOCRATIC THEORY
AND
LOCAL GOVERNMENT

BY

DILYS M. HILL
B.A., Ph.D.

Senior Lecturer in Politics
University of Southampton

London
GEORGE ALLEN & UNWIN LTD
RUSKIN HOUSE   MUSEUM STREET

First published in 1974

© George Allen & Unwin Ltd. 1974

ISBN 0 04 352052 9 hardback
ISBN 0 04 352053 7 paperback

Printed in Great Britain
in 10 point Times New Roman type
by T. & A. Constable Ltd., Edinburgh

In memory of my parents

ACKNOWLEDGEMENTS

I would like to thank Professor P. G. Richards for his helpful encouragement and invaluable advice. I would also like to thank Maurice Hookham, from whose advice and help much of my interest in these ideas originate. I am also grateful to Mrs P. Dunn and Mrs P. Powell for typing the manuscript.

CONTENTS

Chapter I

INTRODUCTION

In this country the debate on local government is conducted mainly in pragmatic, not philosophical, terms: what are the technical problems of providing a particular service; what size of population can be catered for by given numbers of staff and resources; what new demands and developments are neglected and how can this be remedied? The need for local government is not a theoretical one but is the need for an effective means of carrying out important public services which central government could not hope to provide itself.

These arguments are also allied to a defence of 'local democracy' conceived as local self-government within existing traditional boundaries. Local authorities provide the essential ingredients of democratic society: elected representatives who are close to those they serve, and who form an easy channel of communication between public opinion and the council. No other body does this. Parliament and government are remote from everyday life and in many spheres the citizen is governed by impersonal *ad hoc* bodies whose lay members (if any) are nominated, not elected.

In England, as in other countries, powers are divided between different areas and agencies of government according to what Arthur Maass calls the basic values of modern democratic society: liberty, equality and welfare.[1] The values of liberty are promoted by the different tiers of government which protect the citizen from arbitrary rule and over-concentration of power. Equality is aided by giving people the opportunity to vote, and to take part, in as many public bodies as possible. Welfare goals are promoted by allocating power so that government services effectively meet the social and economic needs of society. This has implications for the organisation of government both at the centre and in the localities, since services need to be brought to the individual in his home community.

But this does not mean that we can assume there are 'natural' communities which are always appropriate areas of administration.

The individual's allegiance to his community may, in any event, have little to do with his views of politics and government. It could well be, as Paul Ylvisaker says, that loyalty is created by setting boundaries, not the other way around.[2] In the final analysis, however, the citizen is the judge of the effectiveness of the system. As James W. Felser points out, sound statecraft is that which converges at the point of the individual citizen.[3] The citizen judges this effectiveness in terms of efficiency (the cost and quality of services) and convenience (services should be close and comprehensible). He is also concerned with democratic control, which means that his representatives must be accessible, responsive – and removable.

In this country there is little in the way of *a priori* theory about the principles of local government. There are certain traditions and values – of locality, of liberty, of the right of ratepayers and taxpayers to take part, of local services but national standards, of 'inspectability' – which have grown up over the last 150 years. Today there is a renewed interest in these questions. There is a concern about participation, both of elected representatives and of ordinary people. In the late 1960s, when reform of local government seemed imminent, there was also a revived interest in the difficult questions of local autonomy, local finance and central control.

Other commentators have examined the principles and values of local government against the actual working of local authorities. There are two kinds of concern here. One is the way individuals are treated: equal consideration, justice and fairness are examined in the light of everyday services and the experience and expectations of ordinary people. The other concern is with variations between local authorities as seen against the clashing values of territorial justice and territorial democracy. That is, citizens expect similar services wherever they may live but, at the same time, expect local initiative, flexibility and local control over decisions. Bleddyn Davies asserts, after examining local services in detail, that territorial justice and 'healthy local government' are opposing claims.[4]

These current concerns show the way in which the problems of local government and democracy are intimately related. Since the time of John Stuart Mill local government has been justified as an integral part of democracy. The ordinary person learnt democratic citizenship in his own community and shared in power and influence. The democratic values of liberty, equality and fraternity were made real in the self-governing community.

Democratic theory and local government were related but, in the twentieth century, there were doubts about the ways in which local autonomy and self-government could be reconciled with mass society and the modern welfare state. Local authorities were criticised as inadequate, both as providers of services and as the nursery of democracy. The ordinary man was a citizen of democratic society and national political parties, pressure groups and the mass media expressed his needs and views far better than an outdated local government could do.

These views have been modified in the last decade under the pressure of events. Ordinary people have demanded more say in local issues. They have joined together to protest, to demand change, and to provide new ideas and services. Planning, housing, education, and services for the poor, the elderly, the handicapped are all vigorously debated. Local government is again seen as an essential part of democratic society. This is not because the individual will learn to be a democratic citizen by taking part in community life but because he has a right to expect effective services and to be justly treated.

The need for healthy grass roots is continually emphasised. This does not mean that it is possible to speak of the democratic theory *of* local government. Local and national democracy are one system. There is no such thing as 'local democracy', separate and autonomous, and justified solely in terms of the self-governing community. There is a democratic theory of government and society, in which there are different public and private bodies and a fabric of attitudes, behaviour and expectations. Local government is part of this society.

For these reasons this book is concerned with democratic theory *and* local government. It reflects the current interest in the broader questions of the quality of life in Western societies, of environment and planning, of mobility and leisure, and of the response of governments to the wishes of their citizens. Democratic theory is not just concerned with the citizens' rights and expectations and the seeming defects of modern society to respond quickly, effectively and fairly to rising demands. It is also concerned with the values and behaviour of governors. This book will try to show that the definition of 'democratic local government' is the councillors' and officers' definition. What they do, for all practical purposes, *is* democracy. The internal working of local authorities, the way that councils treat their citizens, and the work of councillors and officers, is thus central.

Democratic theory also gives a central place to communication and one test of the health of democratic society is to examine the openness of government and the amount of information available. Democracy has always been criticised for its defects in these respects.

Governments are too secretive. The mass media provide wide-ranging information but are accused of trivialisation and sensationalism. At local level these criticisms are strengthened by the attitudes of local authorities and the monopoly position of the local press. But information also depends on people's willingness to listen to it and use it. Information is only worthwhile if it can be used. If many people feel that they have no real opportunity to alter what is done then there is little point in listening to what governors have to say.

Participation and communication are thus twin aspects of democratic life; but so too are information and accountability. To hold elected representatives to account means hearing their future plans and past performance. It also means the opportunity to vote them out of office and to do this on informed grounds. Here too, democracy is imperfect. At local level, it is argued, it is particularly imperfect. Low polls, uncontested seats, a paucity of lively electoral information and confrontation, and an unhealthy dominance of national party fortunes all reduce democratic debate. Reform of the local government system is as necessary to cure these defects as much as to alter boundaries and functions.

Throughout the debate, however, the main theme remains. Local government is about the provision of services to local people, in the locality, through an elected council served by a staff of professional officers. The stability of this concern reflects the British tradition of adaptation of existing institutions to fulfil both old and new tasks rather than a complete recasting of the system.

The roots of the British tradition are representative democracy and citizen involvement but there is no modern philosophy to match the tradition. *The Times'* comment on the occasion of the Report Stage of the Local Government Bill in July 1972 is revealing. Though MPS would fight bitterly over particular details as these affected their home areas, it said, it was no use expecting them to debate the broad theme and philosophy of local government, since no such philosophy had been forthcoming.[5] We should not believe, however, that no philosophy exists. It is there, but it is rarely necessary to spell it out. We take the underlying values of the local government system for granted. This is not just British pragmatism and dislike of theorising. It is also a measure of confidence in the worth of the system, in spite of its defects and the calls for reform. It is a true reflection of this approach that traditions and values are only examined, if at all, when reform threatens to upset existing procedures and existing boundaries.

This book looks further than these matters. It examines the roots of the philosophy of local government, the making of these principles in practice, and the future pressures of regionalism and community. We begin by looking at the traditions of democratic theory and local government and how these are related to each other.

NOTES

1. Arthur Maass, 'Division of Powers: an areal analysis' *in* Arthur Maass (ed.), *Area and Power: a theory of local government* (Free Press, 1959), pp. 9-10.
2. Paul Ylvisaker, 'Some Criteria for a "Proper" Areal Division of Powers' *in* Arthur Maass, *ibid.*, p. 37.
3. James W. Felser, *Area and Administration* (University of Alabama Press, 1949), p. 10.
4. Bleddyn Davies, *Social Needs and Resources in Local Services* (Michael Joseph, 1968), pp. 23-5.
5. *The Times* (8 July 1972).

Chapter II

DEMOCRATIC THEORY AND LOCAL SELF-GOVERNMENT

In England local government has long been defended as a vital and integral part of democracy. Local self-government is valued because it is just; it safeguards and enhances the citizen's rights, and it is an important setting for political education. Local representative institutions enable a larger number of people to take an active part in democracy. Local self-government is also a part of the state through which services are brought to people in their home communities, subject to local public opinion and with the benefit of local knowledge.

Democratic theory has, however, a wider concern than that of local self-government. Its true nature has been disputed for centuries and, some would argue, there is no agreed theory of democracy and no precise definition of the word itself. Others claim that complex twentieth-century society differs so radically from previous times that the theory is outdated and must be rewritten to take account of how individuals actually behave (since citizens are far more 'apathetic' than the theory said they should be) and to reflect economic and technological developments. Yet a third line of argument has been that democratic theory does not entail local government and that, furthermore, local government and democracy are opposing forces.

It is currently asserted that if democratic theory is to remain relevant to today's needs then it should be reformulated to prescribe means by which individuals could take a greater part in exercising power at work and in their home communities. This participatory democracy movement of the 1960s, while not rejecting elected local authorities out of hand, calls into question the ability of existing bodies to reflect and represent the whole range of modern interests and values.

DEMOCRATIC THEORY AND VALUES

Democratic theory, as it has evolved from classical liberalism in Victorian times, centres on representative government to fulfil its aims of liberty, equality and fraternity. The basic tenets of representative institutions are: free elections; majority rule; protection of minorities, subject to the majority's final say; and the assumption that government operates on a basis of widespread discussion and a responsiveness to an informed public opinion. Representative institutions are said to be truly democratic when all kinds of people can take part. This means more than having a legal right to be elected since it depends on social and political factors as well – such as time, the relevant skills and knowledge, and so on. Though only a relatively small number of people actually stand for election, or exercise their right to vote, the system and the theory are justified because everyone *can* share in government.

Participation in democratic government is also dependent on understanding the issues involved. Information is essential. Democratic theory places great emphasis on the need for channels of communication and, in practice, politicians and their constituents meet through a diversity of means. Public opinion is created by word of mouth and the influence of personal contacts, particularly among the influential community leaders and their circle. For the majority of people, the highly organised mass media increasingly provide the sole source of informed comment on current events. The danger is, in modern times, that we may become spectators, not getting information in order to take action but merely watching the spectacle of politics.

People's attitudes to each other, and to government and its representatives, are also important. Democratic theory holds that men must treat each other with equal consideration and offer each other equal opportunities in life, to make democracy a reality. Fraternity is as essential as liberty and equality. Majority rule and representative government are central because democratic theory insists that power is legitimate power – those who hold power are elected by, and responsible to, the whole body of their constituents. Local government has a place in the theory because this is a proper arena in which legitimate power can be exercised and held accountable.

The view that local government has such a place is part of the British tradition but it is not an inevitable part of democratic theory. The demands for majority rule, representative institutions, consultation and participation can all be met by a national system of government, while at local level a decentralised bureaucracy administers national services. Democratic government does not necessarily entail locally elected councils. In English thought, however, this logic has been overridden by another established value: the need to encourage people to realise their full potentialities. The dictionary definition of democracy is the rule of the people. In practice, however, representative institutions give power to the politically active: power is theoretically open to all but people must actively avail themselves of it. This, it is said, is more easily and widely achieved at the local level.

Democratic theory is also rooted in the nature of man and his life in society. It is an egalitarian theory; emphasising that although men are never absolutely equal they must be given both equality of opportunity and equality of consideration. But the egalitarianism that comes from man's nature and needs calls for mutual tolerance. Local government provides a unique and vital setting for this necessary political education in all its aspects.

Men learn, by their direct involvement in local affairs, what is possible, practical and expedient. Experience teaches them the use of power and authority and, at the same time, shows them that this calls for consultation and negotiation. They see the claims of other people and groups and the need to justify their own actions. They also learn to curb their extravagant schemes. Common concern, common responsibility, fraternity and tolerance are the marks of democracy.

The justification of local government as political education has had a central place in democratic reasoning from J. S. Mill until recently.[1] A word of caution is necessary. Local government may indeed educate individuals into an appreciation of political life and of the wider democratic society. But so too do other activities, in a wide variety of groups and associations. Some current observers believe that democracy can be better learnt in the factory than in the community.

Political education and discussion are not now the main justifications of local government's place in democratic society. Participation is seen as fundamental. This is not a new concern since Victorian reformers also claimed that every citizen had the right and the duty to share in all levels of government. The modern interest is somewhat different. The existing forms of local government do not, it is argued, encourage the level of participation on which they were founded—polls are low and many seats in local elections (particularly in country areas) are uncontested. The functions and powers of local authorities, and their financial autonomy, need, therefore, to be increased to invigorate public interest. In addition, new forms of participation are already appearing on the local scene and these must be incorporated into both democratic theory and local practice. The prescriptions vary: from calls for wider consultation of citizen groups and greater co-operation on representative bodies to demands for neighbourhood councils controlling their own home areas and varieties of workers' control in industry.

DEMOCRACY AND LOCAL SELF-GOVERNMENT

By local government is generally meant a system of territorial units with defined boundaries, a legal identity, an institutional structure, powers and duties laid down in general and special statutes and a degree of financial and other autonomy. The definition of democracy, on the other hand, is concerned with the national political system based on citizen participation, majority rule, consultation and discussion and the responsibility of leaders to lead.

Historically, there have been three contradictory views of how local government and democracy are related. The first view, that of Toulmin Smith and the mid-Victorian romantics, is that local self-government is a cherished tradition in total opposition to the elected democratic principle. The second view is that the principles of democracy – majority rule, egalitarianism and uniform standards for all – cannot accommodate the claims of local government which is parochial, diverse, varied and potentially oligarchic and corrupt. This critical view of modern local government is well argued by Langrod and Moulin (see below, p. 24 ff). The third view is the John Stuart Mill tradition which holds that democracy and local self-government are necessarily related. Liberty is strongly defended: taxpayers must be allowed a voice in government; be informed and consulted; and people must also be free, in their towns and villages, to manage their own purely local interests.

John Stuart Mill, like Tocqueville, justifies local government as political education and as the unique setting for fraternity. As such it is the prime element in democracy, and has an intrinsic value regardless of the functions it may carry out. This *a priori* reasoning is denied by modern pragmatists who would be more likely to argue, with Whalen, that the division of powers between central and local governments is not a matter of principle. Convention, and the traditional political framework, determines the role of local government in the state and its contribution to democratic society. Hugh Whalen's pragmatic conclusion is that local government is part of political tradition and a way of providing government services rather than self-government.[2]

In practice, local government may not possess the legitimacy which theorists claim for it since the citizen's interest is concerned only with individual problems and grievances and he is otherwise relatively indifferent to its existence. The practical approach then is to see local government as providing services for local inhabitants, and protecting them against an impersonal bureaucracy. Again, this is better achieved locally than centrally since councillors are in a better position to control the expert and judge his advice. Nevertheless, William Thornhill's point is well taken: there is no such thing as 'local democracy', unique and separate from national democracy. The term democracy refers to the state as a whole and local government's vital contribution is that it is a political institution by which people share in government and resolve their differences.[3]

The British value local government as an accepted and necessary part of democratic society. Many European thinkers take the opposite view. The different beliefs are well illustrated by the debate in *Public Administration* in the early 1950s between English, French and Belgian writers. Professor Langrod's views reflect the French tradition of the correct relationship between the centre and the localities. The French local government system differs from the English in that all localities have the same general status (whatever their size or urban/rural characteristics) and powers are given to local authorities according to their ability to carry them out. Central control is strict and is carried out through a system of Prefects, appointed by the centre, who are particularly concerned with finance and budgetary matters. Professor Langrod stated that democracy was concerned with the nation-state as a whole and with majority rule, equality and uniformity. Local self-government, by contrast, was parochial, and was concerned with local differences and separatism. The two were essentially opposed and it was only a historical accident that they had developed together in the nineteenth century.

It was equally false, Langrod declared, to see local government (as Mill had done) as the setting for political education for democracy. Few national leaders come from the local arena and local politics are more likely to reinforce narrow sectional interests than an appreciation of democracy. The citizen was more likely to learn about democracy from national politics and national issues.[4]

A Belgian civil servant, Dr Leo Moulin, also refuted the Mill tradition that local government was an education for democracy. The individual's local involvement is in practice very limited. In any case, central government is so different in its scale as to be different in kind, so that local experience and knowledge were hardly appropriate to national affairs. Like Professor Langrod, he feared that local vested interests and possible venality were inappropriate to a modern democratic society.

The English tradition was defended by Keith Panter-Brick. Democracy was not just majority rule, social and political equality, and uniform standards and provisions. Local government and democracy were not necessarily and inevitably opposed, even if the trend in modern society was to greater centralisation and central control. Local government was still essential to allow the individual to voice his needs. Panter-Brick argues that participation is vital to democracy since it is in the community that people appreciate and tolerate each other's views and learn the art of practical politics. It is doubtful, furthermore, if a country can claim to be democratic if a substantial part of government – i.e. local affairs – is not run in a democratic form. Local self-government, finally, teaches two prime democratic virtues: the justness of one's claims and those of others, and the need to select from among competing claims those that are to be given priority.[5]

THEORIES AND TRADITIONS OF LOCAL GOVERNMENT

Theories of local government emphasise two aspects of political life. One is local self-government in the community. The other is the part which local units play in the state as a whole. In England the local units of parish, shire and borough, and the rule of the vestries and the magistrates, go back to Elizabethan times. But these were not independent sovereign bodies on which the state was based or from which it had evolved. They were subordinate units, subject to the sovereignty of the state. Nor were the local bodies democratically composed of all local inhabitants. Though the vestries were in theory open to all they were, like the boroughs and the magistrates bench, filled in practice by men of established status and wealth, and payment of rates was an essential prerequisite of citizenship from the end of the sixteenth century onwards. Moreover, until the reforms of the 1830s, the central political question was property and its diffusion, not the need for local self-government. As Mackenzie reminds us, nothing was heard of this so-called ancient doctrine of the constitution until after 1832.[6]

The upheavals of the early industrial revolution, with the increase in population and the growth of the towns, brought new thinking about local government. In the early years of the nineteenth century the Utilitarians began to examine the organisation of government in two main ways. One concern was with the centre and the local areas.

The other was with the idea of the superior (directing, controlling) and subordinate (tax-raising, providing services) powers.

Jeremy Bentham, the father of the Utilitarian school, believed in a systematic hierarchy of administrative bodies and it was he who invented the term 'the local government'. His views on local democracy are, however, ambiguous. Local headmen, and local 'sub-legislatures' would be elected but they would also be subject to the control and inspection of central government. The Utilitarians became impatient at the traditional hostility of local bodies to reform. The reformists, led by Chadwick, turned their interest to *ad hoc* bodies and to a Central Board and local boards (for example, for the poor law and for health) rather than to a recast democratic system of local government. Chadwick himself believed that local councils were not examples of true self-government but corrupt 'job-ocracies' which central government must over-rule if necessary reforms were to be made.

The reformers saw local government as the enemy of democracy. The advent of democracy – majority rule in national government, sound and uniform administration and appointment by merit not patronage – would destroy inefficient local self-government in favour of national standards and central supervision. In general, theorising followed in the pragmatic footsteps of Bentham and Chadwick: the criteria were good administration and the abolition of corruption, so that the extension of political rights was intertwined with the need for improved administration.

The stress on efficient administration did not go unchallenged. In the 1850s the imposition of public health measures led Toulmin Smith, in his books *Local Government and Centralisation* (1851) and *The Parish* (1854) to allege that there was a better, traditional doctrine of government. The parish, with its historic obligations on local inhabitants to serve in local office, was the unique unit of self-government which would safeguard interests and foster responsibility. To remove power from selected parish officers, and nominated justices of the peace, in order to hand them over to elected municipal councils – and counties – was a dangerous innovation. Toulmin Smith and the romantics had faith in the unreformed boroughs and parishes of earlier years, and the obligations of service which they embodied.

Later in the century this romanticism gave way to the denunciation of bureaucracy. Local ratepayers and national politicians were also united against Chadwick's autocratic methods and centralising drive and, in the late 1840s, managed to (temporarily) overthrow his central

Board of Health. Local self-government was denounced as a sham, which in practice delegated functions and powers to an 'army of functionaries' and which led to extravagant expenditure, mischievous government interference and an increasing tendency to centralisation. In spite of these beliefs, the conservatives did, reluctantly, accept the changes which brought improved services and were unenthusiastic about unfettered local self-government. But they were equally unhappy with the move to democracy. Many conservatives, of whatever class, saw the vote as a mixed blessing since it meant that by definition you were a ratepayer. And ratepaying was as disliked then, as now.

The ideal of the parish community, however, never entirely disappeared. Later in the century those who called for civic responsibility also believed that popular elected government should be exercised in the smallest possible unit, that is, the parish. The local community was the bedrock of democracy in the sense that it offered participation, discussion and political education to all its inhabitants. Gradually, however, even the enthusiasts conceded that the parish was too small for many important functions.

'Localness' remained a central theme which was held to be crucial to any democratic system of local government. When reforms were suggested, in Victorian times as now, changes in boundaries were debated in terms of natural community and corporate interest. This adherence to the value of primacy of 'localness' persisted through changes in economic and social life, the transportation revolution and increasing governmental activity. The definition of localness and the idea of collections of local people responsible to themselves in their community, remains a continuing part of English thinking on democracy.

J. S. MILL AND REPRESENTATIVE GOVERNMENT

J. S. Mill sees representative government as a great educative force which teaches men to look beyond their own immediate interests and recognise the just demands of other men. By sharing in government, individuals accept the results; this is both a practical and an ethical justification. At local as well as at national level, the same principle applies: since men have to pay for government through their rates and taxes then they should have a voice in public affairs.

Mill recognised that popular government could not guarantee more efficient services. But it did make political liberty a reality by basing government on discussion, and on the sharing of power and responsibility. He thought that local bodies and their members would almost certainly be less knowledgeable and intelligent than central government and accountable to an inferior public opinion. Local government was, nevertheless, an admirable arena for carrying out local, detailed administration and a school of political responsibility. Political education was essential because there was otherwise the danger that, Mill believed, working-class majority rule would mean class legislation – rule in their own interest. Representative government must also, for the same reason, be based on a property franchise and on a system of proportional voting to ensure the rule of those – the ratepayers – most likely to defend the public interest.

The twin aims of nineteenth-century reformers were to establish local responsible bodies and, at the same time, provide for the efficient administration of new services. The movement – though it took almost seventy years to achieve – was for uniform and inclusive administration, that is, local bodies which would provide services to a minimum standard and bring these together under one comprehensive roof. This meant a unified political responsibility – one body of elected representatives to control and guide services. These aims for uniform political and administrative responsibility stemmed from two, sometimes conflicting, demands. One was, from J. S. Mill, the Fabians and early socialists, a theory of democratic popular government at both central and local level. The other, stemming from the Utilitarians and public health reformers, was a theory of efficient administration, based on (as in the case of the Poor Law for example) uniform local units and central government.

The time of J. S. Mill's theorising on representative government was also the period of increasing civil and political liberty. The franchise was widened and, at the same time, a modest expansion of education and other services enabled individuals to begin to take advantage of these liberties. But liberty did not imply a wide range of government services or an active local council. Minimum government, stressing the individual's need to manage his own affairs without help from the state, was the dominant belief. And minimum government was also a creed of legalism: rights and duties, exacting the due letter of the law, and so on. At local level this meant that *ultra vires* was the cardinal principle.

Mill's claim that democracy was the only just form of society and representative government was its best practical expression, did not go unchallenged. The landed interest continued in its traditional opposition to the extension of the franchise. It found support from the middle class who feared the incursions of the mob into political life and who settled into a comfortable conservatism after the heady days of political and administrative reform of the 1830s. The arguments for and against the extension of the franchise were couched, on the eve of the 1867 Reform Act for example, in terms of the fears of working-class domination and of a 'levelling down' of standards.

Democracy, said John Stuart Blackie, was logically fallacious and dangerous in practice. American experience should warn us of the tendencies to corruption and to the inevitable decline of standards towards which its egalitarian values had led. Self-government was a sham, and the search for equality pernicious.[7] Representative government could not solve these evils. The radical, Ernest Jones, in opposing these fears, stressed the need for political liberty and equality to give men the material benefits which they legitimately demanded.[8] The extension of the franchise was the only way to widen the concerns of government and so help the working class to obtain education. The argument should not, therefore, be put the other way around, that working men must be better educated before they could be granted the privilege of the vote.

The late nineteenth century saw the development of equality and fraternity within democratic thought, under the influence of Fabians and socialists, and their gradual (though not total) acceptance in social and economic life as well as in politics. At this time, the Webbs and others favoured local government as a means of giving ordinary people much-needed new and expanded services. These would be locally provided, and 'municipal socialism' would replace private profit with public service, which should be trusted to local control with a minimum of central supervision. The Webbs' vision was of civic responsibility and civic pride. It represents perhaps the high-point of local self-government in radical and socialist thinking.

THE WEBBS AND THE FABIANS

The Fabians and early socialists urged that, if liberty and equality were really to be achieved then the working class must be given the vote, they must stand for election and take their rightful place as governors, and they must promote a programme of social and economic reform. Democracy could not be achieved while government was concerned mainly with law and order and foreign affairs. Greater government intervention should give working people better health and education, and more economic security. Only then could they use their vote effectively and have the necessary time and financial and other support to help them become local councillors and members of parliament.

The franchise was widened and civil and political liberty gradually achieved. But the Webbs and Fabians believed working people must combine together (and with other sympathisers) to work for representation and social reform. This would not be handed to them by the existing ruling classes. The best way of achieving these aims was to pursue the programme of municipal socialism: local self-government, ruled by the majority (not just by property owners) and the provision of a wide range of services, municipally (i.e. publicly owned for the improvement of local life). All this was to be achieved within the – transformed – system of representative government and not by its revolutionary overthrow.

These English 'practitioner-theorists', as W. Hardy Wickwar calls them, believed in six basic principles of local self-government.[9] The first principle was that the group, not the isolated individual, was the basic fact of social and political life. Men came together in many groups – trade unions, co-operatives, voluntary associations and in their home neighbourhoods – and these should be recognised in the organisation of government. Second, local self-government had grown out of traditional community life based on historic local units. Third, these historic communities were more important than special purpose *ad hoc* authorities and could command people's loyalty. But, as the fourth principle stressed, this did not mean that historic boundaries should not be altered to meet new needs; the new technical age now demanded an enlarged scale of operation and resources. The fifth and sixth principles we have already outlined: local authorities should be as free as possible from central control (and from *ultra vires*) and they should be based on a positive municipal socialism. The Fabians believed that these principles would work through a practical fraternity, of men's goodwill and common interests.

During the course of the nineteenth century civil and political liberty was largely achieved as the franchise was widened, the legal system reformed, and corrupt central and local oligarchies gave way to elected government and to professional administration. Equality was also partly realised, with the coming of mass education and other basic reforms. But this was a slow process which was not fully achieved – some would argue it still is not – until greater government intervention brought economic and social reforms to make equality and liberty a reality.

Fraternity was more elusive. The difficulty was that, by bringing men together to defend their common interests, the result might be the resurrection of the old selfish factions in a new form. Fraternity would then mean one pressure group competing against another in which the well-being of the community is lost. The socialists of late Victorian times did not fear this. They did indeed believe that their definition of brotherhood, based on common economic and class position, called for conflict against other groups and a need for working people to join together to win power at town and county hall. In the first half of the twentieth century their opponents were to argue that the result of this reasoning was the introduction of artificial, divisive party politics into the consensus of community life.

The potentially conspiratorial element in fraternity had also, in the twentieth century, been softened by the gradual acceptance of 'lobby democracy'. That is, the acceptance of a great variety of pressure groups, reflecting all aspects of people's work, professional and other concerns, which began to play an active part in government and politics. The democratic process of consultation was widened, not overthrown, by these myriad groups. They were not sinister interests but examples of a practical fraternity allowing compromise among opposing demands and for more informed decision-making.

The belief in fraternity and in the group basis of democratic government was reaffirmed in the 1920s and 1930s by G. D. H. Cole. He believed that group life and brotherly action must be at the centre of a reformulated theory of democratic government. His groups were not middle-class pressure groups trying to influence government but guilds of workers in all trades and professions who would be an integral part of the governmental machinery. Men would control their working lives through the guilds – a kind of workers' control, though without the revolutionary fervour of continental syndicalism. In local government, at ward and communal level, all important social and work groups should be represented. This functional representation – the views of men as producers as well as citizens and consumers – would help people to influence government more effectively.

Cole stressed that men cannot be fully represented just as voters. The important aspects of men's lives – their work and their neighbourhood – need to be directly reflected in councils and governments. Only then will men be truly equal. In practice this has not happened. Functional representation has no place in local government, apart from the limited use of knowledgeable laymen as co-opted members of committees. And class and party, interest group and professional expert, continue to emphasise the divisions between men and their very differing powers and influence.

The Webbs also came to believe that, like Cole, functional representation of men as producers of goods and services was as essential as territorial representation. Local government had concentrated so much on remedying the evils left over from the industrial revolution that it failed to enlarge men's ideas of the good life. Even Labour councillors were unable to improve community well-being. Their main aim was to remove 'municipal degradation' not to promote civic pride as the Florentines, in a golden age of municipal enlightenment, had been able to do.[10]

The Webbs' solution, for directly elected ward committees for each function of the local authority, with a full-time, paid Ward Councillor, was an attempt to introduce ideas of neighbourhood self-government which parallels their ideas of workers' participation in industry. But the exclusively municipal ideal was fading and calls for participation in all spheres was replacing it. At the same period an American, Mary Parker Follett, was also arguing for a democracy based on the everyday groups in which people are involved, particularly in the neighbourhood. This would provide political education and be a practical way of achieving social policies, by contrast to the corrupt party politics of the local council and its vested interests.[11]

Follett's ideas are interesting since they re-emphasise the idea of localness, of community based on common interest and non-party political goals. The Webbs and Cole, by contrast, see group organisation as an essential means of expressing the individual's work and professional interests – men as producers as well as men as inhabitants and voters. This implies conflict and compromise, politics and bargaining. Both ideas – of localness, neighbourhood and consensus, and of functional representation – remain a lively and difficult part of the debate on local government in democratic society.

THE CHALLENGE OF THE TWENTIETH CENTURY

Since the turn of the century democratic theory has had to come to terms with a changing and complex society. Changes in economic and social life gave rise to two kinds of political re-orientation. On the one hand, mass political parties and pressure groups gave individuals many methods, at local and national level, of making their views known, protecting their interests and influencing their political leaders. At the same time, parties and pressure groups organised political opinion: they brought out the vote, channelled demands and brought leaders and led together. These moves were not universally welcomed since, it was claimed, local self-government was undermined by their influence. Party politics should not play a pre-eminent part in local affairs and the pressure groups interfered with, rather than facilitated, the relations between councillors and constituents.

The other aspect of large-scale society which gave cause for concern was the realisation that, as the population grew and the scale of life changed, political man, like economic man, was very different from the ideals suggested by Victorian theorists. Individuals did not vote in great numbers in local elections and seemed generally content with – or apathetic about – the administration of local services. They had little or no detailed knowledge of their council, its elected members or its real contribution to local life. They accepted what was provided, complained when they were personally dissatisfied, and had little interest in local government as such.

These difficulties were explained – or explained away – by the argument that democratic theory was now to be realistically rewritten as the competition between élites (the political parties and leaders) for the people's vote in periodic elections. The political élite will still be responsible and accountable, even if people are apathetic, since it will anticipate the voter's reactions and rule in the light of public demands.

Democracy is, then, what men actually do rather than what they ought to do. Local government is still democratic, in this view, since councillors rule in the light of what they anticipate local voters expect and what officials, like civil servants, can foresee (or perhaps forestall) of individual and group demands. A minority of citizens are, of course, still actively concerned and as long as there are adequate means for them to organise and to influence, then power will be effectively dispersed. The tyranny of autocratic, unresponsive government is avoided and the essential balance and compromise of democracy is maintained.

The 1960s saw a threefold attack on this attempted reformulation of democratic theory. The idea that the theory needed to be rewritten in the light of events ignored the fact that governments were secretive, hard to make accountable and often unresponsive. It would be as realistic to make the actual operations of governments, parties and pressure groups more democratic – that is more open and more accountable – as it would be to rewrite the theory. This also applied to the so-called apathetic elector. His apathy should not be accepted but questioned; and society and its institutions re-examined to see if individuals would wish to take a greater part in society and if so, how this could be accomplished.

B

Finally, the ready acceptance of the view that active citizens formed a pressure group movement which prevented power from being concentrated and tyrannical was, it was argued, too complacent. The poor, the elderly, the unorganised, and the discriminated against, had no voice in this middle-class pressure group democracy and the danger was that the mid-twentieth century would repeat all the evils of Victorian vested interests. The result would be that no one ruled in the name of the community as a whole.

These reactions helped to pave the way for the search for new institutions, and new theories, to help individuals take a greater and more effective part in government. In this, local self-government was a renewed focus of attention. Two points should, however, be noted. The renewed interest in local government was not just a search for increased individual participation in the sense of a call for greater consultation. The aim was to help individuals grasp greater power, to say what should be done and how goods and services should be distributed. The second point is that the concern with localness sometimes seems like special pleading for the under-privileged so that participatory democracy in the community is in practice the self-government of the ghetto or the poor neighbourhood.

In this country, though the ideas of neighbourhood self-help and of general participation have gained some acceptance, the tradition of representative local government is vigorously defended. Power is centralised in the local council and the parties, not dispersed through bargaining pressure groups and special *ad hoc* public bodies. This is responsible and accountable power and, moreover, it enables local councils to get things done. Local authorities are not stalemated by conflict, but provide services in a democratic manner.

A rather different argument is that, in the welfare state, elected local authorities have a relatively modest place in the total pattern of central and local administration. Nor are they self-governing in any deep sense since the quality, quantity and type of services they provide are all determined from the centre. Their self-governing nature is also circumscribed by the standards set by the professional officers and their associations. This has arisen from the twentieth-century problem that, impatient at local traditionalism, central governments have turned to other means of bringing new services to local areas.

The problems of the interwar years, and the Keynesian revolution in economic thinking, brought increasing government intervention in social and economic affairs and an impatience with the seeming intransigence of local authorities. At the same time the increasing technical scale of operations and the need for a broader financial base also led governments to look for new or improved means of organising public services. In the 1930s the London Passenger Transport Board provided a new form – decentralisation to area boards of the public corporation kind – as an alternative to hiving off more central powers to local elected bodies. And, after the war, local authorities lost their gas and electricity services to nationalised public industries based on regional areas and with nominated, not elected, governing Boards. Democratic local government seemed a secondary cause.

A further difficulty is that, even if theory could describe the place of local government in the modern state and a necessary minimum of self-government, it would still be impossible to establish a comprehensive explanation of the individual's behaviour and beliefs. The citizen's attitude to his local community is complex and based on a variety of factors: his need for services; his relative indifference to 'the council' as such; his acceptance of the *status quo* or his 'apathy'; and, above all, the alternative calls on his loyalty.

These alternative ties – of trade union or professional group, of leisure interest, of family life, of voluntary associations – cut across local administrative boundaries. They relate man to man, and man to society, in ways which bypass local government. Any theory of democratic self-government must, therefore, recognise the interests that people have and their attitudes to them. And this could mean rejecting the local community as a way of making democracy more effective in favour of reorganising national politics, changing the internal organisation of trade unions and professional bodies, and democratising the work-place through 'workers' control' and other means.

These changing attitudes have another, potentially embarrassing, implication for any attempt at theorising. New loyalties, and their expression through powerful associations, might leave local government behind as a relatively minor focus of people's lives. But this affects different people in different ways. The middle class, the managers and professional people, the 'cosmopolitans' of A. H. Birch's study of Glossop, for example, look to national politics and to their work and its professional bodies for their main interests.[12]

To these men real political power lies outside the community and they have no need, and no interest, in standing for the local council or seeking to influence what it does. For the elderly and the poor, however, the local council may still be a significant focus of attention because its decisions affect their homes, their standard of life, and their daily well-being. And again, as studies such as Glossop show, the long-term residents, the 'locals' as opposed to the socially and geographically mobile 'cosmopolitans', are more likely to be lower middle or working class, small shopkeepers and so on. These long-standing local residents are more concerned with the council and its ways – and they may have a relatively narrow and parochial outlook. Any theory of 'local self-government' is, therefore, in danger of overlooking this divergence of attitudes and concerns. It may, if it stresses the desirability of increased local autonomy too strongly, increase a tendency towards the defence of the *status quo* and towards parochialism.

PARTICIPATION AND COMMUNITY

Some twentieth-century writers have also challenged the legacy of liberal democracy which they criticise as a theory based on the economic order of the market place. The theory must be reformulated to reflect the changes in modern economic life and people must be given greater equality if they are to take part in society. In this view, Mill, T. H. Green and the English idealists were naïve to believe that all men could take an equal part as voters and elected representatives when they were manifestly unequal in other respects. More social and economic equality is needed in order to give equal participation to all citizens.

It is also argued that this call for more equality reflects the world-wide rising demands for the good life for all people and that this, in turn, demands greater 'grass roots' discussion and participation. In some underdeveloped societies, and in Yugoslavia, there is a great stress on local consultation and self-government. In Yugoslavia, for example, there is a complex system of small, elected groups at neighbourhood, village and city level and functional works groups and councils. These societies, it is claimed, offer examples for our own country because we, like they, must meet rising demands both for goods and services and for more genuine consultation. This leads to the wider view, stated by Carole Pateman, that only by experiencing democratic society, especially at work, can individuals learn to take part effectively in politics.[13] If people's working experience mainly consists of carrying out orders given by others, in set ways and with unquestioned objectives, then they are very ill-equipped to take any real part in making decisions in public life, even at the local level.

The English tradition is sometimes also compared with the greater opportunities for participation and expression of opinion that are available in the United States. The American system, however, can hardly be called local government at all in the English sense. It is made up of a variety of separately elected boards (such as education), commissions and agencies (planning and housing) and with a local authority with minimal public health, basic services and law and order functions. In recent years, however, the American ideas about participatory democracy have influenced English thought and practice. The 'participatory democracy' movement began in the early 1960s, in response to civil rights demands and the urban crisis. In return for federal aid – in the War on Poverty, Economic Opportunity and Model Cities programmes – the federal administration demanded greater local involvement for local recipients. The people who would benefit from better services – the poor, the black, the unemployed – would sit on the boards to run the programmes, work as welfare helpers and so on. Decentralisation of decision-making was crucial to theory and practice alike.

The programmes were much criticised. Local politicians and city hall behaved much as before, and the demands for greater participation turned into demands for benefits, jobs and actual services instead of 'talking shops'. The problems of the cities seemed overwhelming. But an important legacy remains for English local government, as later chapters will show. Participation was greatly debated and its place in social work and in planning was advocated by English inquiries, such as Seebohm and Skeffington. It became an integral part of the Urban Aid programme in this country and of planning legislation. The second theme which this country has taken from the participatory democracy movement is the interest in the group and the neighbourhood as an arena for genuine democratic participation. Popular demand for ordinary people to have a greater say has arisen because of dissatisfactions with government: leaders seemed too remote, they could not be controlled and they did not consult or inform the electorate before they acted.

Participatory democracy, however, also claims to enrich men's individual personalities and happiness and to develop their potentialities. Though contemporary representative democracy also claims to be politically educative, in practice it is not concerned with the effects on the individual but with procedures and with the working of government. The defenders of participatory democracy state that by contrast it alone, like the classical theories of the eighteenth and nineteenth centuries, is based on moral purpose – how men live together to achieve the good society. Its paramount values – equality, participation and local control – are paramount and *a priori*, not deduced from men's imperfect behaviour in an imperfect society.

MODERN ATTEMPTS AT THEORISING

Modern theorising has not given us one legal or social philosophy by which to decide the nature and form of local government. There are, however, various implicit assumptions about how people behave and a recognition of three broad elements of local government: nationally determined but locally provided services; a need to explore 'community' ideas and ideals; and a concern with administrative efficiency as defined by technical criteria.

The coming of the welfare state has made central government very concerned with the quality and quantity of local services but indifferent to whether these are provided by democratically elected bodies or other agencies. This relative indifference is, however, mitigated by practical politics. Local knowledge and information are essential if services are to work well and local bodies are, therefore, convenient and useful. They prevent services becoming dangerously remote and isolated from local influence and opinion and they provide valuable intelligence feedback for central departments and political leaders. Political reality also reduces governmental indifference to the question of democratic versus purely administrative local bodies. This arises from the fact that local councils are a focus for party politics. Local party organisation is vital to national politics and sustains and is sustained by the continued life of local elected councils.

Theorising is a difficult task because people's lives, attitudes and beliefs are not only different from those of their great-grandparents, but they differ as between locals and cosmopolitans, working and middle class, long-term residents and the mobile. People who have lived in an area for many years, those whose social status is very much like that of their parents, and working-class people, are all likely to have an attachment to their home area and the local political community. Those who are more middle class, who have lived in the area for shorter periods of time, and who are more socially and geographically mobile, have wider horizons and take less interest in local political and social affairs. There is also the recognition that the individual's community life has two different dimensions. One is his family and friends, his 'home' neighbourhood. The other dimension corresponds to his need for work, leisure, shopping and for public services, and will range over a wide area. We live, as it were, in a whole series of areas, from the neighbourhood to the region, and political and administrative organisation must reflect this fact. We are no longer just citizens of one community, but of many, to which our loyalties are varied and changing.

Throughout these changes, however, the predominant value on which theorising has rested is that people who live in the same (administrative or politically defined) place and are dependent on common services should have a democratic body through which they can express their demands. At the other extreme the pragmatists have taken local government as a 'given' which, whatever its place in democratic theory, provides a means of administering public services. As such, the system itself needs to be reformed according to criteria of efficiency and effectiveness. This ignores, as the earlier theorists themselves had tended to ignore, the reality that the self-governing community (however defined and however dominated by the centre) is a political arena. It is characterised by conflict – over schools, traffic, housing, redevelopment and roads – and this conflict is resolved by a series of decisions following a process of discussion and compromise. In a word, by a process which is normally known as politics.

In this political process other factors besides community, area, administration and efficiency must be allowed a full part: communication, seeking and leading local opinion, and negotiation. It also involves a wider arena than that of the council chamber, and covers other local public bodies, business and industry, and voluntary groups. It is crucially affected by relations with other local authorities and with central government. In this situation the theory and practice of local self-government will be more concerned with central/local relations, with financial autonomy and with the influence of professional officers and the management revolution than with elections, representation or the accountability of leaders to led. These latter problems continue to be important but are, temporarily perhaps, overshadowed by central/local relations.

W. J. M. Mackenzie suggests that modern thinking is based on three values. First, local government is justified as a traditional institution which still commands loyalty. Second, it is an effective and convenient way to provide certain services. Finally, it is of value because it is a means of political education – or ancient rights, modern services and active citizenship.[14] L. J. Sharpe argues that modern attempts at theory – based on concepts such as liberty, equality, participation, or efficiency, for example – are not very successful at determining what is or should be the key principle or value. He concludes that the strongest justification for local government is its claim as an efficient provider of services, not as a defender of liberty or democracy.[15]

The claim of local authorities to be an efficient provider and co-ordinator of services – in spite of some criticisms of unequal standards – is threefold. First, they are democratic bodies subject to a local electorate and not wholly subordinate agents of the centre. Second, they are also a source of consumer pressure *vis-à-vis* the centre which, in the case of some groups – the poor and the elderly, for example – is an essential democratic function since these people are not protected by powerful organisations. Finally, local government is, unlike the market system and its price mechanism or the rigidity of the public corporation, flexible, humane, and responsive. Local government is uniquely able to respond to rising demands for services – such as education, welfare and so on – without succumbing to bureaucracy or the 'incipient syndicalism' of professionals set on their own objectives.[16]

Local government is the setting for the conflicting aims of representative and popular democracy. The former is based on elections and on councillors who take the responsibility for decisions in the light of electoral support. The latter demands popular access and adequate communication so that citizens know what is done in their name and have proper means of getting their grievances remedied. Our insight into the working of democratic society is enhanced by the way local authorities accommodate these conflicting aims.

The attitudes of local people to democratic local government are expressed in the practicalities of finding out what is happening and then doing something about if it need be. But democratic local government must also recognise a further, and problematic, set of values. These are the extent to which the issues that councillors think are important in fact coincide with the priorities of the electorate. This is a weak element in English local government, where councillors are accountable for what they have done in *ex poste facto* terms and where there is little citizen participation in the early stages of decision-making.

THE CONTINUING DEBATE

In this country, democracy has never been argued out. The aim in the nineteenth century was middle-class representation and, once the fear of uneducated mob rule was ended, the extension of the franchise and the gradual introduction of social reforms. The main concern was with good administration, not democratic ideals, and local government was to be reformed – or bypassed – to improve the standards of state services. At the same time representative institutions went on much as before, though their work was greatly increased and was supported by a growing variety of professional expertise. The stress on good administration overlooks, however, the inevitable division of interests in democratic society. Democracy's claim is that it alone provides criteria for resolving conflict in ways that treat citizens with justice and fairness.

It is the problem of planning – social, economic and land-use planning – which has been largely responsible for the renewed interest in local democratic forms and procedures and the principles behind them. The second strand of modern thinking is the proper place of the expert and how to control him, without sacrificing efficiency. Unless effective services can be achieved, and operated justly and fairly, then participation is meaningless and self-government gives way to bureaucracy.

These difficulties can never be resolved completely, because circumstances – including our needs and our attitudes – change. The nature of the problem is well illustrated by the work of the Royal Commission on Local Government in England, which reported in 1969. The Royal Commission defined the purpose of local government as the efficient provision of services, the focusing of national attention on local problems, and as 'a viable system of local democracy' which retained people's interest.[17] Local government gives people a common purpose in the exercise of power, to influence what is done, and to accept the consequences of their actions. Rule through elected members is its paramount feature, uniquely close to the people it serves and an essential part of the 'fabric of democratic government'.

None of this, however, gives us a hard and fast principle by which to define size, areas and functions in absolute and *a priori* terms, although it did call, in the Commission's eyes, for interdependence of town and county. But it also leads to the paradox that the implications to be drawn from the Royal Commission's views on local democracy is the need for small units, while their recommendations call for larger local units on the grounds of efficiency and the demand for services. The problem is in part recognised by the Note of Reservation from two members of the Commission. The Note argues that democratic viability has a large subjective element to it and the practical test at any given moment is not abstract theory but 'what public opinion will stand or can be persuaded to accept'.[18]

In the period from 1969, when the Report was published, until the passing of the Local Government Act in 1972, the national party political debate was only marginally concerned with the principle and was primarily a conflict over structure and function (and over detailed proposals within individual constituencies). Both sides called for more – if vague – local autonomy and freedom from central control. There were fears that reducing the numbers of councillors would undermine democratic representation and localness. Participation and effective services were, it was argued, twin elements of democratic local government and the former had no claim to override the latter. Others believed that there was a great need for better links between governors and governed, whatever the size of the area; ordinary people must have ready access to those who took the decisions. Until people understood what local government did for them and who was responsible for decisions then local democracy would not flourish. Those who opposed the dominance of the criteria of efficiency also held that local self-government in relatively small or unchanged local areas was essential to counteract bureaucracy on the one hand and 'government by protest demonstration' on the other.

In the early 1970s national politicians were also concerned at the seeming disillusion among voters with party politics and the growth of 'community politics' in many forms. The Labour politician, Anthony Wedgewood Benn, and Liberals' Jo Grimond took up this theme, arguing that local government must accommodate and encourage community projects and neighbourhood councils.

The difficulty is, however, to define and defend community in today's mobile society. As we have suggested, people may look to local, regional and national work and leisure associations for action and influence rather than to their local areas. It may be a mistake, therefore, to give small-scale community activity an increased part in local government or to regard it as a necessary element of a reformulated theory.

The problem is not, however, disposed of so simply. Jo Grimond's suggestions – that representation must be different for different purposes, and that fraternalism must be actively increased by greater individual participation in decision-making – both have implications for government.[19] Both of these ideas suggest changes of theory and practice. In English local government, representation is the democratic principle. In practical terms, members represent electors, constituents and inhabitants, that is, they are elected from particular electoral divisions and by a local (but general) electorate. Though people can sit as co-opted members on local council committees there is no special representation. The current criticism of this tradition appears to be similar to that of G. D. H. Cole, that some kind of functional representation should supplement traditional elected membership of local councils. For example, in the health service or in local government, individuals who are interested or affected – as consumers or clients – should be allowed to put forward their own spokesman to sit on these committees.

In this country the ideas of additional or alternative forms of representation have been rejected, on three main grounds. First, that the need for such special representation can be met by existing (if need be, improved) councillors, parties, committees and councils. Second, special representation tends to vested self-interest; someone must decide priorities, mediate conflict and speak for the unorganised. Only elected members who are responsible to all electors can, or should, do this. Finally, the community or public interest is not left, in English theory or practice, to competition between functional groups but lodged in the hands of an elected, comprehensive local authority which is both responsible to the whole body of electors and responsible for co-ordinating community services.

The second strand of recent debate – the need for greater individual involvement in decision-making at work and in the local community – must be treated with equal caution. Participation is not a new phenomenon but describes the well-known political process: voting in elections, standing for the council, working for local political parties, joining in local groups to press for better services. If participation is to be improved, and more and more people involved in decisions which affect their lives, it does not follow that new forms are needed. The question in fact confuses the problems of power, authority, consultation and accountability (which are dealt with in later chapters). 'Who governs', on what grounds and in what ways, continues to be the main concern. Community or functional groups may in practice turn out to be yet more middle-class pressure groups, not fraternities.

There is also, as Geraint Parry notes, the demand for 'good decisions' as well as the call for 'deciding for yourself'.[20] The question is not only 'who governs', but also 'to what purpose?'. That is, men demand justice and fairness from their governments and also equality and action – goods and services to sustain and enrich daily life.

The evidence suggests that the elector is becoming more 'consumerist' or 'instrumental' in his approach – demanding goods and services and judging politicians and governments on their ability to

meet these demands – rather than clamouring for a more participatory society. Many councillors and officials, for their part, have a
strong sense of public service and see themselves as responsible for
carrying out duties in the name of the whole community, guided by
given standards and by expectations that services should be fairly
and justly administered. They are generally hostile, as Anthony
Barker stresses, to sovereign 'communities', whether geographically
or functionally defined. Democracy is in large part what these active
community leaders use as their day-to-day working definition.[21]
Participation – actual involvement in the design and delivery of
policies – should not be confused with demands for more consultation or better redress of grievances.

In order to meet the goals of democratic theory, participation and
the intervention of local groups (of whatever kind) will always be
present. The support for the large political parties may be changing
and there may be a need for fresh forms of opposition both inside and
outside local councils. The expert is more and more dominant in
policy-making. There is the problem that, even in democratic society,
inequalities between men may be justified on the basis of merit and
the need for expertise. But these are perennial, well-recognised
dangers and ones which representative government must meet by
more open decision-making. The extent to which this occurs will
depend on the kinds of demands which people make, and theorising
will, no doubt, reflect these changing attitudes.

NOTES

1. See, for example, C. H. Wilson, *Essays on Local Government* (Basil Blackwell, 1948), pp. 11-24.
2. Hugh Whalen, 'Ideology, Democracy and the Foundations of Local Self-Government', *The Canadian Journal of Economics and Political Science*, Vol. 26, No. 3 (1960), pp. 390-4.
3. W. Thornhill, *The Growth and Reform of English Local Government* (Weidenfeld & Nicholson, 1971), pp. 29-30.
4. Professor Georges Langrod, 'Local Government and Democracy', *Public Administration*, Vol. 31 (1953), pp. 26-31.
5. Keith Panter-Brick, 'Local Government and Democracy – A Rejoinder', *Public Administration*, Vol. 31 (1953), pp. 344-7 and Vol. 32 (1954), pp. 438-40.
6. W. J. M. Mackenzie, 'Theories of Local Government', L.S.E., *Greater London Papers*, No. 2 (1961), p. 7.
7. John Stuart Blackie, *On Democracy* (Edinburgh, Edmonston & Douglas, 1867), pp. 13-14.
8. Ernest Jones, *Democracy Vindicated* (Edinburgh, Andrew Elliott, 1867), pp. 11-18.

9. W. Hardy Wickwar, *The Political Theory of Local Government* (University of South Carolina Press, 1970), p. 52.
10. Sidney and Beatrice Webb, *A Constitution for a Socialist Commonwealth of Great Britain* (S. & B. Webb, 1920), p. 207.
11. Mary Parker Follett, *The New State* (Longmans, Green & Co., 1920), pp. 245-6.
12. A. H. Birch, *Small-Town Politics*, (Oxford University Press, 1959).
13. Carole Pateman, *Participation and Democratic Theory* (Cambridge University Press, 1970), pp. 105-8.
14. W. J. M. Mackenzie, *op. cit.*, pp. 14 and 18.
15. L. J. Sharpe, 'Theories and Values of Local Government', *Political Studies*, Vol. 18, No. 2 (June 1970), p. 168.
16. L. J. Sharpe, *op. cit.*, pp. 171-4.
17. Royal Commission on Local Government in England, *Report*, Cmnd. 4040 (1969), pp. 10-11.
18. Sir Francis Hill and R. C. Wallis, 'Note of Reservation' *in* Royal Commission Report, *ibid.*, p. 148.
19. Jo Grimond, 'Community Politics', *Government and Opposition*, Vol. 7, No. 2 (1972), pp. 141-4.
20. Geraint Parry, 'The Revolt against "Normal Politics": a comment on Mr Grimond's Paper', *Government and Opposition*, Vol. 7, No. 2 (1972), p. 152.
21. Anthony Barker, 'Communities and "Normal Politics": a further comment', *Government and Opposition*, Vol. 7, No. 2 (1972), pp. 160-1.

Chapter III

THE DEVELOPMENT OF DEMOCRATIC THOUGHT
IN RELATION TO EVENTS

LIBERTY, EQUALITY AND FRATERNITY

The nineteenth century saw the establishment of representative government. The franchise was widened and local government, the legal system, and other institutions were gradually reformed. For many years, however, liberty had the limited meaning of freedom from arbitrary rule. This was a period of minimum government, in which the state's main task was to provide law and order and national defence. These attitudes gradually changed under the pressing problems of town life which called for collective action and public money. To this end, responsibility had to be placed in the hands of reliable and accountable local bodies.

The vote was given to more and more men (if not to women). The new voters had to be educated, and the worst evils of poverty and urban squalor remedied, if class rule or class warfare was to be avoided. The drive for equality was, therefore, more complex than that for liberty. Education and other services had to give equal access for those with equal claims – as voters, residents, ratepayers or whatever. But equality of opportunity, and local services which went beyond a basic minimum to make town life tolerable, meant redistributing goods and services. This called for increasing government intervention in the economy. Thus equality was bound up, in the development of democratic thought, with socialist ideas and met with great resistance. In the process local government became, for the twenty years between the final establishment of the structure in 1894 to the First World War, the centre of political and philosophical attention.

The weakest element in the democratic debate was the idea of fraternity. The idea implied that some criteria could be found by which men's brotherly actions could be judged, and this in turn led to conflicts between opposing ideologies. For example, the socialists stressed that only their beliefs encouraged true brotherhood. Their opponents believed that men could only respect the claims of others if they themselves had a large degree of freedom from state interference, and could work together on a basis of mutual tolerance.

As a result of these conflicts, theorising about fraternity was inconclusive and centred on practical issues. Two examples are the acrimonious debate on municipal trading or 'socialism' in late Victorian times and the conflict over town planning, which continues into the present day. Definitions of the community or of public interest that emerged from this debate have been equally pragmatic. The public interest, for example, is that which results from bargaining between sectional interests and which governments can persuade people to accept at any given time.

The fraternal, self-governing community does have, however, alternative roots in English tradition. The idea of place, of localness, stretches back to antiquity and vestiges of 'direct democracy' have survived into our own age. The parish meeting – the annual meeting of all parish electors – is perhaps the best-known example. The idea of limited communities directly responsible for their own affairs can also be seen in Private Bill provisions for public meetings and town polls (local referenda). Similar provisions were embodied in the Sunday Entertainments Act of 1932, the Licensing (Scotland) Act 1959 and the Licensing Act 1961 (with regard to Sunday opening in Wales). The election of borough auditors, and the right to be heard by auditors are further remnants of the old ideas of direct democracy.

If local self-government contains elements of a historical community ideal it is nevertheless profoundly the child of modern mass society and of its demands for effective and efficient administration. Uniform standards, justly and fairly administered, are of prime importance. The development of complex, large-scale industrial society, with its parties and pressure groups, changed the nature of democratic government. Democratic mass society was a bargaining society: between parties and pressure groups, elected representatives and officers, the centre and the localities. And equality and fraternity became competing, if not opposing, forces.

THE IMPACT OF VICTORIAN REFORMS

In the early years of the nineteenth century the need for reform – in poor law administration, in town government, and in public health services – was overwhelming. The struggle to provide the basic necessities of orderly community life placed a great strain on the borough, the vestry and the magistrates' bench.

Reform began, under the impending outcries of ratepayer and magistrate, with the re-organisation of the Poor Law in 1834. Industrialisation and urban growth had overwhelmed the old parish system which was both costly and ineffective. The 1834 Poor Law (Amendment) Act created a new area, the Poor Law union, based on geographical and administrative convenience. It only remained true to historic boundaries insofar as the parish was the unit of formation. The poor law reforms were, in fact, the only ones to incorporate Benthamite principles: local representative bodies (the Poor Law Guardians); a central Poor Law Board and 'inspectability'; administration through paid local officers; and areas based on utility and convenience.

The new poor law introduced the principle of election into community affairs. The Poor Law Guardians were elected by and from among qualified ratepayers. The traditional oligarchy did not disappear entirely, since Justices of the Peace continued to sit as *ex officio* members. The system also introduced, ominously, the system of audit. This was supervised and directed by the central Board of Poor Law Commissioners and the auditors had disallowance and surcharge powers. The elective principle was a step towards democracy. But central control, inspection and audit were opposing forces, which threatened local autonomy (including the freedom to do nothing).

In later years the poor law reforms were criticised on other grounds. The relief of poverty was put on a local, elected, rational footing but was outside the local government system of parish and borough. It was government by *ad hoc* bodies and, though efficient, it was not an integral part of comprehensive, community self-government. The 1835 Municipal Corporations Act, by contrast, offered little contribution to general theory. The reforms, which applied to less than 200 boroughs, nevertheless introduced a broader local franchise. This was in fact more democratic than the parliamentary franchise of the time, since all ratepayer inhabitants were included. But the Act laid no new duties or powers on the municipal corporations and they thus made little general impact on the community as a whole.

The poor law and municipal reforms differed in another respect. The poor law was governed by the new utilitarian spirit of centralisation, with local bodies as virtual agents of the centre. The borough reforms, by contrast, gave new life to the old tradition that local inhabitants had a constitutional right to manage their own affairs. But the Act did nothing about powers or areas – the old historic boundaries, however anomalous, remained intact. The countryside surrounding the reformed towns was also untouched by these changes and the magistrates and vestries continued to be accountable only to themselves. Throughout the century town areas remained within historic boundaries unless the council chose to expand by means of Private Bill. There were no general rules or acts of Parliament to set out the territorial divisions or how these might be changed.

The Municipal Corporation Act of 1835 established that the municipal corporation was the legal personification of the community. This replaced the self-selected oligarchy using corporation funds to its own ends and primarily concerned with the return of members to parliament. The new councils were elected by the ratepayers, meetings were open to the public, accounts audited yearly, and the administration of justice separated from municipal affairs. The appointment of a Town Clerk and a Treasurer were made obligatory. Towns of more than 6,000 inhabitants were divided into wards, each with three councillors. Aldermen formed one quarter of the council, so that the fully democratic representative goal was not achieved. And although central supervision was confined to Treasury sanction for raising loans, it did enshrine a principle which was to burgeon in the future.

The 1835 Act deprived individual councillors of their interest in corporate property and laid down that income was to go into the Borough Fund. After such payments (debts, salaries, etc.) which had prime claim on the Funds, then the surplus was to be spent for the general benefit of the inhabitants, and for the improvement of the Borough. This democratic freedom was, however, restricted by subsequent events. The Act of 1835 referred to the Fund's surplus: there was normally no surplus and the boroughs had to use the statutory power which the Act gave them to raise a rate to meet expenditure. This meant that their freedom was constrained by the – lively – concern of the ratepayers and, increasingly, by the imposition of statutory functions by central government.

Of course, local initiative was not entirely lacking. Local authorities used private Bills to promote new services. The great Public Health measure of 1875, for example, was based on the twenty-year experience of a mass of local Private Bill legislation. Thus although local authorities were not able to make full use of the freedom which the 1835 Act had given them, they were, by means of private Bills, able to demonstrate their initiative.

The Poor Law Amendment Act of 1834 and the Municipal Corporations Act of 1835 did more than set the administrative pattern of local government. In addition they established the belief that a local authority's prime duty is as the trustee of public funds. This had a lasting effect on local government, leading to supervision through the courts who prohibited any expenditure which was not *intra vires*, that is, specifically set out in some Act of Parliament. *Ultra vires* reinforced the restrictive air of local government. *Ultra vires* was originally a device to protect railway shareholders and traders who faced competition from these privileged limited liability companies, by insisting that the companies could only carry out those activities set out in their statutes of incorporation. Any activity outside these terms was illegal, hence *ultra vires*. Thus, since Municipal Corporations were corporate bodies, then the same principle could be applied – though the situation with regard to borough councils created by royal charter was ambiguous. Gradually the principle was extended to the whole of local government.

Local authority activity, therefore, had to be covered by the express words of some act of Parliament. These limitations to the self-governing community were further reinforced by the existence of the district audit. Where a local authority acted *ultra vires* then the district auditor could surcharge the individual councillor to recover the money so spent. The 1972 legislation changes the situation to some degree. The doctrine of *ultra vires* remains, as does the ability of local authorities to spend a small amount on the interests of their area and its inhabitants (the product of 2p in the pound rate). But the 1972 Act does appear to remove some of the previous restrictions. In future, where audit is conducted by the district auditor, then if he judges that an item of account is contrary to law, he may apply to the High Court for declaration. It then lies within the court's power, not that of the district auditor, to judge the matter and, if necessary, order repayment. If the sum involved is over £2,000 the court may order the councillor to be disqualified from council membership. The removal of the district auditor's power to surcharge, though commendable, is largely replaced by control in another form. Nearly 150 years of local government have not removed the fear of possible impropriety.

The reform of 1835 had another crucial effect on the growth of democracy, since the Act became a model for future administrative and structural reform. The form of municipal councils, as well as their methods of working, were used for other bodies, including the county and district councils in the 1880s and 1890s. By the end of the century the whole of local government had become 'municipalised' and there was little attempt to find new forms for new conditions.

THE INFLUENCE OF PUBLIC HEALTH LEGISLATION

The period from 1834 saw a dual philosophy of government. On the one hand the local Board of Guardians embodied central control and local administration. On the other there was the virtual independence, though virtual inactivity, of the municipal corporations and of the Justices of the Peace in Quarter Sessions. A possible third way was offered by local boards of health. To some extent, the public health legislation was a victory for a different concept of local self-government. Instead of the stress on economy and efficiency there was set the expansionist idea of improved services for all the community.

The Municipal Corporations Act of 1835 had not swept away the Improvement Commissioners, set up under private local Acts, nor vested their functions in the new borough councils. The boroughs varied too greatly in size and in their problems to make them suitable for all-purpose government. There was also the fear that corruption would result if too many functions were concentrated in one body. The 1835 Act enabled, but did not compel, Improvement Commissioners and other *ad hoc* bodies to transfer their powers to the reformed municipal councils. It was the great public health measures, culminating in the great reforms of the 1870s, which finally compelled the concentration of services in the hands of all-purpose local authorities.

The public health legislation of mid-Victorian times also changed local powers in another way. Instead of the autonomous council, seeking improvements through private local Acts, national legislation set up a central authority (a Board of Health) and laid specific powers and duties on all local councils, according to type – borough, district, parish. This idea gradually pervaded the whole of local government. From the 1848 Public Health Act onwards the general trend was to adopt the town council as the sanitary authority, where possible, instead of creating separate local boards of health.

The 1848 Act laid functions on municipal borough councils, who also became responsible for highways. But the Act was adoptive and outside the boroughs the central Board of Health could only create local health districts and boards on petition of the ratepayers. The exception was in communities with very high mortality rates, where the Board could compel the setting up of a local health district. The life of the central Board was short (it was dissolved in 1854) and only some 200 boards had been established in that time. But the 1848 Act is important because it introduced representative local bodies into these communities (outside the boroughs) for the first time.

The anti-Chadwick, anti-centralisation reaction to the public health movement was far more vigorous than that against the Poor Law which, after all, was meant to save, not spend, ratepayers' money. As a result there was a chaos of permissive legislation, borough councils and *ad hoc* local boards of health, rather than a uniform system. One consequence was that, when attempts were made in the 1870s to wrest order out of this chaos, more detailed central supervision, not less, was enforced.

The public health measures of the 1860s and 1870s had a creative impact on local authority services. 'Public health' was defined so widely that it became an umbrella for a variety of services and this in turn helped the development of the omnibus authority. By 1871-2 this trend had been officially recognised. The Royal Sanitary Commission of 1868-71 saw local self-government as the essence of English government. But the principle of local administration, locally financed, was undermined by the small size of some local units and by haphazard and sometimes conflicting laws. The only way to strengthen and simplify local administration was to bring all local services together under the control of a single local town council.

The reforms of 1871 (when a central, powerful Local Government Board was established) and 1875 (when local responsibilities were re-allocated) followed this thinking. The municipal boroughs were again treated differently. In the municipal boroughs the town council was the health authority. In other areas, with 3,000 people or more, the single governing body was a local board. In the remaining rural areas the Poor Law Union would be the administrative area and the Guardians the ruling body.

The influence of J. S. Mill's thinking was evident in these reforms. His views had helped to weaken resistance to central control. But a fully-fledged local representative democracy took longer to establish. Governments and party leaders were not yet ready to agree that all local authorities should be elected by popular vote, though the first seeds of this movement were set by the expansion of the franchise after 1867 (see below, pp. 56 ff).

THE CALL FOR REPRESENTATIVE GOVERNMENT

The call for representative government raised the twin questions of who should be represented and by what means. In practice, the first question was answered by giving elected power to men of property, the ratepayers. Later the franchise was gradually extended to other groups so that the local resident replaced the ratepayer as the citizen qualified to vote and stand for election. The second question was answered, very slowly, by the practical tendency towards the elected, all-purpose local authority to replace the *ad hoc* special purpose body.

By the end of the century the Victorians had gone a long way towards the modern democratic belief that, in the name of liberty and equality, all citizens must have equal access to public office. What had changed in the period after 1835 was that 'citizen' ceased to mean 'ratepayer', uniquely qualified to rule because of his direct interest in good government. Sixty years later it was argued that the qualifications for the local council were knowledge, commonsense, probity, and the representation of a significant number of local inhabitants and of a definite party political philosophy.

The property, ratepayer principle had stemmed from the reform of the open parish vestries in order to set poor law administration on a sound footing. The mass meetings of the vestries were prototype democracies but, in the nineteenth century, they were increasingly replaced by closed or select vestries ruled by a self-perpetuating ratepayer oligarchy. After the Sturge Bourne Acts of 1818 and 1819 some 3,000 parishes adopted the system of electing a parish committee to administer the poor law and employ a paid overseer of the poor. Thus the eighteenth-century legal rights of all inhabitants to share in parish business was superceded, as were the corresponding duties to act as constable, churchwarden, overseer of the poor and surveyor of highways.

The ratepayer principle, established by the Municipal Corporations Act 1835, excluded the working class. After the mid-century, however, the property qualification was not always strictly enforced, especially in the large industrial towns. There, with the financial support of trade union and trades councils, a handful of working-class councillors were elected. The Municipal Corporations Act of 1882 removed the general property qualification but retained it for those living in a seven to fifteen mile radius of a town. These people remained eligible, on a property but not a burgess roll qualification, for council membership. In the towns anyone on the burgess roll could stand for election as councillor or alderman. The old rules applied, however, in the countryside. It was not until the 1894 Local Government Act that, for the first time, those who did not pay rates could be elected members of county districts, of their Boards of Guardians, and of the parish councils.

Council membership based on the property principle for the other categories of local authority was not finally relinquished until 1914 when the County and Borough Councils (Qualification) Act substituted one year's residence for the ratepayer qualification. The modern principle of democratic representation based on residence as the voting and membership qualification was established.

The struggle for democratic local government also had to define how selected representatives should behave. Councillors had to have local knowledge and contact with local opinion, but by late Victorian times the electorate was also demanding that councillors should decide on policies and priorities. This demand could not be divorced from the search for responsible men to carry out the policies and, increasingly, party philosophy and party organisation sought out and promoted candidates. The radicals attacked corrupt local oligarchies of wealth and privilege and demanded their replacement by democratic councils. The conservatives, for their part, feared democracy and its threat to the settled rule of landowners and rate-payers alike. They argued that only those who paid taxes and rates had a right to rule; the working class had no incentive to keep down expenditure and, worse still, would rule in their own interest and not that of the community as a whole. These fears slowed down the move to democracy.

The reform of county and borough government in the 1888 Local Government Act again extended local democracy. It divided the counties into electoral districts, gave ratepayers the vote, elevated towns of 50,000 population into county boroughs, and provided for district audit. The 1888 Local Government Act was essentially an extension of the principles of the Municipal Corporations Act of 1835 to the counties, not a rethinking of what local democratic institutions should be or should exist to provide. After 1888, there-fore, although there might be some sense of a local self-governing community in the towns, this feeling was absent in the far-flung areas of the counties. In the towns there were more opportunities for men from different classes to come together in the common interests of the area, without travelling very far. In the counties there was a lack of common interests in the community sense and the need to travel to county hall was a barrier for all but the man of leisure in the age before motorised transport. The result of the nineteenth-century reforms was to give a more tangible and visible form of government in the towns than in the counties. The structure itself was thus a con-servative force and though the suffrage had been extended in 1884, representation remained narrow. The new institutions which followed at the end of the decade retained the old boundaries and still relied heavily on the unpaid service of the leisured class.

The extension of the franchise did not, in the event, greatly change the composition of the governing class. The old Quarter Sessions did not abdicate but transformed themselves into constitutional rulers. J. P. Dunbabin shows that the Conservatives' hope that there would be no drastic changes in the governing class was, for many years, a justified one.[1] At the first elections for the new councils, only half the seats were contested. J.Ps. succeeded in winning half the councillor seats and eventually rather more than half the Aldermanic bench. Traditional leadership in the countryside remained largely unchanged until the First World War eroded the traditional respect for these men and also changed social and political conditions.

In the last quarter of the century the idea of reviving the parish assembly sprang up, culminating in Gladstone's Parish Councils Act of 1894. By this time it was too late to revive the full powers of community self-government. The individual no longer lived all his life within such a small boundary and modern communications had extended his horizons far beyond the parish. The parish survived, however, as a pressure group and as a setting for local amenity activity.

The Parish Councils Act of 1894 introduced local self-government into the rural parishes. At the same time the old urban and rural sanitary authorities became urban and rural district councils and they and the Boards of Guardians were all to be elected on the same franchise. After 1894 the whole of England was covered by popularly elected bodies and, subject to central control, local self-government was created.

THE EXTENSION OF THE FRANCHISE: POLITICAL LIBERTY AND EQUALITY

Two conflicting forces governed the extension of the franchise. One was the right of every individual to take part in government on the simple basis of citizenship. The opposing idea was that property alone gave men that direct interest on which to base responsible participation. It was also thought right to distinguish between the local and the national franchise since whereas national taxation and legislation affected everyone, local administration impinged on the ratepayer to a greater extent than on other inhabitants. This belief persisted into the twentieth century; up to 1945 the qualification for the local vote was ownership or occupation of land or buildings.

The new poor law and the reformed boroughs established rate-payer qualification. The Sturge Bourne Acts of 1818 and 1819 were similarly based, but they also introduced the system of plural voting into local government. Those who paid more rates had proportionally more votes. Hobhouse's Act of 1831, by contrast, appeared more egalitarian. Everyone who paid rates, both men and women, were given one vote whatever their rateable assessment. And voting was by ballot, not show of hands. Hobhouse's Act also provided for annual elections, with one-third of the council retiring each year. This became a permanent feature of local representation.

From 1835 until the late 1850s the working classes did not have the vote and could not sit on local councils. In addition, if rates were paid by the landlord, not the tenant, the occupier was disqualified. In 1850 new legislation allowed compounding of rates. This placed the onus to pay rates on the landlord who then recouped the money through the tenant's rent. As a result the municipal franchise was greatly extended since householders had the vote even when they did not pay rates directly. By contrast the parliamentary vote stayed as it was in 1832 and was thus less egalitarian than the municipal vote. In 1867 the parliamentary and municipal franchise was extended and in 1869 the Municipal Franchise Act reduced the residence qualification from two and a half years to one year. It also gave the vote to women, though the courts subsequently held that this applied only to single women (i.e. ratepayers and householders), not to the wives or daughters of qualified voters.

In the countryside self-government remained an unrealised goal. There was, however, a growing demand that political rights be extended to the country dweller. At the same time, it was denied that only property owners should have the vote: men should be given the vote because they were citizens with an interest in the quality of local services. Ratepayer exclusiveness was also challenged on the grounds that local authority services were increasingly financed from national taxation as well as from the rates, so that a purely rate-payers' democracy could no longer be justified.

The 1884 Reform Act gave a uniform household suffrage in county and borough constituencies. Lodgers were included, as were occupiers of land or tenements to a yearly annual value of £10. By the 1880s a reluctant Conservative government was under pressure to establish a system of elected county authorities to which new services could be entrusted and to which the same central supervision would apply as in the towns. In addition, local services increasingly called for government grants. As long as the unrepresentative Quarter Sessions remained then the government could not easily meet the landowners' demands for rate relief. The prosperous farmers were also demanding a voice in local affairs. The fear of democracy, and the reluctance to relinquish their right to rule, gave way before these pressures.

By 1894 representative government had democraticised town and county alike. But 'one man, one vote, one value' was still not achieved. Majority rule was tempered by the electoral system: for example, in the cumulative voting for the School Board elections. The 1870 Education Act provided that in districts where there were no voluntary schools, School Boards could be formed. The local boards were elected on a cumulative vote – each voter had as many votes as there were candidates and could give them all to one candidate if he chose – to safeguard religious minorities. From 1879 School Boards were elected every three years and this raised a further question of democratic control.

The system of partial renewal in local elections (one third of the members retiring as a body) had passed from Hobhouse's Act of 1831 into the reformed boroughs after 1835. But little thought was given to this as a general principle. It was not until 1879 when the Education Act gave the school boards triennial, not annual, elections that the rival merits of the two systems were considered. Both principles were embodied in the 1888 reform of county government. The 'general election' feature of triennial election applied to the counties while county boroughs had annual elections – and both embodied the 'continuity' element of the aldermanic bench.

The course of the nineteenth century shows a move from fear of unrestricted democracy to the notion that every man, of whatever condition, should have a voice in government. At the same time, there were attempts to prevent the unrestricted effect of pure majority. In the earlier period this was achieved by such devices as plural voting, and by making a two-thirds or three-quarters majority necessary for some kinds of business (the setting up of select vestries, Inspectors for lighting and watching of a parish, and so on). Later, the effect of elected majority rule was softened by the inclusion of ex officio Justices of the Peace on Boards of Guardians. Similarly, when the franchise was further extended in 1867 and 1884, the electorate could still not overthrow the council by its votes. The aldermanic bench (whose members served for six years instead of three) was established on the grounds of continuity of administration, experience and stability.

The principle of plural voting was not finally eliminated from local government until the Local Government Act of 1894 gave the vote to all county and parliamentary electors. Plural voting for the Guardians was abolished together with the property qualifications and the ex officio guardians.

The local government franchise was rationalised into an equal franchise for men and women by the Representation of the People Act of 1918. The local government vote was given to men and women who had occupied property for six months, and to the occupier's wife (subject to a lower age limit of 30 years). The Representation of the People (Equal Franchise) Act of 1928 finally enfranchised women on the same terms as men. Not until 1945, however, was a fully democratic system achieved, when the Representation of the People Act of that year gave the parliamentary elector a vote in local government elections. The 1945 Reform was, initially at least, a matter of expediency: to create a local government register separate from the parliamentary register was thought to be a waste of resources. Even then, the special local government franchise was retained whereby, through ownership or occupation of business premises in a town, a vote on that account could be obtained.

THE GROWTH OF FRATERNITY

Each extension of the franchise – to the middle class in 1832, to the urban working class in 1867, and to the agricultural labourer in 1884 – was followed by structural and administrative changes in local government. The 1830s and 1840s saw the reform of town government and of the poor law. The next two decades brought the great public health improvements. The establishment of the central Local Government Board in 1871 marked the increasing formalisation of the system. The 1884 extension of the franchise ushered in the beginnings of mass democracy and was followed by the 1888 Local Government Act which reformed county government.

The ideals of liberty and equality were met, to a significant degree, by this establishment of representative government. The idea of fraternity has had a lesser place in democratic theory and practice. Fraternity involves ties of sentiment and feeling which, it is argued, are easier to express in the local, rather than the national, setting. But in the nineteenth century common sentiment did not necessarily – if at all – mean extensive community services for all. This can be seen in the development of housing, and the town planning services.

The Royal Commission on the Housing of the Poor, which reported in 1885, took a typically practical approach to problems which in other countries might have been argued in terms of fraternity and distributive justice. Real progress depended, said the Royal Commission, not on more legislation but on firm and vigorous administration. By contrast to this administrative approach any principle of fraternity was slow to emerge. Such principles had little practical impact on services such as town planning for example, since there was no compulsion to stop the operation of market forces. Planning was a by-product of building by-laws, working-class housing legislation, and basic public health measures, rather than a means of improving the community as such.

The Public Health Act of 1875 gave the first hope of coping with the overcrowded towns by its provision for the general adoption of building by-laws. But it still did little or nothing to initiate new facilities and there continued to be a marked disparity between working-class and middle-class districts. The need for more collective action, as opposed to individual or commercial self-interest, was only slowly recognised. After the 1850s general reform was imperative; but the form it took was severely limited by individualistic, as opposed to collective, philosophies. Thus the building by-laws, when they came, were limited to essential public health measures since wider regulations would have been an invasion of property rights. Even then town improvement had to be weighed in the balance of profit and loss.

The development of collective solutions to urban squalor grew out of very different roots. Public health legislation, though important, was circumscribed and palliative rather than forceful and positive. A more active approach came from the housing societies and the philanthropists. But the houses still had to show a return on invest-ment, and the overcrowding continued. It was the philanthropists, however, who brought a more wide-ranging perspective, even though they were often concerned mainly with their own workpeople and not with the whole community. But they were interested in living conditions in the broadest sense, with amenity and open space as well as with better housing.

The early efforts of local authorities were less comprehensive. By the turn of the century they were prepared to tackle the slums and saw the need for more open space. But they did not believe that the two were interrelated. It was easier, as transport improved, to allow urban sprawl. This had two main effects. The local authorities were, temporarily, relieved of the need to engage in comprehensive planning. But this in turn left them with the most intractable problems from which the better-off had fled.

The Housing, Town Planning, etc. Act of 1909 applied mainly to new suburban development and gave local authorities no powers to control built-up areas. Local authorities could not, like some of their European counterparts, compulsorily acquire land for expansion. Compulsory purchase powers were limited to provisions for working-class housing and public health measures. The pragmatic ratepayer philosophy continued. Town planning legislation in the early years

of this century followed only very slowly in the footsteps of a vision-
ary like Patrick Geddes who was developing a wider concern with the
whole quality of life in towns. Local authorities were slow to use their
powers and planning was still seen as the prevention of nuisances.
Their motives were not fraternal or egalitarian but ameliorative.

The Town Planning Act of 1919, like the Housing Act of 1923, was
mainly concerned with the new development of land. The Town
Planning Act of 1925 (which made planning compulsory) and that of
1932 both consolidated the law and extended planning powers to all
built-up areas and to the countryside. Right up to the Second World
War, however, local authorities were not effectively compelled to
make plans. They had few powers of control and little effective,
comprehensive planning took place. Local authorities were also
impeded by the continued suspicion that planning was dangerous
because it interfered with the individual's right to do what he liked
with his own property. Planning represented, from one aspect, a
potential move to greater economic and social equality. It was also,
from another point of view, a conflict of competing sectional
demands, not a force for the common good.

The permissive and limited nature of planning legislation was a
twofold impediment to improved community living. The ideals of
equality and fraternity suffered when, as the middle classes retreated
to the new suburbs, local authorities were left with the poor and
underprivileged inner city areas. Planning had to cope with the Victorian legacy rather than set principles for the new life. This was not
the only problem. On the one hand, town expansion cut across old
boundaries and renewed the town/countryside conflict. On the other,
there was severe economic dislocation in some regions while others
prospered. The existing planning legislation was only marginally
useful in these situations. This brought central government increasingly into the local scene.

INDIVIDUAL AND COMMUNITY RIGHTS

The 1947 and subsequent Town and Country Planning Acts finally
embodied some consensus on what was acceptable planning, though
its central provision – the betterment levy – was contentious. A
second force was a growing body of professional and expert opinion.
In between were the lay councillors and the different pressures from
competing local claims which they had to face. The post-war legislation, by requiring that development plans should be based on
physical, social and economic surveys of the area, moved away from

the pre-war notion of planning primarily in terms of amenity and convenience into planning on the basis of obtaining proper control over land use.

Democratic planning interferes with individual rights and compensation is thus a central question. Ever since the 1909 Act planning has been beset by the twin problems of compensation and betterment. On the one hand owners whose property is reduced in value by planning decisions demand recompense. On the other, there is the question of justice for the community, since some owners find their property increases in value by the same process.

Very limited compensation was provided in early town planning legislation but pre-war attempts to recover the value which accrued to individuals as a result of planning legislation – what in general terms is referred to as betterment – were unsuccessful. The wartime government appointed the Uthwatt Committee to consider the problem and recommended what was, in effect, the nationalisation of development rights in land outside the towns. The 1947 Town and Country Planning Act embodied this recommendation and also extended it into built-up land in the towns. The right to develop land was strictly controlled, compensation for compulsory purchase was limited to existing use value and, if permission to develop were granted, the landowner had to pay a development charge. These procedures were widely criticised. They were finally revoked in 1954 by the Conservative government and retrospective compensation was given to those who suffered loss due to the development charge and the limitation of compensation to existing use value.

The debate on the balance of justice – to individuals, local authorities and the community – continued. When Labour returned to power in 1964 the question of compensation and betterment was re-examined. The Land Commission Act of 1967 set up a central body with powers to acquire land at current use value plus a part of the development value. A betterment levy was imposed which covered some 40 per cent of the development value. A. E. Telling states that the owner thus retained some of this value, unlike the development change made under the 1947 legislation.[2] However, the scheme did not work with the speed and smoothness which would have made it generally acceptable and the Conservative government abolished the Commission, and the betterment levies, when it returned to power in 1970. But public disquiet about land and property values, and their deployment by local authorities and private owners alike, is still heard.

The coherent development of town planning was slow because of the conflicts of principle between individual rights and community well-being. Conflicts over individual versus collective rights were also exemplified by the progress of municipal trading at the end of the Victorian period. Some believed that municipal trading, and other forms of collective enterprise, were always harmful and provided for only sectional interests. Others believed that vigorous local self-government would check vested sectional interests and work for community ends.

The growth of services had always implied an increased restriction on individual freedom, especially on the unfettered use of property rights and on the individual's right to provide only for himself. He had to pay, for example, for services such as education or housing which might only benefit other people. But this was accepted as prudent reform. There were those, however, who feared that municipal trading introduced a new socialist ideology which forced local government into a collectivist mould rather than expressing civic pride. Municipal socialism advocated that ratepayers' money should be spent on services which rightly belonged in private hands.

This was one side of the coin. On the other side was the fact that trading services had existed for a long time – not as attempts at socialism, but as responses to the real needs of town life. The public utility services of local authorities grew up piecemeal, not as part of a collectivist philosophy, but as a matter of local utility. Some safeguard was provided by the uniformity of the 'Model Clauses' Acts whereby standard provisions could be incorporated into a Private Bill whenever a local authority set up a municipal service.

Nineteenth-century legislation also made it easy for local authorities to take private trading utilities over on advantageous terms. This caused resentment. But since tramways, gas, electricity and water were usually local monopolies, whose owners could charge what they liked with no means of controlling the services they provided, municipalisation was thought to be justified. The Fabians had a different motive: socialism by municipal ownership and control. The Fabians believed that 'Gas and Water Socialism' was a just distribution of society's goods and services and a way of bringing people into government as consumers and producers. And it was this philosophy which brought forth the opposition.

But municipal trading did not have a profound effect on local boundaries or on local management. The collective ownership and management of trading services was perfectly consonant with existing forms of local government. There was no great influx of working men into the councils, nor was there any sign of new attempts at self-governing of the services by those who manned them. The democratic control of local enterprise did not necessarily lead to a broad benevolent community spirit. Councillors were still obsessed by the pressure of ratepayer opinion which made them clearly aware of the need to avoid entrepreneurial risk and commercial boldness. Another fear was that municipal trading would mean that more and more lower middle-class voters would be salaried employees of the local authority and thus voters in their own cause – a variant of class legislation. Those in favour of local enterprise pointed out that the charge of its corrupting influence could be equally well applied to the existence of brewers and publicans on local councils and directors of companies supplying the corporation with services. Moreover, the fear that municipal employees would be voters in their own cause was exaggerated: they were organised into much more traditional sectional interests and had no identity as 'local government employees'. At the same time a similar argument surrounded direct labour and the use of direct labour departments. From their inception the argument divided those (as it does now) who saw this as an economic use of the benefits of large-scale operation and those who saw it as an ideological party attempt to undermine the proper sphere of private enterprise.

After the First World War and with the growth of the organised Labour vote, concern for municipal socialism gave way to interest in national solutions to the questions of production and the distribution of services. The Labour Party did, however, continue to support municipal enterprise and showed its faith (while in opposition in parliament at least) in local initiative by pressing for local authority enabling bills (eight times in the twenty-year period from 1921 to 1939). All these attempts to replace costly and time-consuming Private Bills by one national legislative measure, failed.

SOME VESTIGES OF DIRECT DEMOCRACY

By the turn of the century, English local government was moving into the collectivist age. Now only vestiges of an earlier, self-governing community ideal survive. Here we give three examples. These are the testing of local opinion through town meetings and local polls in Private local Bill procedure; the local options for Sunday entertainment and licensing hours; and the right to appear before the district auditor.

Referenda were introduced into local government by the Sturge Bourne Act of 1819 which allowed a poll of ratepayers to decide

questions of land purchase and the building of workhouses. The
1850 Public Libraries Act made similar provisions. The Public
Health Act of 1875 provided for town polls and town meetings, since
parliament believed that a locality had to argue a good case for new
powers beyond those conferred by general legislation. Local
councils, even though ruled by democratic majorities, had to be
restrained.

The Borough Funds Act of 1872 which gave local authorities
power to promote Private Bills and to spend money on opposing
those of private companies – an outcome of the controversy over
water, gas and other basic services – again forced local councils to
consult their inhabitants before acting on their own (presumably
majority) decisions. The Act required that, in order to promote a
Private Bill, a local council must pass a majority resolution at two
successive council meetings. And a poll of owners and ratepayers had
to be taken through a public meeting or, if demanded, a vote. And,
as Keith-Lucas shows, the effect of the poll, based on a system of
plural voting which favoured the richer owners and occupiers, gave
the real power to them rather than to the local council.[3]

The situation remained in this difficult position until the 1903
Borough Funds Act laid down that the referendum was to be of the
whole electorate, not of the ratepayers and owners alone. It is
noticeable that the counties were not required to hold referenda: it
was in the towns, where municipal trading was still a threat, that
these attempts to circumscribe democratic decision-making were still
believed to be necessary. The Local Government Act of 1933
perpetuated the town meeting and referenda requirements surrounding local councils' promotion of Private Bills long after the original
bogey of municipal trading had passed away. These provisions add
little to the quality of democratic procedures. It is costly; few people
bother to vote, and it encourages sectional and vested opposition
rather than democratic debate. Now, however, this vestige of direct
democracy is to disappear. It will no longer be necessary, under the
1972 Local Government Act, for a local authority to obtain the
Minister's consent to the promotion of a Private Bill and town
meetings and polls are abolished. Instead, there must be thirty, not
ten, days' notice before the full council meeting at which the resolution to promote or oppose a Private Bill is taken.

An area in which local referenda, it can be argued, does allow for
genuine local opinion is in the field of liquor licensing and Sunday
entertainment. The Sunday Entertainments Act of 1932 allowed local
option on cinema opening through public meeting and the poll pro-

cedures. Local plebiscites are also provided in the Licensing Act (for Sunday opening in Wales) and the veto poll in the Licensing (Scotland) Act 1959.

Auditing procedure is also interesting because the provision for elected borough auditors is a remnant of earlier ideas of community democracy. The Poor Law Amendment Act of 1834 contained provision for audit and the 1844 Poor Law Amendment Act created an 'auditor of the district' who had power to disallow items of unauthorised expenditure and to surcharge members of the Boards of Guardians. But the reformed Municipal Corporations of 1835 were exempt from District Audit. It was felt that democratic elections were a sufficient check on administration. In addition to the normal internal audit carried out by their own officers the boroughs had their accounts audited either by professional auditors or by three borough auditors. Two of these borough auditors – the elective auditors – were elected on the municipal franchise. The third – the mayor's auditor – was appointed by the mayor from among council members.

Under the twin influences of the 1844 Poor Law Amendment Act and the Public Health Acts of 1848 and 1872, district audit was gradually applied to all the new local authorities which came into being from the mid-century onwards. But the boroughs remained in their unique position. Gradually, however, certain borough services (and particularly after the turn of the century, county borough services) were subject to audit. Under the 1870 Education Act the District Audit came to audit School Boards' accounts and when the 1902 Education Act transferred the education service to local authorities then County Borough education accounts were subject to district audit. The 1925 Rating and Valuation Act applied the same principle to rating and valuation accounts.

The 1933 Local Government Act codified the law on district audit and applied it to all county councils, to London (at both county and metropolitan district level), urban and rural districts and to the accounts of parish meetings and parish councils. The 1933 Act also provided that municipal corporations could resolve to adopt either district audit or professional audit. In addition, post-war legislation relating to particular services (for example education, child care, rating) made these accounts subject to district audit for all local authorities, including the Boroughs, responsible for that service.

In the twentieth century then, as municipal corporations adopted district or professional audit, there were virtually no elective auditors left. In the few cases where they remain the turnout of voters to elect

c

them has for many years been very low. Elective auditors are now of marginal significance in democratic control and accountability.

Similarly, the right of electors to appear before auditors, and to inspect the accounts, while valuable in principle are now also relatively unimportant in the maintenance of citizen rights. Nevertheless the rights themselves are re-enacted in the 1972 Local Government Act. The Act allows local authorities to choose professional audit instead of district audit. Under district audit, the elector or his representatives may attend before the auditor. If professional auditors are used then an aggrieved elector may ask the Secretary of State to direct a district auditor to hold an extraordinary audit. Aggrieved individuals also have the right to be given the reasons for the decisions which have been taken, if necessary in writing. The individual can then appeal to the court if he wishes and the court can make or refuse a declaration, vary, confirm or quash a decision or issue a certificate of account. These provisions are interesting not so much because of their championing of ancient rights but because they appear to be a potential safeguard as the district audit system gives way to professional audit.

THE GROWTH OF PARTY POLITICS

J. S. Mill believed that the proper duties of representative bodies were discussion, criticism and overall control of administration. Since his day representative government has changed profoundly with the coming of modern mass political parties and pressure groups which threatened to turn elected bodies into machines for registering decisions taken elsewhere. This was already a fear in late Victorian times when the growth of conflict within and between parties and pressure groups threatened to dilute the central position of representative bodies in democratic theory and action.

After the excitement of reform in the 1830s electoral activity waned except for the largest boroughs. Community spirit, and the concomitant party activity, was also discouraged by the chaos of areas and public bodies. There was no all-purpose elected local authority to focus energy and goodwill. The zeal of the middle-class reformers also faded once the worse evils had been remedied. The electoral contest was revived by the extension of the franchise in the 1860s and by the controversy introduced by the public health measures. These brought conflict between the 'improvers' on the one hand and a variety of Ratepayer Associations led by small property owners, the 'economisers', on the other.

The extension of the franchise in 1867 impelled the parties to develop local organisations. The pattern was set by the Birmingham Liberal party under Joseph Chamberlain's leadership. Soon the Conservatives followed suit and by the end of the century nearly all the large towns were fought on party lines for municipal and school board elections. Conservative and Liberal party managers defended party politics: it helped, rather than hindered, the recruitment of able councillors. It also increased the voter's interest in council affairs. The opposing view was that party politics introduced artificial divisions and diverted the council from its real job of providing efficient services for all.

The growth of the party system meant potential conflict between different interests but it did not necessarily imply divisions over policy. Before the advent of Chamberlain's 'Birmingham Caucus' and the threats of municipal socialism, divisions in the council chamber were a question of personality, tradition and religion, rather than of issues. The new Fabian ideas, and the sectarian conflict spilled over into other aspects of municipal affairs so that there were two opposing camps: Tory, Anglican, restrictive attitudes on the one hand facing liberal, non-confirmist, expansionist views on the other.

Even so, in school board and town council, the real conflict was over who should control power, not necessarily over what policies should be pursued once political power had been won. The emergence of the Labour party, with its defined philosophy and programme, meant a different set of aims. After 1900, and most importantly, after 1918 when the changed constitution promoted the growth of local parties, the Labour party aimed to gain power, and increase expenditure, particularly on poor law relief. This met with bitter opposition from the other parties. After 1919 the belief that party politics should have no place in council work achieved new impetus as a defence mechanism against the Labour party. The non-socialists also feared that the working class would be an unknown and reliable element: unused to the conventions of council procedure and prone to extravagant innovation born of socialist ideology rather than local necessity.

In the event, these fears were groundless. Working-class Labour councillors followed the existing system and *ultra vires* effectively inhibited any dramatic local innovation. Another fear – of national party influence on local policies and procedures – was more difficult to set at rest. In the 1930s the Labour party produced a set of model Standing Orders for the organisation and behaviour of party groups on local councils. These were not mandatory but gradually the majority of Labour groups did adopt them. The Conservatives, Liberals and Independents claimed that this was undemocratic. They argued that (in spite of the fact that the model Standing Orders related to procedure and organisation rather than policies) local Labour parties were obviously subject to national directives. How could local ratepayers be sure that their interests were being protected, the non-socialist parties argued, if local Labour councillors had to follow procedures laid down by the national headquarters of the party and vote according to the party whip instead of their own consciences?

In spite of these fears, other councillors gradually organised into more formal party groups, although it was not until after 1946 that this became widespread. Even then, in many councils, especially in the countryside, party politics played little overt part in council and committee work. The question of one party dominance, however, remained a problem for any ideal of democratic government. It weakened effective opposition and, in some cases, alternative ideas and initiative. This situation arose from the structure of local government itself. The setting up of the counties and county boroughs produced socially homogeneous areas which returned one party or group of individuals to power for long periods—Labour in the large industrial towns, Conservatives or Independents in the countryside. This became a permanent feature of English local government. A diminution of democracy, of open debate, might be said to have been a consequence of these structural reforms of the late Victorian period.

The style of local party politics depends, as J. G. Bulpitt shows, on the number and size of the opposing groups on the council, the degree of patronage which they exercise, the operation of standing orders by the Labour Party, and so on.[4] This political style has consequences for the democratic process at many significant points. Where the two main parties operate a fully 'political' system, contesting elections and so on, then there is a more open government in which there is at least a strong likelihood that debate is public, and important issues are aired in the council chamber, reported in the press, and reflected in local election campaigns. The opposite process tends to be true where a council is dominated by one party for long periods. Over the last hundred years party politics has been mainly an urban phenomenon. Party politics was slow to develop in the counties, matching the slow decline in the influence of the landowners and the dominance of 'localness'.

Today, while party politics is a part of local life, several doubts still remain. Burke's view, that a political party is a body of men 'united for promoting by their joint endeavours the national interest, upon some particular principle in which they are all agreed', may be regarded as applicable to national, but not local, affairs. National government is concerned with 'principles', with policies and their embodiment in legislation. It is the job of local authorities to put these principles or policies into operation: they are concerned with administration. Party politics has no part, in this view, in the day-to-day work of the councillor to serve the community as a whole, not some organised section of it. The councillor is an elected representative, responsible to his constituents, not a mandated delegate from the political party organisation. Locally, then, the old dictum of Lord Halifax – that party is at best a kind of conspiracy against the rest of the nation and party discipline incompatible with the liberty of private opinion – has lingered long after it disappeared at national level.

Party politics is also inappropriate in local administration, it is suggested, because it prevents committee and council matters being decided on their merits. The important decisions are taken in private, in party group meetings which are closed to officers of the local authority. It is feared that this has two defects. One is that the party group lacks the advice of the council's professional experts, which is a potentially harmful (or at least embarrassing) situation. The other defect is that decisions taken in group meetings may be in effect minority decisions. For example, if a Labour group meeting is conducted according to a strict interpretation of the party's Model Standing Orders then where a decision is taken to the vote it must then be followed by all members. Thus a decision could be taken by a majority of the party group which in fact is only a minority of the council considered as a whole.

The party caucus is also criticised as undemocratic on other grounds. First, in the case of the Labour party, the Model Standing Orders lay down that decisions taken by the group (after due procedures) should be binding on the individual member who should then not embarrass his fellow group members by putting questions or raising issues in committee or council without first clearing this with the party leaders. This, it can be argued, is a serious restriction on the councillor's freedom of debate and on his abilities to defend his constituents' needs and demands.

The second criticism of the party caucus is that it is undemocratic because the group meetings include people who are not members of the council. The Labour party Standing Orders, for example, provide that three representatives of the local party's General Management Committee, plus the local party secretary or agent, may attend the group meetings (though they have no voting powers). The situation is not so formal on the Conservative side though outsiders do attend such meetings.

The disquiet about the influence of the local party organisation goes further than this. The General Management Committee of the local Labour party is responsible for the selection of the candidates to stand in local elections and it, not the party group on the council, is also responsible for the policy document on which the elections are fought. The rejoinder to this criticism is that the membership of the council and the General Management Committee overlap, that councillors normally form the greater party of the body which draws up the election manifesto, and that the local party trusts its councillors and the work which they do in council affairs.

These difficulties can in practice be said to be overcome by tolerance and good sense. Councillors are party men but they act in good faith and are judged as such. The difficulty is not that party politics exists but that it is so secretive. Any group of people united by a common aim and interest will try to behave in a coherent and consistent manner and will be motivated by a loyalty to the group and opposed to other groups. Nor is the influence of outside groups necessarily pernicious; such influences have existed – and do exist – in many forms and it is a matter of opinion whether they are regarded as either the impact of a multitude of local views or as an undemocratic, sinister influence.

The discussion of the proper place of party politics has been concerned with the influence of party on day-to-day administration and the possible undue influence of outside party organisation. There has been, in addition, the criticism that party politics inhibits good candidates from coming forward into local government. Such people are, it is said, deterred by party labels or, alternatively, see council membership as hopeless since they do not belong to the party which is normally in the majority locally. On the other side party politics has been defended as helping to increase interest in council affairs. Without political parties there would be more uncontested seats and lower polls; parties also help to recruit more working-class and younger candidates on to local councils. Those who defended party in council work also hold that it gives coherence and clarity to elected representatives more, not less responsible to the public since it helps electors to judge their performance and their promises. The difficulty is that, as has been suggested, this party competition works imperfectly, given the inbuilt permanent majority in certain areas, which reduces the opportunity to reject the majority party at the polls.

Local government is political in the broad sense because there are issues and policies which are properly the subject of discussion, debate and opposing views and interests. It becomes party political because, given that these functions and issues do exist, then the parties will regard them as matters of party political conflict. Party politics is now a permanent part of council business as well as of local election platforms. What should be of continuing concern is the extent to which this process is open and knowable rather than secretive and inward looking.

INDUSTRIAL DEMOCRACY IN LOCAL GOVERNMENT

The twentieth century also saw the growth of industrial democracy (the emergence of professional associations and trade unions amongst local government employees) which altered the old traditions of local authorities responsible to local ratepayers for the employment and payment of local authority staff.

In the nineteenth century the unpaid public service of parishioners gradually gave way to the appointment of full-time officials, paid for out of the rates. The Poor Law Amendment Act 1834 set the pace with its relieving officers, medical officers and workhouse master. From 1848 onwards the real foundations of a paid local government service were laid under the impetus of government pressure on the more reluctant public health authorities. This had already started in 1835 when the Municipal Corporations Act made the salaries of officers a first charge on borough funds. At the same time, paid police services were made mandatory (a position realised in the counties in 1839). Local authorities were free, outside the requirements to hire a Treasurer and a Clerk, to employ their own staff and lay down qualifications, levels of pay and other conditions of employment. Over the next sixty years this was dramatically changed by the growth of professionalism and of trade union bargaining.

The twentieth century saw a great growth of staff associations, the most extensive being NALGO (the National and Local Government Officers' Association). Founded in 1905, it had succeeded in organising some 80 per cent of its potential membership by the end of the nineteen-thirties. At the same time the Local Government Act of 1933 codified the position of local authorities as employers by enabling them to appoint such officers as they thought fit (while requiring the appointment of the clerk, treasurer, and medical officer of health). Section 121 of the Local Government Act 1933 also replaced employment 'at the council's pleasure' with 'reasonable notice'.

The ability of a local authority to employ its own staff, while still characteristic of English local government, was affected from the First World War onwards by the growth of national negotiating machinery for salaries and conditions of service. In 1917 'The Committee on the Relations between Employers and Employed' (more familiarly, the Whitley Committee after its Chairman, J. H. Whitley, an M.P. and later Speaker of the House of Commons), recommended the voluntary formation of national and district industrial councils of employers' and workers' representatives.

The response of local authority associations and the trade unions was swift. A National Joint Council held its first formal meeting in February 1920 – and its last meeting at the end of that year. The work lapsed in the depression years but late in 1936 another National Joint Council was formed. This covered relatively few officers since the teachers, police, engineers, fire brigade staff, mental hospital officers and local government manual workers had separate arrangements.

Before the full development of the Whitley Council system local authorities were still constrained by the fact that rate of pay had to be 'reasonable', that is, not markedly higher than for similar kinds of employment. If they disobeyed this requirement, then they could be acting *ultra vires* and individual councillors could be surcharged by the District Auditor. This position was reaffirmed by the famous Poplar case, in which the manual workers' wage rates paid by the Board of Guardians exceeded the market rate. After a lengthy legal process, the right of the District Auditor to surcharge on this basis was confirmed and the unrepentant Board members, led by George Lansbury, went to prison. Although the principle was never directly applied to the clerical and administrative officers of local authorities, opinion at the time believed that there were probably limits to the rates of remuneration which local authorities could pay.

In spite of this constraint, and the statutory requirement to appoint to certain designated posts, local authorities nevertheless enjoyed a wide freedom. They had complete discretion on qualifications and training, pay and conditions, tenure and superannuation, in spite of the growing influence of NALGO and the compulsory superannuation provision of 1937. The position was only finally altered to a significant degree by the coming of the national Whitley machinery in 1946 and the operation of the 1944 Education Act which gave the Minister of Education power to require Local Education Authorities to pay teachers the scales laid down by the Burnham Committee.

The wartime emphasis of good industrial relations boosted Whitleyism, and in 1943 the local authority associations agreed to the creation of a National Joint Council for local authority Administrative, Professional, Technical and Clerical services (the NJC). This set in being a national scheme of salaries and conditions which became known as the 'Charter', which came into force in April 1946. The Charter laid down desirable conditions for recruitment and training, salaries and suggestions for the good conduct of officials. There are now over twenty national negotiating or similar bodies wholly or mainly engaged in the field of local government employment. Co-ordination is obtained through the Local Authorities Conditions of Service Advisory Board, which enables the local authority associations to survey the field as a whole.

The theory of democratic local government, however, still holds that it is the local council which is collectively responsible to the electors. And local authorities are free, under the 1933 and now the 1972 Local Government Acts, to appoint such officers as are necessary and pay them a reasonable remuneration. This freedom is in practice circumscribed by central prescription and by the Whitley machinery and its standardisation.

Whitleyism has meant that salary negotiations are largely in the hands of representatives of the local authority Associations and thus uncontrolled by individual authorities who effectively delegate power to these negotiators. Trade unionism is a powerful force in these negotiations. Though the two sides consult and confront each other at provincial and local Whitley council level, effective decisions are taken nationally. The ratepayers' influence on expenditure, of which wages and salaries form a large part, is an illusion. The local community must trust that elected members will be fair and just employers who are also vigilant guardians of the public interest.

Officers are, nevertheless, legally the servants of the council and must work under its directions. They must in general act under the council's orders, except where statute lays specific duties on them personally, and they have no direct responsibility to the electors. In this way the principle of representative government is preserved.

SOME CONTINUING PROBLEMS

It can be argued that practice is a better guide than philosophy to the present state of democratic local government. Theory leaves open the question of commitment, of the extent to which anyone should be prepared to defend the underlying principles. The idea of the local community managing its own affairs has its roots in Mill and de Tocqueville. In the twentieth century the question has been: what do we want local administration to do? Democracy is a difficult concept which involves a number of practical problems. For example, it depends on people's knowledge of public affairs and yet, though in practice this knowledge is imperfect, government still works. Is there some sense, therefore, in which government is less democratic than it 'should' be? Many people would agree that this is so, and that we should positively strive, for example, to increase the numbers of people going to the poll, improve the level of knowledge and interest, and so obtain a more lively local democracy.

Another problem has been the role of opposition in democracy. At the local level, this has at times been particularly acute, since in large towns one-party rule has continued for long periods, and the countryside has been dominated by no-party but conservative rule, with little effective criticism within the council chamber – and few spontaneous sources of opposition from outside. This leads to a further difficulty. What kinds of action are permissible – or desirable – in a democratic society and what attitude should we take to protest of various kinds? Finally, there is the stumbling block of uniformity: local democracy is part of public decision-making and local variations may be further reduced. (The problem of the possible clash between equality and fraternity is dealt with in Chapter V.) In spite of all these difficulties the consensus appears to be that democratic forms of government are preferable. Even if it is not self-evident that local authorities should be democratically elected, it is widely assumed that citizens will find their democratically elected council more comprehensible, accessible and responsive.

The question still remains open as to what is, or ought to be, the relation between local self-government and democracy. The problem is not just one of law, of government structures, or of pure theory. It is also one of atmosphere, of trust and confidence within which the whole system operates and this is still, in England, a matter of representative government as the basic justification. Administration at the local level – whatever the disputes about area, boundaries, and tiers of government – is still seen as administration under the choice and influence of electors, citizens and inhabitants.

Local government is essentially committee government, which is justified because elected lay members bring common sense and local knowledge to bear on the way services are administered. But committee government has had another effect. It has meant that the council's responsibility to the local electorate is diffused and difficult to grasp. Responsibility, A. Dunsire asserts, becomes an *ex post facto* accountability of committees to the council, who are then responsible to the electorate through the party system.[5] Where committees take decisions, it is difficult for the citizen to find out what is being done or to pinpoint responsibility. Although this gap is in theory filled by the political parties, there are difficulties. Problems of democratic administration, and of the role of parties, are dealt with in the next chapter.

NOTES

1. J. P. Dunbabin, 'Expectations of the New County Councils and their Realization', *The Historical Journal*, Vol. VIII, No. 3 (1965), pp. 353-79.
2. A. E. Telling, *Planning Law and Procedure*, 3rd edition (Butterworth, 1970), p. 293.
3. Bryan Keith-Lucas, *The English Local Government Franchise* (Basil Blackwell, 1952), p. 206.
4. J. G. Bulpitt, *Party Politics in English Local Government* (Longmans, 1967), pp. 102-3.
5. A. Dunsire, 'Accountability in Local Government', *Administration*, Vol. 4, No. 3 (Autumn 1956), pp. 85-7.

Chapter IV

DEMOCRATIC ADMINISTRATION

DEMOCRACY AT WORK

A local authority's internal organisation and day-to-day conduct of business is not defined in a single Act of Parliament. The main constitutional framework, the 1933 Local Government Act, has now been replaced by the 1972 Act. This now defines a local authority, its government by the whole body of members (the council), the establishment of committees, the broad duty of the officers, the amount of delegation allowed, and so on. Other Acts, relating to individual services, make certain requirements, notably the establishment of particular committees and the employment of certain chief officers.

Internal organisation is a mixture of these different statutory measures and of tradition and precedent. W. J. M. Mackenzie shows how, although set firmly in a framework of national policies and standards, the effective work of an authority depends on local factors. These fall into five broad groups: the attitude of the electorate; the quality of councillors; the quality of officers; the relations between the two; and the relations of that local authority to Westminster and Whitehall.[1] Local administration thus operates within a three-dimensional environment: the overall national framework of government; the conduct of business through members and officers; and the climate of local public opinion.

The image which the local authority presents reflects this situation. Primarily, local government is committee government, firmly constrained by the central government and conducted through a local professional public service. To the ordinary man, this may appear bureaucratic and confusing; it is difficult to see how decisions are made and officials, not councillors, may seem to dominate the service.

Democratic theorists have been concerned at the potential clash between bureaucracy and democracy. In Victorian times this fear was directed against the public official and his threat to individual liberty and self-reliance. Today, though such fears have not entirely disappeared, bureaucracy is seen as a tool to bring beneficial services to everyone, not merely to the (deserving) poor of former times. Although the Victorians believed bureaucracy was a real danger to self-government and to liberty, they also believed that this was less so at local level. Local self-government, responsible to an immediate public opinion, reduced the potential power of officials. As the modern committee system developed the belief also grew up that democratic control was made a reality through the councillors' close supervision of council work. This control was reinforced and perpetuated by the operation of *ultra vires* and district audit. The councillors, collectively, were responsible for detailed administration and could be individually surcharged if they allowed expenditure on items not expressly contained in the relevant statutes.

The view that committees made democratic control a reality was at its height up to the First World War (and perhaps romanticised in the literature for a longer period). Since the Second World War, however, renewed fears aroused by a bureaucratic Welfare State have put committees in a very different light. Committees, like Bagehot's Boards, are criticised as screens behind which the real business is conducted by professional officers. Councillors can only marginally affect what is done, either by special pleading for individual cases, or through a strict party political line on certain issues.

The idea that committees are examples of democracy at work, or alternatively are mere facades, has been influenced by the debate on the nature of policy and administration. There has been a long and unsuccessful search for an agreed definition of these terms and a means of distinguishing between them. The nature of this debate has now changed. It is no longer said that councillors (or national politicians) make policy and officers (or civil servants) carry it out. The business of government is seen as a complex political process with a diversity of aims. Traditionally, certain procedures and customs are followed, governed by the council's standing orders, past precedents and the established collaboration between members and officers. The democratic safeguard here is that the officers must know to whom they can go for decisions in awkward cases, and this should be the elected representatives sitting in committee. Public or semi-public discussion in council and committee is itself some safeguard of democratic decision-making: the public has a right to know how business is conducted as well as the outcome of particular issues.

D. N. Chester suggests that there are three main elements of local administration. First, there are the major policy decisions, including such things as development plans, the annual rate levy, or the decision to re-organise secondary education. Second, there are routine matters, where established procedures are followed and there is no political controversy. Finally, there are issues which are currently controversial. These are not necessarily questions of policy or party conflict and can centre around personalities, particularly localities, or the treatment of individual cases.[2]

Any attempt to distinguish between major policy and routine administration is misleading. The problem is that what may currently seem to be merely routine detail may in the long term add up to commitments to certain policies. This means that councillors cannot afford to ignore 'mere details' and concentrate on 'policy'. Nor can the burden of routine work be solved by calling for more delegation to officers. Detailed work, followed by policy decision, is characteristic of almost all local services and members and party groups must be involved from the beginning.

THE DEVELOPMENT OF COMMITTEES

Committee government grew out of Victorian efforts to solve the problems of urban and industrial society while retaining popular control and protecting individual liberty. Reforms were piecemeal, as each service (the poor law, the police, the health services and highways) were dealt with in turn. And, in turn, the device of the special board for each separate service, with varying degrees of central supervision and grant-aid, was established. From these separate boards have grown our modern committees, and the habit of defining what local authorities do according to distinct functions.

There were moments, however, when radical rethinking might have been attempted – the reform of the boroughs in 1835 or the establishment of the local government structure between 1885 and 1895. These were missed opportunities; not because of the English dislike of theory but because of the sheer pressure of events in a changing society. Historically, then, the reformed Poor Law of 1834 established the principle of a separate, elected Board to manage a particular service, to raise a rate and to hire paid officials. The work of the Board of Guardians was defined by parliament and under central direction and inspection. Similar specialised activities were to be found in the Improvement Commissioners who were tackling basic services in the towns.

The Municipal Corporations Act of 1835 was, by contrast, a potential alternative. It dealt with a single authority responsible to the whole community. It also allowed the establishment of committees to carry the burden of work but only one, the Watch Committee, was mandatory. The reformed corporations, however, although empowered to make by-laws for good rule and government, were not thought of, or trusted, as omnicompetent local authorities. Separate bodies for special services continued and the situation was further reinforced by the public health legislation of 1848 onwards. In the municipal boroughs themselves, the setting up of a Watch Committee, and the government's specific grants under the Police Act 1856, helped to establish the tradition of a separate committee, and a separate department, for each service.

The piecemeal approach to problems not only set the basis for future committee administration but tied this to the controversy over area. The poor law reform had produced an administratively convenient area; the other reforms did not, and local boards were fitted into the complexities of boroughs, poor law unions, and petty sessional divisions. The administrative logic was simple: define the problem and devise a solution to meet this immediate need without worrying too much if the area is suitable for the purpose.

The Highway Act 1862 is a good example of this principle. Quarter Sessions were empowered, under this Act, to combine parishes into highway districts under highway boards. Because of the anomalous definition of local public health boards in the 1858 Local Government Act, many small parishes evaded this amalgamation by adopting the Act's (permissive) powers to appoint a local health board. The Highways Act of 1863 halted this process by excluding parishes of less than 3,000 people. But the *ad hoc* tradition remained – and the Highway Act showed that a problem could still be solved by setting up a special board for a separate function, however small the area of the authority.

The public health measures did gradually help to change this situation. Although set originally in the same mould of a separate board for a single service, public health legislation gradually brought services together into a conglomerate, if not an organic, whole. By the Public Health Act of 1872, consolidated in the 1875 Act, England was divided into urban and rural sanitary districts and local administration rationalised. This process was further consolidated by the reform of local government in the 1880s and 1890s, which brought services together – and their inherited administrative traditions. In many cases the personnel – both members and officers – were absorbed and Boards re-emerged as committees. The same principles applied when a local authority took over a local trading company or promoted a private Bill to obtain parliamentary permission for a new service. Thus the *ad hoc* tradition helped to produce functional committees within multi-purpose authorities.

Functionally separate services were not all due to precedent or pragmatism. Central government was a major influence. Parliament proceeded cautiously in extending general legislation and based this on the practices of the previous Boards or of existing Private Bill powers. Governments were also conservative in their piecemeal approach and reinforced the idea of a separate committee for a separate service. In this way legal responsibility could be properly defined and located, and central supervision clarified. *Ultra vires* also played a major part. In order to show they were not exceeding their statutory powers, it was desirable to appoint a responsible committee for those particular duties. This would ensure that elected members were collectively answerable to the whole council and that their committee worked under the guidelines of standing orders.

The committee was an excellent device for allocating responsibility but the conjunction of specialisation and the *ultra vires* doctrine turned local administration into an over-cautious and detailed process. Councillors were responsible for what was done in their name; they came to believe that this meant close supervision of day-to-day business. In Victorian times they were perhaps justified in this belief: officers were not always well chosen, trained or well paid. Detailed supervision was necessary and the committee, collectively rather than as individuals, was a sensible way of achieving it.

The problem is not that the Victorians responded in this way but that their pragmatism became hardened into principles. The 1933 Local Government Act, the specialised legislation of the Welfare State after 1945, and the retention of certain obligatory standing committees by the 1972 Local Government Act have perpetuated the form and spirit of Victorian provisions. It is hard not to conclude that committees must be necessary and admirable by virtue of their survival capacity alone.

The constitutional position of committees, and their procedures, can be traced from the Municipal Corporations Acts of 1835 and 1882, and the Local Government Acts of 1888, 1933 and 1972. The major theme is a regular pattern of council meetings (at first quarterly and then at more frequent intervals) and, where a general power to appoint committees is given, the proviso that the approval of the full council is needed for all committee activities. The other main theme is that of financial procedure: the levying of the rate, the establishment and use of borough funds, the raising of loans and the payment of officers.

In 1835 the Municipal Corporations Act established the full council as the governing body with committees as subordinate and largely advisory bodies. Three factors altered the situation: the growth of functions; the trend to omnibus authorities; and the provisions for delegation contained in the public health legislation. Discretionary powers had to be given to committees if councils were not to be overwhelmed. The eventual result was that democratic accountability was in practice not that of elected council to the public but of committees to the whole council, who were in turn only periodically and indirectly responsible to the local electorate.

The 1888 Local Government Act marks an important point in this process by its definition of council/committee relations. The Act empowered county and county borough councils to regulate committees and their procedure. But while Section 82(2) repeated earlier requirements that every committee should report to the full council they were not, as they had been under the Municipal Corporations Act of 1882, automatically required to submit all their acts and proceedings. The extent and form of their report was determined by the council itself. This laid the foundation for the future high degree of independence of committees. As business increased, councils came to require less and less detailed minutes and reports.

The 1933 Local Government Act put the final seal on this change by giving councils a general power to delegate to committees. It was also reinforced by conventions which grew up as the work load increased: committee minutes accepted in council with little or no debate; committee expenditure allowed within their due allocation without further debate or ratification (up to specified amounts) and selective, and full, minutes and reports. Even wider powers are now embodied in the 1972 Act which allows delegation to officers and to sub-committees – thus ending the tradition that the delegate could not delegate, *delatus non potest delegare*.

The twentieth-century refinements of the Victorian legacy have largely been acclaimed as beneficial. The committee system, said Harold J. Laski, was one of the 'fundamental English contributions to the difficult art of self-government'. It evoked an enthusiasm which, under the leadership of chairmen who could draw together lay and official knowledge, made for real progress.[3] In recent times this enthusiasm has waned. The committee system has been criticised for its delays, secretiveness, party control, officer tyranny and rival jealousies. The orthodox rejoinder is that committees divide the work into manageable parts and ensure that elected members are collectively responsible for the council's services. In this way electors' views are not merely heard, they are represented in the making of decisions. Committees also safeguard against bureaucracy because collective rather than individual responsibility ensures against arbitrary or corrupt decisions or undue reliance on officials. This is a major defence of democratic government since committees draw in as many people as possible.

The belief that administration is made more democratic by the involvement of councillors in the whole range of council business has been extended to draw in non-elected local citizens as well. The Local Government Act of 1933 gave local authorities a general power to co-opt outsiders on to council committees (with the exception of finance). This practice is continued by the 1972 Act. Certain other Acts, in the education and welfare fields, permitted councils to include local people as additional members of committees. In all cases the majority of committee places must be filled by local council members.

Co-option is criticised, largely on the grounds that local authorities make little use of it or else choose additional members on party grounds rather than on grounds of knowledge and experience. It is not seen as undemocratic – local councils have always been able to consult with whom they choose – but too narrow and ineffective. On occasions there may also be fears that the co-opted members prevent the councillors from exercising proper control. A recent case was that of an Education Committee where, because of internal dissension between the two main parties, co-opted members had a crucial say in the selection of the committee's chairman. The situation was only finally resolved when the Minister of Education and Science intervened to allow the authority to disband and reconstitute its Education Committee. But such an *impasse* is rare.

The democratic composition of committees is not the main difficulty. The major criticism of committees is that they are, on the one hand, narrowly preoccupied with detail and short-term issues. On the other hand it is said that they are too autonomous and powerful. Some committees, such as education or social services, have executive powers conferred on them by the parent Act so that it is virtually the committee, not the council, which is the local authority for that service. The extreme case is that of the police. The 1964 Police Act makes the local police authority responsible (though giving it no powers of direction) for the service but the Watch Committee, which is composed of councillors and magistrates, remains outside the council's control.

Following the Maud Committee on Management of Local Government Report it was hoped that the dangers of autonomous committees would be removed by freeing local authorities from the statutory requirements to set up certain committees. This would enable services to be regrouped and committees streamlined and allow overall policy control and direction. These hopes were reduced by the 1970 Social Services Act which made a separate committee and chief officer mandatory and by the 1972 Local Government Act provisions for committees for Education, Social Services, National Parks, Police, Regional Planning in the children's service, and for the purposes of Superannuation.

It appeared that, in spite of the promises for more local autonomy, central governments still held to the old Whitehall view that specific statutory committees were needed to ensure that duties were actually carried out. This view has support in some professional fields also; the original intention of the Local Government Bill to remove the requirement for a specific committee for Education was defeated by protests from educationalists and administrators.

COMMITTEE MEMBERS, CHAIRMEN AND OFFICERS

The increasing complexity of local administration is changing the traditional roles of councillors and officers. H. Hugh Heclo states that, to a great extent, the old position is reversed so that the official is the policy-maker, and the councillor carries out routine administration in committee.[4] Alan P. Brier has stressed the need to recognise that local politics and administration depend on traditions of conflict or co-operation between different groups and interests which in turn stem from the socio-economic life of the area.[5] Councillors' attitudes also affect the way that committees work, and this, and their alleged deficiencies, have been fiercely debated in recent years. Maud noted that attitudes and competence were as important as the legal framework. Local administration depended on the attitudes of members, the traditions of local government generally and of each area in particular.[6]

In K. C. Wheare's well-known terms, committees are judged by their competence and relevance. That is, they must be duly constituted according to the council's rules and have the power to decide the questions for which they were set up, i.e. they should not be screens for decisions taken elsewhere. The committee member must be competent, but he should also have the essential additional qualities of a questioning outlook, interest in the work and an ability to change his mind if need be.[7] The fact that he has a particular interest or point of view will not detract from democratic administration as long as this interest is well known and, if financial, is safeguarded by known rules.

Committee and council decision-making is, as the 1933 and now the 1972 Local Government Act (Schedule 12, Part VI, 39) emphasise, a collective and not an individual responsibility. All acts of a local authority 'shall be done and decided by a majority of the members of the local authority present and voting thereon at a meeting of the local authority'. Though decision-making is delegated to committees to a substantial degree, the collective principle permeates the work of the authority. Decision-making is also collective in another sense since, with rare exceptions, committees are made up of all shades of opinion on the council.

Committee membership depends on such things as the size of the council and the number of committees and on the political balance, the seniority of members, and individual preferences. Normally, a local authority will have a special Selection Committee to determine committee membership and again, where party politics is a dominant force then party patronage and pre-selection will play a large part in this process.

Party patronage is also an important influence on the selection of chairmen, though committees generally enjoy the right of electing their own chairmen. It is usual for an individual to be chairman of only one committee, particularly in the larger authorities. And council standing orders lay down how long he may remain as chairman, though usually there are provisions for re-appointment. The committee chairman is an influential figure: leader and spokesman, co-ordinator, and, with his officers and members, a decision-maker. This eminence stems from his primary function of conducting orderly business and controlling the agenda but it is enhanced by the fact that, in the eyes of the public and his colleagues, the committee is 'his' committee. Constitutionally, decisions are made collectively by committees and council. In practice, chairmen and officers play a leading role in a complex political process dominated by party, faction and personality.

H. V. Wiseman has shown how this process works in a large city. Many members like to keep in touch with details, even where officials could appropriately deal with such matters. Chairmen and party leaders, for their part, have a forum for discussion and collective direction of council work through the party group. But this too has its traditions, rules and conventions, and it is by no means the case that chairmen can be remote or dictatorial.[8]

If the chairman is both leader and co-ordinator of his committee's work then the committee member has to be equally versatile. In local government, policy and minute detail are both dealt with in the same committee process. This gives rise to the explanation that the councillor's job is mainly supervisory: to see that services are administered justly and fairly as well as efficiently. Others would deny that the councillor is, in this way, ensuring democratic administration. Instead, he is allowing officers to make policy while he administers. The only way in which this can be remedied is to remove policy-making to a central 'cabinet' while backbench councillors fill in a more advisory and ombudsman role. Unfortunately, there is little evidence that most councillors wish to spend all their time on policy. The Maud Committee on Management of Local Government Report clearly shows that councillors gain most satisfaction from their detailed committee work because they feel that, in this way, they are helping to provide people with real benefits and helping to solve concrete problems.

COMMITTEES AS POLICY BODIES

Committee government is also a source of policy. This process depends on the existence of parties and of an overall 'cabinet'. Such a policy committee may be a party group or some smaller body – such as a committee of chairmen – within it. Alternatively, the policy body may be an official committee of the council. The officially recognised policy committee, as opposed to the informal party group, is now widely welcomed. It allows policy-making to operate with the benefit of full professional advice. But there are difficulties. Committees still continue to make policy through their own detailed work: if they are prevented from doing this they may become impotent or irresponsible. They may avoid the major questions and the attention to detail may increase, not decrease. The policy committee may also find that it is reduced to a buffer between conflicting committees rather than a source of new ideas.

The use of the policy committee also raises questions of relations between committees and the full council. The Maud Report advocated a management board, acting as a policy committee and standing between (advisory only) committees and the full council. Local authorities rejected this in favour of policy committees set over (executive) committees. But the effectiveness of committees depends on their powers, and on their relations with the full council. The adequacy of a committee's authority depends on the council's own powers and this in turn is dependent on central/local relations. If councils have no real discretion then committees lack genuine authority and deteriorate into mere advisors, through the council, of central government. The ineffectiveness of committees may thus stem from too much central control.

The opposite danger is that, since councils give committees a great deal of delegated power, what emerges is not committee administration but government by virtually *ad hoc* bodies. Their real accountability is then to the local party group and to the central government for the standard of its services, not to the council or to local citizens as such.

The effective performance of committees must also be judged in terms of their relations with officials. The officials' expertise is basic to good administration, but they must also have an active belief in government by discussion and in the need for laymen as well as for specialists. This can be endangered by the experts' claim that certain issues are purely 'technical' or 'administrative' and that they have the sole right to take such decisions. In the course of their work officials become very committed to their own specialisations and standards so that actions may become inevitable and leave too little room for alternative choices.

Councillors too may become over-committed as a result of their claim to exclusively relevant knowledge. Commitment plays a valuable part in decision-making but it can lead to a resentment of criticism and to the use of committees as screens against adverse publicity.

The call for streamlining and separate policy-making also tends to overlook the impact of party traditions and the way that this varies from place to place. How committees operate, and where policy is finally decided, depends on the extent of party politics. We have already noted that policy-making is incremental, that is, it builds up from day-to-day decisions and precedents. But it is also political in the broadest sense, that is, it depends on the conflicts and alliances within the council. Where a council is divided on strict party lines then policy-making takes place within a definite framework. This is made up of the majority party's programme, its control of patronage including all the key committee posts, its discipline, and its use of formal co-ordinating bodies such as a central policy committee or an informal caucus group.

Where the caucus operates it is often criticised as an undemocratic feature of local government. The party caucus, which local council officers may not attend and advise, can include local city or constituency party members. These outsiders, while having no vote, do open up the possibility of influence from non-council sources. Both main parties deny this, arguing that it keeps the council members sensitive to electoral opinion.

The importance of party control and controversy should be seen in perspective. English local government operates in an atmosphere of relatively low public interest and party conflict is normally muted. As a result council work is not dominated by questions of ideology or party principle but by administrative politics. That is, the arguments are about methods, procedures, standards of service and the application of rules and precedents to individual cases. Any controversy is dealt with around the committee table, not in public. Partly this is due to the pre-eminence of the officers and their professional autonomy but it is also due, as Michael J. Hill notes, to their attitude to party dogma and controversy.

Officers are much closer to the elected laymen than their Whitehall counterparts and feel that public political conflict threatens their position and their advice. Political conflict and compromise still exists, dominated by the councillor's defence of his constituents' interests and anticipation of voting reactions. This is not so important, however, as the dominant role of the official who has the initiative in administrative bargaining and also consults with a wide variety of interests.[9]

Local officers, particularly chief officers, are in touch with a broad spectrum of local opinion and are, as would be expected, broadly reflective of the professional and middle classes to which they belong. Michael Hill suggests that there may be a potential danger in this situation. Leading officers, used to consulting informally with local elites, believe that they are behaving quite properly and do not see that they are consulting a minority opinion. In a similar way they may regard councillors as one among many general sources of public opinion rather than as the single voice of the public will. A few senior councillors, by contrast, are drawn into the officers' world; they are, as Michael Lee showed over a decade ago, in effect co-opted as a kind of administrator into official decision-making.[10] This situation is particularly evident where party political divisions are narrow or absent.

The administrative style of politics is reinforced by the fact that councillors prefer to concentrate on routine rather than key issues. This attitude will not be changed by a mere reduction in this burden of routine since these councillors are unlikely to transfer their interest to policy making. An interest in policy-making comes, for the majority of councillors, when party conflict dominates council work.

PROFESSIONALS AND PROFESSIONALISM

In local government issues come forward for decision from central government, individual councillors and party groups, officers, and through public demands and grievances. But the majority of issues come from officials and this gives a network of close contacts between officers, committees and members which is unique to local government.

The question of the nature of the professional's role in decision making centres on his control of information. The calibre of committee deliberations depends on those officers and chairmen who control the flow of information. Obviously, the crucial cases are those where the information itself is highly technical. Two possible avenues are open to the officer (assuming that he does not abuse this particular situation). One is to try to show the committee what the consequences of action will be. Or – and the two are closely linked – alternatives are put to the committee in such a way that genuine choices are open to members.

The Bains report, on management and structure in the new local authorities, recognised the need for members to be kept fully informed. There was some evidence that officers withheld information from opposition members. Other examples, however, showed that access to information differed according to attitudes, with some councillors wanting a strict 'either/or' government versus opposition situation.[11]

The officers' dominance of the channels of communication may be challenged, to varying degrees, by the cohesion of party machinery. Nevertheless, his professional control of information is a powerful base of his influence. The rise of this professional eminence stems from the historical development of the local government service. The growth of paid employment in the reformed boroughs after 1835 was influenced by the developments in the poor law and in public health and made specialised professional officers the core of higher administration. This set the tone for the rest of the service since in late Victorian England there was a great upsurge of professional associations which all aimed to set standards, control qualifications and entry, and influence salaries and conditions of service.

It has been suggested that the degree of professionalism in local government has been a mixed blessing. At best it has produced highly competent and professional staff: the Hadow Report of 1934 commented on the rising standards of service which the associations had encouraged. But it has also resulted in the employment of specialists who have to pick up the art of administration, unaided, during their professional career. This is now changing as administration and 'management' are recognised as relevant professional skills.

A different kind of criticism is that professional values, which may in fact be inexplicable to outsiders, are not seen as needing any justification. When this is combined with the inertia of bureaucratic routine – once techniques are developed to deal with a problem it is hard to stop – there is a real danger that professionals may become blinded by their own skill. This is why feedback from lay committees is vital and why professionals must be able to justify their technical advice.

The influence of professional values on administration does not, however, operate in a monolithic way. Just as there is a wide range of local authority services so there is also great diversity in what officers do. An obvious distinction, for example, is between services which are more consumer-orientated (personal social services, education) and those which give priority to technical needs (roads, financial budgeting). These differences also affect the officers' expectations that councillors will offer knowledgeable and relevant comments.

Perhaps the most controversial area of professionalism is town planning. Planners are accused, variously, of being secretive, dilatory, inflexible and over-committed to techniques. Democratic procedures designed to protect both the individual and the community (through the publication of plans, public inquiries and so on) are lengthy and confusing. The faults should not all be laid at the doors of professionalism: democratic control by elected members remains the main, and seemingly intractable, problem.

THE SEARCH FOR EFFICIENCY

Over the last decade the search for efficiency in local authority administration has taken several different approaches. This section deals with four of the main problems: the use of manpower; aids to management; the debate on management reform from Maud to Bains; and the concern with centralised policy making.

(i) *The use of manpower*
The best use of scarce manpower is a central part of efficient administration. Two main factors stand out. One is the argument, elucidated in the Mallaby Report of 1967, that skilled staff are in short supply and local authorities suffer harmful shortages. The other dominant

factor is the view that new skills are rapidly being demanded as governmental services expand. The claim that there is a manpower crisis is a familiar one. So too are the remedies. The Mallaby Committee recommendations, like its predecessors, were set firmly within traditional skills (even the call for chief executives with greater administrative experience was to be found in the Hadow Report of 1934). The Mallaby Report rejected a single, national local government service and recommended instead a Central Staffing Organisation with responsibilities for publicity and the oversight of training needs. The body was never established but the Local Government Training Board now fulfils these tasks to some extent.

The Local Government Training Board, a voluntary body set up by the Local Authority Associations and the GLC in 1967, paralleled the statutory Training Boards established for certain sectors of industry by the 1964 Labour Government. The LGTB operates on a financial basis of raising levies from member authorities and distributing grants for training purposes. It incorporates the work of the old Local Government Examinations Board, established in 1946 by the Local Authority Associations. With the re-organisation of industrial training introduced by the Conservative government in 1972, and the demise of the levy/grant system for the industrial boards, the future of the LGTB is problematic. Re-organisation of local government may impel a return to local authority responsibility and the end of the voluntary levy and grant system, though the need for a central body to oversee and advise on manpower and training seems as necessary as ever.

(ii) *Aids to management*
Management aids and services have grown from the use of the computer in the early 1960s, aided by the collaborative efforts of local authorities. The Local Government Computer Committee was transformed in 1967 to the Local Authorities Management Services and Computer Committee, LAMSAC, to provide a comprehensive national advisory service. LAMSAC also undertakes research in such areas as job evaluation, clerical work measurements, and the preparation of productivity agreements. Cost-benefit analysis, organisation and methods, operational research, strategic path analysis, are all now familiar tools which financial and planning experts in local government are using – and with which administrators must be familiar. But they are not mere tools: they reinforce centralisation within a local authority and use of the 'team approach'.

PPBS has a similar effect. PPBS – planning, programming, budgeting systems – is a means of allocating resources through a series of 'programmes' or plans. PPB must relate the budgetary process (for the coming financial year) with the planning process (normally over five years) and then analyse the outcome of the programmes. Its main aim is to relate resources to problems, not to committees, and it makes for greater centralisation since it necessarily cuts across existing boundaries and demands an overall directing body.

By 1971 some forty of the larger local authorities, including the GLC, were looking at PPB. But the extensive use of this approach is problematic. Smaller authorities think that it is not for them, and many councillors undoubtedly also fear that there is again a tendency to shift decision making from members to officers.

(iii) *The management debate from Maud to Bains*
The democratic dilemma in local administration is to strike a balance between efficiency and the interests of the individual. The Maud Committee on Management of Local Government showed that the debate on efficiency is strongly influenced by councillors' beliefs that it is more *democratic* for them to decide cases individually than to establish general policy rules for officers to pursue.[12] However, as the Maud research suggests, this belief may be more populist than democratic – a fear of what neighbours may say rather than of defeat in local elections – so that it is individual and group pressures which affect a councillor's actions rather than democratic accountability.

The councillor's concern with detail may also stem from the difficulties he has in understanding complex issues and deciding policy based upon them. These may be realistic, not obscurantist, attitudes since councillors have no choice but to trust their officials. Committee members are also ill-equipped to chase the progress of issues or supervise the machinery. It is difficult to dismiss officers or monitor what they do. This difficulty may, in some authorities, be overcome by the power and status of individual chairmen – but with the paradoxical outcome that this then denies the 'democratic' nature of committee deliberation in which all members are equal and decisions are made collectively.

The attitudes and experience of officers also affect the search for efficiency. Departments, like committees, are grouped around the professional skills of officers. Particular technical and administrative jobs have to be done, and will be tackled in much the same manner as always, whatever new committee structures or management techniques are introduced. In fact, in spite of these constraints, officers have in general welcomed the introduction of new aids and services.

Finally, there are the expectations and attitudes of the public itself. Councillors may not be driven to seek for new methods if in fact their constituents care little about policy but regard the local authority as a kind of consumer body to help with individual problems. Such constituents, says R. J. Buxton, see councillors as 'oilers of the wheels of administration' rather than policy-makers.[13]

The search for efficiency has centred on the twin problems of co-ordination and policy planning. Co-ordination has, traditionally, been carried out by the council itself, by horizontal senior committees such as Finance, by the estimates and budgetary process, by party control, and by informal working groups of officers. But in recent years local authorities have felt the need to go further in their search for comprehensive administration, and have considered the advantages of a specific co-ordinating committee.

The Maud Report suggestion for a co-ordinating body, the management board made up of representatives of all parties on the council, did not find favour in the local government world. It demoted functional committees, responsible for day-to-day running of services, to the status of advisory bodies whose deliberations could only be channelled to the full council through the management board. Two years later the Redcliffe-Maud Royal Commission on Local Government in England proposed that service committees would be the main initiators of policy, but there should also be a central committee to co-ordinate policy and overall planning.

Co-ordination should not be seen, however, as a goal in itself. The need for co-ordination arises, first of all, when new or expanded services are being planned and priorities determined. Co-ordination is important in a second way. This is in the day-to-day running of services and in the implementation of plans. Although policy co-ordination currently excites greatest attention, the second need, for everyday collaboration, is probably harder to achieve. Forward planning is exciting: people come together willingly to set up new ventures or, just as eagerly, to protect their interests. But everyday co-operation involves professional and committee jealousies and suffers from the sheer size and variety of different parts of the administration. Making sure the services fit together for the benefit of the public may thus swing between the extreme of informal contacts on the one hand, to rigid formal procedures on the other.

The integrated, co-ordinated approach continued when, in May 1971, the then Secretary of State for the Environment (Mr Peter Walker) appointed, jointly with the Local Authority Associations, a Study Group on management structures. The Group consisted of a steering committee under Sir Frank Marshall, chairman of the AMC, and a Working Group chaired by Mr M. A. Bains, Clerk of Kent County Council. The Report of the Group (the Bains Report) was published in September 1972.

The Bains Report advocated a central policy and resources committee (matched by a management team at officer level) to co-ordinate policy review with control of finance, manpower and land. Bains denied that this was a powerful central committee which reduced the influence of ordinary councillors. Councillors would sit on the 'resources sub-committees' of the central body and this militated against frustrated backbenchers and charges of over-centralised power. The Report also suggested that a 'Performance Review Sub-Committee' would act as an independent watchdog, while the programme committees would be regular monitors of their own programmes.[14] Bains, like Maud, favoured minority party representation on the Policy and Resources Committee even though recognising that this might place it in a subordinate position to the party caucus. The 'apolitical' nature of Bains was a major weakness since it implied that the management process could be divorced from party politics.

Bains' other suggestions were more helpful. It argued that the committee structure should be based on a 'programme' concept with committees serviced by several departments. These would be implemented by joint working groups and informal councillor groups. This combination of the traditional 'vertical' structure and the 'horizontal' working group (known as the matrix form of organisation) is, Bains suggested, a flexible, adaptive and multi-disciplinary approach. Royston Greenwood and J. D. Stewart have claimed, however, that the co-operative matrix organisation faces strong centrifugal forces from professionalism and professionally orientated departments.[15]

Bains was advisory, not mandatory. It was weak, therefore, in delimiting roles and functions, particularly that of the local authority's Chief Officer vis-à-vis other chief officers. The Chief Officer was, it suggested, primarily the leader of a management team and the local authority's chief advisor but his position could not be formalised: 'There is much to be said for allowing the man himself to develop his own interpretation of the job within a fairly broad framework.'[16]

Bains did, however, stress once more the need for a total 'community' approach. This was sensible, but co-operation of this kind was, and is, difficult. It was also hampered by the actual reform of local services, since the government re-organised these on a fourfold basis: county and county district authorities, area health boards and regional water authorities. The 'community' approach was also problematic because of the uncertainties surrounding the county and district agency arrangements. Bains recommended that there should be (in addition to the agency agreements) joint (advisory) committees of county and district members for each district to co-ordinate functions and policies. At county level there would also be a joint committee of leading policy and resources committee members from the county and from each district. This would be a basis on which to build joint planning; it would meet two or three times a year.[17]

Such procedures appear necessary to allow for co-operation but they can be time-consuming and costly and their exact place in the new agency arrangement was unclear. They cast serious doubts on the wisdom and practicality of local government reforms which appeared to be workable only on the basis of such elaborate informal arrangements.

(iv) *The concern with centralised policy-making*

In recent years there has been a growing interest in 'corporate management' or 'corporate planning' which cuts across the old divisions between services and committees and takes an overall approach with some kind of central policy body to control current work and plan for the future. Two themes are central. On the one hand, policy planning and corporate management seek efficient use of resources and manpower, bringing local officials into closer collaboration with each other. On the other hand, J. K. Friend and W. N. Jessop show how democratic decision-making must allow councillors real choices between alternatives presented to them in intelligent and intelligible ways.[18] At present councillors find it difficult to get clear guidance on complex issues and so tend to refer problems back to officers on the one hand or to the leaders of majority party groups on the other. That is, choices are either sidestepped or dealt with in wider party political terms. If a central policy committee is to solve this situation then it must have a positive, initiating role and not be merely an advisory body.

Professor Stewart stresses a similar need for the overall planning of priorities within a corporate team approach led by a chief executive, and the need for effective information feedback and the monitoring of performance. Setting objectives and analysing alternatives are the core of local authority policy planning. And this in turn means a central policy planning unit responsible to a chief officers group.[19] Stewart is thus advocating a policy committee which does more than merely control the capital budget. It must be responsible for overall policy and supported by a corporate management team of officers. Any changes in the committee structure are subsidiary to the need to develop the interdisciplinary team approach. He recognises that any tools to generate alternatives, such as the PPB system, must fit into the political process. The councillors' desire to control the process is legitimate and they must have better information and methods of evaluating what management achieves.

But there are problems which must be recognised when calls for more integrated services, and centralised policy control, are made. The call for the integration of physical and social services, for example, may be misleading in relation to what local authorities actually do. There is the danger that the provision of social services is confused with the planning of the social environment and integration becomes an end in itself. And the use of policy planning approaches may bring fears of greater central power in council work and of domination by officers. Moreover, the search for effective decision-making does not take place in a political vacuum. It has been argued, for example, that Labour councillors may distrust managerial changes which may threaten lay control, while Conservative councillors may be more likely to press for such changes in the name of efficiency. Conservatives, campaigning against 'extravagance', have been impressed with the managerial revolution in business and commerce and wish to see it imported into local government.

THE RESPONSE FROM LOCAL AUTHORITIES

The ideas and the new approaches all influenced the ways in which local authorities organised their internal affairs. There appears to have been a general consensus that the Maud Committee on Management of Local Government was right to argue that the whole council is not capable of acting as a managerial body, even though the use of a smaller unit means a departure from the principle that all members must be involved in decision-making. Most local authorities, however, have up to now followed the line of the Wheatley dissent to Maud which favoured retaining standing committees and saw the Management Board as a central policy committee. The Maud and Mallaby ideas of the Town Clerk as the chief executive officer have gained ground in local government.

Reform of the structure has also impinged on the approach to new methods. Alan Norton shows that, after the Black County reorganisations of the mid-1960s, there was a slow adaptation to the new scale of business. Paradoxically, total committee manhours decreased while individual committee meetings became long and exhausting. Significantly, councillors in the new larger authorities needed guidance on how to exercise control through greater delegation, removal of individual grievance items from committees, and concentration on key decisions.[20]

Local authorities are also experimenting with management teams, and with policy committees. There are various kinds of Chief Officer Groups, and some authorities have grouped council departments under directorates of officers working in conjunction with a policy committee. By 1972 Greenwood et al. estimated that at least twenty county councils, thirty-five county boroughs and eighteen London Boroughs had policy committees.[21] The counties favoured a multi-party composition for the policy committee but it seems likely that, in future, the one-party policy committee will predominate since it has the advantage of linking policy to political co-ordination. A form of central policy body seems inevitable, though councils are unlikely to replace executive committees entirely since they reject a system which would relegate some councillors to 'back-bench' advisory positions. A resulting problem has been that the central policy body is merely an additional layer on top of existing committees. If, in addition, it is in fact the old finance committee writ large then its initiatory function may be very small.

A more encouraging sign is the substantial reduction in the number of committees; ten to fifteen is now the normal complement, though the device of additional working parties and working groups is still widely used. The reduction in the number of committees has occurred, as Greenwood et al. show, regardless of the size of the town.[22] The common aim seems to have been to retain committees as executive bodies, but with less involvement in routine detail, with an extended committee cycle and fewer meetings. County councils have made similar changes, though not quite on the same scale, and Greenwood et al. demonstrate that they continue to rely on the traditional use of overlapping committee memberships, rather than policy committees, as the integrating force.[23]

Reduction in the numbers and size of committees will not completely transform local administration. Councillors tend to be highly satisfied with their existing roles and fear changes which may threaten their contact with everyday issues. Councils have, in consequence, been cautious in extending delegated powers to officers, and in regrouping departmental responsibilities. This may now change as the 1972 Local Government Act allows wider powers of delegation

to committees, sub-committees and officers. Wider delegation may
lead to potentially undesirable fragmentation, but this is counter-
acted by the increasing role of the chief officer as co-ordinator of
policy and planning. The chief executive officer, leading a management team of chief officers, has emerged in the big county boroughs
and London boroughs, and to a lesser extent in the county councils.
The management teams, of five to eight people, are mostly concerned
with capital programmes and with co-ordination.

There is still disquiet, however, that the new methods have had a
strong centralising effect at a time when, outside the council, there
are increasing demands for greater decentralisation and for more
popular control. These demands are potentially as strong as those for
efficiency. The advocates of new management structures do not
concede that their proposals may run counter to the need for
democratic administration. As Jeffrey Stanyer warns, however,
councillors cannot be selected to fill a set of previously prescribed
managerial roles.[24] Councillors are nominated and elected by a party
political system within a local social structure and their abilities will
reflect these factors, not the needs of 'rational' management. The
position of elected representatives makes the application of
management ideas to local government very difficult and a better
solution is to fit the job to the councillor and to his values and perceptions.

Stanyer's stimulating argument is a necessary warning but his
definition of management may be too narrowly conceived. The
management of a local authority demands the combined co-operative
action of councillors and officers and in this broad sense, Peter Self
rejoined, councillors are automatically managers.[25] Their managerial
role is not separate from, but necessarily tied to, their political role.
Councillors approach these questions from a variety of standpoints.
Some see their role as watchdog for the community, others as
managers and policy-makers, yet others as solving individual
problems. Given this variety, the 'management' demands for effective
leadership appear to be well met, especially within larger authorities.
Peter Self also argues that, where the trend is to larger local authorities and to managerial roles, there is an equal need for functional or
consumer representation at the more local area level.[26]

CORRUPTION – A FOOTNOTE

The Local Government Act 1972 (sections 94-98), provides that a
councillor with a direct or indirect pecuniary interest must declare it

D

and must not speak or vote on any question touching on that interest. The Minister can grant dispensations and, since 1967, a general dispensation enables council tenants to take full part in discussion of general housing policy. Section 117 of the 1972 Act covers the pecuniary interests of officers, and debars them from accepting fees or rewards. One difficulty with this situation is that the law does not insist on the disclosure of a councillor's pecuniary interest unless he is present when a matter in which he has such an interest is under discussion. He may, if he chooses, make a general declaration under s. 96 of the 1972 Act but this is not compulsory. The main problems arise from councillors' access to information of value to developers and contractors. This is not itself illegal, though, as D. E. Regan and A. J. A. Morris point out, it may be thought to be against the general or community interest. There also appears to be a small, but persistent, number of illegal expenditure irregularities by officers.[27]

But doubts still arise in planning: in 1972 Lord Henley, the chairman of the Council for the Protection of Rural England warned of a possible growth in 'systematic corruption' in local planning decisions[28] and the membership of local planning committees continues to give rise to some disquiet. In the last two or three years the number of convictions of councillors and officers for corruption offences, mainly in connection with the placing of contracts and in planning, have increased.

Greater publicity is needed (however much councils may say this would be inimical to planning decisions) so that public confidence can be reassured. There have been suggestions for a code of conduct for councillors by which they would declare their interests and a register of these would be kept for inspection by the press or the public. But the risk of conflicting interests in council work is almost unavoidable and it is difficult to draw a hard line, especially if a strictly enforced code would drive out valuable members.

In the summer of 1973 *The Times* published the results of a survey which it had commissioned into the public's attitudes towards local councils and councillors. A high proportion (some 80 per cent of those questioned) would like to see all committees and meetings open to the press and radio and also favoured the idea of a register of councillors' financial and business interests. But a majority still believed that major planning decisions should remain the responsibility of local authorities. The survey showed that people's views on the financial integrity of councillors were ambivalent. While four out of ten voters had doubts about councillors' honesty, two out of every three agreed with the view that 'most local councillors are honest and responsible people' and they also felt that councillors tackled local problems adequately.[29]

On the same day *The Times* devoted its first leader, entitled 'Where There Is No Trust' to the subject and called for a standing tribunal or commission to examine the problem. This gave rise to a lengthy, and heated, debate in the paper's correspondence columns, including vigorous rejoinders from both the Chairman of the Association of Municipal Corporations and the Chairman of the County Councils Association. Correspondents accused the mass media of exaggeration and distortion.

English local government is both free, to a very large extent, from dishonesty and corruption and it is believed to be so by the majority of local people. Doubts and difficulties exist in any system and though a register of councillors' interest would help, the system must operate on trust and confidence. Publicity continues to be essential.

DEMOCRATIC ADMINISTRATION?

The question of who is responsible for decisions, and in what ways, is still paramount but the simple dichotomy between elected policy-makers and official executors is no longer believed to be a *sine qua non* of true democracy. At the same time there has been a concern over the qualities which both elected members and officers should possess. The idea has grown up that, since officials are not 'mere tools', then it is desirable for them to be sensitive and outward looking rather than a remote priestly caste. The sensitivity and responsiveness of officials is, however, less of a problem than their accountability. The former confidence in the power of elected representatives and committees has been eroded. Critics argue that officials are irresponsible: committees cannot control them in any real sense. The need for technical expertise, and the effects of modern management practice, make the layman's comments either superficial or irrelevant.

Today, it is argued, the main way in which officials can be held responsible is through the non-legal, conventional operation of professional standards. The officer is accountable to his fellow officers within the authority and to the body of knowledge and standards set by his profession as a whole. The officer remains legally accountable to his council and works within the priorities set by it and by the committees. His own views about for what and to whom he is responsible are equally important. In day-to-day administration, therefore, there is a great reliance on the officers' values, their standards of professional responsibility and their loyalty to the council and its services. For the most part, of course, this works well. But the problem is that elected members are ill-equipped, because of the part-time unpaid nature of the work and the inadequacies of the committee system, to either change or control this situation.

These two criticisms – that officials are, strictly speaking, irresponsible, and that the inadequacies of committee administration prevent democratic control – have been countered by radical solutions. Officials must be made more responsible by allowing greater discussion of their work in public; by making participation a reality; and by enforcing better remedies both through the courts and through an extension of the Ombudsman system. If officers had to provide more public information, defend their professional decisions and consult more often with individuals and groups then they would be, it is claimed, more accountable to local citizens. If necessary, new legislation should define the officer's responsibilities more closely and this could also be achieved by a stricter use of a local council's standing orders.

The other set of remedies calls for a dramatically recast committee system. Administration must be streamlined and the work of committees, and departments, more effectively co-ordinated. Policy, planning and control must be given prime place. Councillors must be adequately rewarded for their work, even if a full salary is thought inappropriate, and they must be given greatly enhanced supporting and information services.

There are difficulties with both sets of remedies. More citizen access, information and participation are desirable but they do not solve the question of democratic control and accountability. If this is sought through more formal control of officials, either by the local council or the courts, then there are dangers of delays and of over-caution. The second set of solutions – for a more streamlined committee system – overlooks an important aspect of council work. Policy is not a matter of grand theory but grows out of day-to-day problems and issues. Councillors enjoy this attention to the particular and the immediate and their experience of such work is part of the development of policy.

Council work is continually evolving to meet criticisms and new demands. In the last twenty-five years allegations of bureaucracy have been countered by the recognition that administration works in practice through mutual trust and confidence, and the influence of high values and standards, rather than by formal, rigid controls. The safeguards are the democratic values of fairness, openness and responsiveness and the stress on professional (but humane) competence. These values are not always met in full but their importance is now recognised alongside more formal provisions for accountable administration.

There is still a need for vigilance, however, over the potential clash between bureaucracy and representative democracy. The argument is about power – who has what, when, and how – and its distribution. Bureaucracy concentrates power in the hands of relatively few experts while representative democracy aims to dispense power (however imperfectly) among elected representatives, voters and organised opinion. In modern times, it is argued, the balance has slipped too far in favour of the administrators and power is concentrated in too few hands. It must be remedied by giving more power back to the people, locally organised in neighbourhood and other groups, so that they can then run certain local services for themselves. Then they will not need the bureaucrats. Radical solutions of this kind have not been adopted but elements of the thinking, and the practice, are already influencing local administration.

The real question is, however, that of democratic (and therefore political) control. Democratic administration as such has little to say about end results (all citizens may, for example, suffer equally from the democratic application of a low level of service). Value judgements have to be made about the desirability of different courses of action and then political priorities must be set out and defended. Modern administration is compatible with democratic values but only if the distribution of services and the redress of citizens' grievances are seen as part of one political process rather than as policy versus administration.

In practice, policy and administration are reflected in the inter-locking of the democratic and administrative elements. The cycle of elections, the work of councillors, and the feedback of local public opinion are intimately related to the management process. The two cannot be divorced. Any attempts to change the internal working of a local authority should not, therefore, replace the old policy/administration fallacy with a new democracy/management division in which 'democracy' is met by defining it as the mere existence of councillors in committee.

Local services affect the daily lives and freedoms of ordinary people. Political sensitivity must, therefore, surround actual administration. This calls for the continual – if not necessarily detailed – involvement of councillors and makes it difficult to insist that they should have purely 'policy' roles or sit on merely 'advisory' committees.

It is equally mistaken to assume that, because politics, policy and administration are one process, the existing committee and departmental structures are adequately democratic. Current reforms reflect the need to harmonise democratic discussion and debate with the demands of management by bringing people together into working groups and management teams which cut across the committee structure at both member and officer level.

The general consensus seems to be that reforms are necessary but that the underlying principle – committee discussion followed by decision, under the overall control of council and party – is still valid. The extent to which administration is becoming more or less democratic is not only a question of structures, procedures and values. To a significant degree it can also be judged by the democratic criteria of equality and justice and it is to this problem that we now turn.

NOTES

1. W. J. M. Mackenzie, 'The Conventions of Local Government', *Public Administration*, Vol. 29 (Winter 1951), p. 345.
2. D. N. Chester, 'Local Democracy and the Internal Organisation of Local Authorities', *Public Administration*, Vol. 46 (Autumn 1968), pp. 287-91.
3. Harold J. Laski (ed.), *A Century of Municipal Progress, 1835-1935* (Allen and Unwin, 1935), pp. 91-7.
4. H. Hugh Heclo, 'The Councillor's Job', *Public Administration*, Vol. 47 (Spring 1969), p. 188.
5. Alan P. Brier, 'The Decision Process in Local Government: a case study of fluoridation in Hull', *Public Administration*, Vol. 48 (Summer 1970), p. 153.
6. Committee on Management of Local Government, *Report* (1967), para. 92.
7. K. C. Wheare, *Government By Committee* (Clarendon Press, 1955), p. 23.
8. H. Victor Wiseman, *Local Government at Work* (Routledge & Kegan Paul, 1967), pp. 52-3 and pp. 92-7.
9. Michael J. Hill, *The Sociology of Public Administration* (Weidenfeld & Nicholson, 1972), pp. 215-23.
10. J. M. Lee, *Social Leaders and Public Persons* (Clarendon Press, 1963), pp. 190-1 and p. 211.
11. 'The New Local Authorities: management and structure', Department of the Environment Local Authority Association Study Group, *Report* (1972), pp. 11-12.
12. 'Local Government Administration in England and Wales', Committee on Management of Local Government, Vol. 5 (1967), Ch. 9, para. 41.
13. R. J. Buxton, *Local Government* (Penguin, 1970), p. 83.
14. The Bains *Report, op. cit.,* pp. 25-26.
15. Royston Greenwood and J. D. Stewart, 'Corporate Planning and Management Organisation', *Local Government Studies*, Vol. 3, Oct. 1972, p. 37.
16. The Bains *Report, op. cit.,* p. 41.
17. The Bains *Report, op. cit.,* pp. 93-4.

18. J. K. Friend and W. N. Jessop, *Local Government and Strategic Choice* (Tavistock Publications, 1969), p. xix.
19. J. D. Stewart, *Management in Local Government: a viewpoint* (Charles Knight, 1971), pp. 64-5 and pp. 168-71.
20. Alan Norton, 'Lessons from Reorganisation in the 1960s: extended notes on a research project, Part 1', *Local Government Studies*, Vol. 2 (October 1972), p. 55.
21. R. Greenwood, J. D. Stewart and A. D. Smith, 'The Policy Committee in English Local Government', *Public Administration*, Vol. 50 (Summer 1972), pp. 162-6.
22. R. Greenwood, A. L. Norton and J. D. Stewart, 'Recent changes in the internal organisation of County Boroughs: Part 1, Committees', *Public Administration*, Vol. 47 (Summer 1969), pp. 161-4.
23. R. Greenwood, A. L. Norton and J. D. Stewart, 'Recent Reforms in Management Structure of Local Authorities – the County Councils', *Occasional Paper 3, Series A* (Inlogov, 1969), pp. 32-6.
24. Jeffrey Stanyer, 'Elected Representatives and Management in Local Government: a case of applied sociology and applied economics', *Public Administration*, Vol. 49 (Spring 1971), p. 85.
25. Peter Self, 'Elected Representatives and Management in Local Government: an alternative analysis', *Public Administration*, Vol. 49 (Autumn 1971), p. 271.
26. Peter Self, *op. cit.*, p. 277.
27. D. E. Regan and A. J. A. Morris, 'Local Government Corruption and Public Confidence', *Public Law* (1969), pp. 139-40.
28. Lord Henley, letter to *The Times* (10 March 1972).
29. 'Public Want Measures to End Council Corruption' (*The Times*, 6 August 1973) and 'Where There Is No Trust' (*The Times*, 6 August 1973).

Chapter V

EQUALITY

THE IDEAL OF EQUALITY

The opening chapters suggested that the ideals of liberty, equality and fraternity were still a useful measure of democratic local government. Local authorities restrict individual liberty in the name of the community. At the same time collective services provide the basis for the enjoyment of the good life: law and order, a healthy environment, freedom from nuisance and so on. Questions of equality arise in many ways: the introduction of new policies which may benefit some groups rather than others; the need to treat all citizens with the same claims on fair and equal grounds; and the just administration of everyday services.

Local authorities' social policies, for example, involve questions of discrimination (in favour of the less well off) and priorities. The introduction of comprehensive secondary schooling, on the other hand, may arouse opposition on the grounds that it is based on inappropriate demands for social equality while in fact disadvantaging the most intelligent children. The personal services may be criticised, for their part, on the grounds that they do not treat all individuals as equally worthy citizens. This charge is laid, for example, against social services which do not treat the poor man as a full citizen but as a suppliant who has to petition for help and for his rights since these will not be given to him automatically in his role as citizen.[1]

These practical problems draw attention to the central question: in what ways are citizens equal and what does this imply for the way they are treated? This is a complex question which has been lengthily debated among democratic theorists. S. I. Benn and R. S. Peters show that, in modern times, the main stress is on equality as equal consideration. To say that all men are equal is to say that they ought to be treated alike, not that they are identical.[2] Any distinctions that are made must then be based on relevant differences which can be known and defended on logical and impartial grounds. Discrimination may be a fact but it is the ways in which we discriminate that must be defended on known criteria. The egalitarian ideal has another side. The defence of equality must make clear what inequalities it is refuting. Historically, this has been the main impetus to social change, as reformers campaigned against injustice and political and social inequality. In modern times this has become a demand for more equality of opportunity. This too is a difficult concept which is constantly refined by shifts in public demand. We accept differences of opportunity if we see the point of them but not otherwise.

Equality cannot be considered in isolation but must be seen in the social context in which it arises. To J. S. Mill, political equality (equal citizen rights and duties) was an end in itself which needed little further justification. But this is not the case with questions of economic and social equality which have become more prominent in this century as governments intervened in all aspects of life. Now, equality has become a principle of social justice, and a foundation of civilised society.

It must be recognised, John Rees states, that equality is not the sole measure of a democratic society, which depends on equally important values such as liberty, stability, individual merit, rewards and incentives.[3] Nevertheless since no system of government is perfect then it will always be necessary to fight against exploitation and the unequal distribution of power in society. In so doing the English tradition has been that of R. H. Tawney's ideal society: humanitarian, possessing a large measure of economic equality through positive social policy, and with equality of consideration.

Today the stress on government intervention to redress gross inequalities has resulted in a new idea of 'positive discrimination'. The idea first appears in official documents in the Plowden Report on Primary Education of 1967, on which the Education Priority Areas were based. The idea behind this term is that in certain cases inequality – more resources to one area rather than to another – is justified in order to bring the least well off up to the standards of the rest. In local government problems of equality are both difficult to define and politically sensitive. A further difficulty is that, to a large extent, the nineteenth century has left such a great legacy of inequality and disadvantage that a lot of time is spent in merely redressing past problems. The practical impact of the desire for equality is the battle against past inequalities and their present-day consequences.

The history of local government gives a clear picture of improvement, both materially and philosophically. The original municipal ethos of ratepayer and property-owner and its restrictive air gave way to more egalitarian beliefs in the citizen-consumer and in the need for expanded services. These developments had consequences for the nature and extent of local services and also produced political parties with differing philosophies. Though both Labour and Conservatives were actively concerned with local improvement they differed on the extent to which this should be done by public services or private efforts and on the need to restrict or expand rate-borne expenditure. This too has had concrete implications for the standards and range of services and for the ways in which these may vary from place to place and for one category of citizens compared to another.

The old ratepayer philosophy, which still has a place in local politics and administration, is a product of Victorian thought and practice. Between the wars it was reinforced by the period of municipal economy, unrelieved, as even the Victorian stringency had been, by civic beneficence. The old 'Improvers' were defeated by the 'Economisers'. 'Municipal economy' was finally defeated by the coming of the Welfare State and the central government's insistence on minimum provisions and national standards. Two problems, however, remain. One is the continued variation in standards and the other is the difficulty of devising acceptable criteria of 'need' in a climate of continually rising expectations.

Other problems of equality concern particular inequalities, or allegations of unequal treatment, in education, housing and the social services. In planning, questions of equality affect the distribution of resources among different sections of the community and restrictions on individual freedoms. Finally, equality cannot be considered without asking the basic question: does central control now make local autonomy an illusion? If so, does this improve equality by imposing territorial justice instead of unacceptable variations between authorities and services?

VARIATIONS BETWEEN LOCAL AUTHORITIES

It is frequently argued that real local discretion and initiative have long been subservient to the national standards of the welfare state. But recent research suggests that there are still significant, and possibly unjustified, differences between local authorities. Evidence is difficult to obtain and to evaluate. Material collected for the Royal Commission on Local Government in England, for example, found a relation between local services and certain characteristics of their areas, but did not pursue the political and administrative factors, though they did recognise these were significant.[4] In education, counties varied according to characteristics of their area but a third of the difference between county boroughs was accounted for by other factors – which were not examined further. And health, welfare and children's services appeared to be barely influenced at all by type of area. All of this points to the probable variation caused by political and personal factors, including administrative discretion and councillors' attitudes.

The variation in general financial expenditure, considered as a whole, is hard to evaluate. F. R. Oliver and J. S. Stanyer, for example, show how difficult it is to distinguish between the influence of Labour party philosophy and of the relative poverty of a town. Wide variations in expenditure can be explained to some extent by economic differences. These influence both the problems facing the council and the likelihood of it being Labour controlled. Heavy industrial areas tend to have strong Labour parties while residential areas, with a larger share of their rateable value in domestic property, have weak (i.e. minority) Labour parties. But nevertheless Oliver and Stanyer conclude that socio-economic factors, rather than strong party influences, are most influential.[5] James Alt comes to somewhat different conclusions. Labour-controlled county boroughs spend more on housing, education and health services and less on other services such as the police. And party control is the most important factor in variations in housing expenditure.[6]

Noal Boaden and Robert R. Alford suggest a way out of these contradictory findings. Local authorities should be judged on their objective needs, their different resources, and their varying dispositions to take action.[7] They conclude that the differences between local authorities mainly arise from three factors: the social composition of the area, the direction of party control and the nature of the local tax base (of which central grants are an important, but not paramount, part). Noal Boaden has further developed the analysis of needs, dispositions and resources. He concludes that variations in expenditure contradicts traditional beliefs that central control is too heavy and too uniform.[8] Local authorities allocate resources on grounds of social justice and political feasibility and this is just as important as central standardisation.

Councillors and administrators have definite views about local needs. These views are influenced by parties and pressure groups, by the relations between councillors and officers, and by the reactions of the voters, the consumers and the general public. These influences vary from one service to another. Party policy plays a large part in education whereas the pressure of social needs appears as the main factor in housing. In health and welfare, councillors' views, and officers' professional values, are decisive. Social needs are equally pressing. The poorest authorities – those with the smallest tax base in relation to need – in fact are the ones most likely to spend on expensive social services. This reflects the pressures their services have to meet.

Boaden concludes, however, that the main variations between authorities arise from party politics. Labour spends more on the bigger services and those which appear to benefit their traditional supporters. There is some controversy about the correct interpretation of this kind of statistical comparison of local authority services. The general conclusions seem, nevertheless, clear: social conditions and a council's views about them are closely related and determine what level of service is provided. This is confirmed by recent research into services for the elderly, and into the children's service. How local authorities respond to need, and how services are provided, depends on the influence of party control.[9]

Variations between local services, then, cannot be put down simply to variations in size or resources. The revelation that social and political factors are important has reinforced the growing protest against such variations. Certain issues in the welfare field – provisions for the disabled, for the homeless, for the elderly – have provoked wide publicity. Such differences are, it is argued, unwarrantable and amount to social imbalance. Positive action, in the form of specific central grants and guidance, and greater publicity, are urgently needed.

VARIATIONS BETWEEN CITIZENS

Unequal treatment of people living in the same local area is justified because they have different needs and make different contributions. Not everyone living in the community has the same demands, and not everyone makes the same contribution through rates, rents and taxes. But then the problem becomes one of the definition and recognition of these differing needs – which may only be resolved through political conflict and the ballot box.

The debate about variations in treatment between citizens is a complex one. Here we concentrate, in the sections that follow, on three main issues. First, there are differences that arise from questions of policy. Examples are comprehensive education, the sale of council houses, and the operation of the 1972 Housing Finance Act. We call this area of concern 'policy problems'. The next section deals directly with the needs of the deprived areas of our towns and the poorer groups in the population. These highlight the difficulty of defining 'need'. And, in the ultimate case, do we treat all citizens with equal justice? What of race relations and the case of the gypsies? We have called this section 'The needs of special groups and areas'. By contrast, our final set of examples, in the section entitled 'Equal citizen rights – planning' considers the principle that all inhabitants expect equal consideration. Reconciling the needs of each with the needs of all is the greatest democratic problem.

(i) *Policy problems in local government*
The first example relates to secondary education. Education policy is always political and controversial. The main argument in recent years has been about the removal of 'selection' at 11+, which leads to different kinds of secondary schooling, in favour of the comprehensive school. On the other hand there is the objection that education policy is being used for spurious egalitarian ends, so that academic standards may be threatened.

Opinion within the political parties and the teaching profession is not monolithic; and these diverging opinions have themselves made for different solutions in different areas of the country. The introduction of comprehensive education had taken place on a small scale before 1964 but it was Labour's Circular 10/65 which saw the attempt to encourage wider adoption. Whether parents understood or approved of the comprehensive idea is difficult to establish. The testing of opinion seemed to show that parents were dissatisfied with secondary modern schools, not necessarily in favour of comprehensives.

Labour's Circular 10/65 did not compel action by local authorities but the Minister made it clear that there would be no financial aid for new school buildings which were not comprehensive. The Minister's only legal power to encourage new comprehensive schemes, however, was the 1944 Education Act proviso that the Minister had to approve the change of use of any local authority maintained school. The change of government in 1970 did not completely reverse the policy. The Conservative Minister released authorities from the requirement to submit comprehensive schemes and encouraged support for grammar, and for direct grant schools (including increased finance), but did not completely debar comprehensive schools. But emphasis did shift to primary schools and to nursery education, since research had shown that many educational inequalities between children had already been permanently established by the age of seven years.

The introduction of comprehensive schooling has been a slow

process in which a high degree of local authority variation has occurred. There are now some 30 per cent of secondary school-children in comprehensive schools. The problem, then, might be thought to be a relatively straightforward one in which consultation, and variation, allowed for the gradual implementation of a policy which was gaining a wide measure of acceptance among professional opinion. But it is not so simple. The conflict of opinion also contains arguments about the need to remove past inequalities caused by selection, differing school resources and so on. In this argument the opposing sides may clash over 'social equality' versus 'educational' aims. The dialogue has to proceed on the democratic procedures of consultation and compromise. But this may not resolve the clash of opinion; national legislation (a lengthy process) may then be needed to resolve it in one direction or the other. In 1973 Labour's attitude appeared to harden in favour of new legislation for compulsory comprehensive education.

The question of equality of consideration and treatment does not 'end there. The consultation requirement in the 1944 Act still gives rise to controversy. In the 1960s it became apparent that consultation with parents favours the articulate middle class. The parents of 85 per cent of secondary schoolchildren who go on to secondary modern or unselected schools, were imperfectly 'consulted' and their choice remained in practice as virtually non-existent as before.

Parents who have looked to s.76 of the 1944 Act to preserve or extend their wishes for their children's education at particular schools have not fared too well. Legal judgements have laid down that a local authority must have regard to the general principle of parental choice but can have regard to other things as well. It can, and does, evaluate the wishes of more than one group of parents. It appears, however, that parents are increasingly demanding a say in their children's education. The difficulties of doing this are well illustrated by the Enfield case. There, a group of parents argued that by changing a grammar school's status, without due notice and consultation, the local authority had 'ceased to maintain' it and so transgressed section 13 of the 1944 Act. The Court of Appeal, reluctant to be involved in questions of politics, did suggest that complaints should be made to the Ministry about the publicity and consultation requirements. But the statutory framework for education does not give real parental control and administrators have wide discretion; in this respect the Enfield litigation achieved little.

The second example of the problem of equal consideration and the demands of the community as a whole, and their policy outcomes, is the sale of council houses. Local authorities have provided public housing, at relatively low cost, since before the First World War. After both World Wars, local authorities were under great pressure to provide homes. 'Rationing' of the demand was left to the discretion of each local authority, who selected its own tenants. Most authorities behaved justly and impartially by using a 'points' system based on family need and length of residence. But in some areas such decisions might be by (arbitrary) committees, and subject to an individual councillor's bias. Secrecy, and suspicion, added to the problem.

By the 1960s these questions had receded and different questions were being put. It was felt that, in an increasingly affluent society, resources should be diverted from indiscriminate council house building to slum clearance and specialised housing for the elderly and the handicapped. At the same time, as wage levels rose and attitudes changed, selling council houses to sitting tenants was seen as both just and sensible. It is also argued that the sale of council houses helps to provide money to build more council houses, though this is a debatable argument. The Housing Act 1957 gave authorities a general power to sell or lease houses, but it was Conservative-controlled local councils who, after Conservative victories in 1966-7, accelerated sales. Some Labour councils also sold council houses, though this was later restricted by the Labour government. In 1970 the Conservative government encouraged sales and stressed the existing discretionary power of a local authority to give a discount of up to 20 per cent of the market value to a sitting tenant. The discount system is justified, in broad terms, because the local authority has the right to buy at the original sale price if the owner sells within five years (with credits for improvement and maintenance).

What are the implications and results of these policy changes? In overall terms, the changes are slight, since the numbers involved are relatively small. But, some critics have argued, the community still needs a pool of rented accommodation. On the other hand, it can be argued, the reasons for setting up large council house estates no longer exist: social conditions have changed dramatically in the last seventy years and local authorities need no longer play such a big part in the housing market. The need for local authority discretion seems to be paramount; some urban areas cannot, in the immediate future, see an end to the demand for public rented housing while others can feasibly offer houses to tenants.

Local policy-making in the field of housing must work within the framework of national legislation. Housing policy as a whole (the finance and building of houses to let) is now more directly controlled by the Housing Finance Act 1972. In the late 1960s the underlying problem of housing finance was the rising cost of government subsidies and the uses to which these should be put. When the Conservative government was returned to power in 1970, it announced its intention, in the White Paper 'Fair Deal for Housing' (*Cmnd.* 4728) to phase out general subsidies to local housing authorities, and, as a result, council house rents would rise to a 'fair rent' level.

The system of controlled rents in the private sector would also be gradually phased out, so that all tenants would be treated alike and the poorest would be helped not by controlling rent levels but by offering rent allowances. The Labour party was hostile to these proposals which it believed penalised council tenants while leaving the tax relief of owner-occupier mortgages untouched. The Act allowed fair rents to be introduced by annual steps and redetermined every three years. Local authorities were required to apply the national rent rebate scheme. Initial government subsidies for rent rebates would be gradually phased out.

On the other side of the balance sheet, the government subsidy for slum clearance would meet at least 75 per cent of the loss to the general rate fund incurred through slum clearance. But some local authorities, instead of receiving subsidies for housing, would find themselves paying money back to the government. Authorities with a large stock of council houses would find, after the rise to 'fair rents', that they had a surplus on their housing revenue account which would in part go to the national Exchequer. The total effect of the changes is to cut back the rapidly increasing levels of subsidies so as to maintain them at 1972 levels.

The government, in the White Paper 'Fair Deal for Housing' had justified its actions by showing that 90 per cent of the Exchequer housing subsidies in 1970-1 (together with local authority subventions from the rates) went to reduce general rent levels. As a result, ratepayers were making a heavy contribution to the housing costs of others. There was also injustice in the system because an unfair pattern of rents existed between different authorities, based on the historical accident of when council housing was built.

Here, then, was the clash of principle. The Act's supporters claimed that owner-occupiers were unfairly expected to support council tenants. There were other inequities which should be remedied, particularly those of unfurnished private tenants and landlords of controlled tenancies, who were both suffering from a distorted market in housing. In 1973 the Furnished Lettings (Rent Allowances)

Act extended the provisions by allowing rebates to some 500,000 tenants in furnished accommodation.

Opponents of the Act also based their views on claims of equity and justice. Local authorities should remain free to decide appropriate rents and rebates. It was not unjust to subsidise council housing from rates and taxes: housing was a basic human need which the community should provide. This need had not been removed by 'affluence'; rising property values and inflation made it as necessary as ever to maintain the stock of public sector housing at reasonable rents.

The move to 'fair rents', even with the rebates to poorer tenants, was arguably inequitable in another sense. When the scheme was fully operational, rebates would come out of the Housing Revenue account and council tenants, not the community as a whole, would be subsidising the poorest amongst them. There would thus, arguably, be greater equity as among council tenants as a whole but an element of inequity in separating tenants – for this purpose – from other sections of the community. Another serious charge was that the democratic rights of local authorities to make policy would be substantially reduced since they would be subject to local rent scrutiny committees. These committees, not the local council, would determine the level of rents, their fairness, and their redetermination. They meet in private and are accountable to nobody.

Tenants would also be treated undemocratically because they would have no right of appeal, unlike private tenants in the existing rent arbitration procedure, against the rent level set by the Rent Scrutiny Board. And their right to make representations (both to the local authority on the original assessment and to the Rent Scrutiny Board) also depends on their ability to submit written requests. This is a highly technical task. The Citizens Rights Office of the Child Poverty Action Group has now produced sample letters for use by Tenants Associations and individuals.[10]

Another feature of the administration of the rebate scheme also gives cause for concern. The rebate takes the form of a money allowance, rather than an automatic advance reduction in the rent paid. The Department of the Environment Circular 74/72 ('Housing Finance Act 1972: Rent Rebate and Rent Allowance Schemes', August 16, 1972) emphasised that local authorities should help tenants by paying rebates through Giro or by other similar means. This cannot be a lump sum: the allowance must be paid as frequently as the rent and not for longer periods.[11] The net result is that the individual has to be charged, and pay, the full fair rent equally with his fellow tenants. The rebate is to help him pay, not to reduce his rent. The disincentive of this procedure for the poorest and least educated citizen is already well recognised in other welfare benefit areas. The other side argued that this all obscured the real issue. The burden of housing finance would be more equitably distributed and there would be a real boost for slum clearance.

Housing problems do not stop there. Two points should be noted. The changes in housing finance, and the support for tenants in the private as well as the public sector, has highlighted questions of security of tenancies. The other question centres around the potential misuse of public grants given for householders to improve their homes, so that more rehabilitation of property rather than its eventual demolition, could be encouraged.

The Francis Committee, set up in 1969 by the Labour Government to study the Rent Acts, came out against any change in the law on security of tenancies on the grounds that it would further reduce the letting market. The Furnished Lettings (Rent Allowances) Act 1973 does not solve this problem, and there is still evidence of landlords putting pressure on tenants to quit as rising property values offer large profits. Council tenants, for their part, have better protection than formerly. The 1838 Small Tenements Recovery Act had given local authorities unique powers of eviction. This is remedied by the repeal of the Act in October 1972; local authorities now have to apply to the county court before they can evict and the tenant has the right to be represented.

Questions of equity also arise in relation to the improvement of housing. The Housing Act 1969 encouraged local authorities to give improvement grants and enabled them to declare 'general improvement areas' in their towns. These were predominantly residential areas in which a local authority considered conditions should be improved. Two results have followed. One is that house improvement grants have led to abuses by owners or landlords reselling at high profits. As a result the community, and poorer tenants, suffer. The other is that, in general improvement areas, problems of delay and consultation have caused blighting and decay in some cases, with the needs of inhabitants – who might have in fact preferred redevelopment rather than preservation – ignored.

These examples show that the attempts by local authorities to encourage one section of housing may have unintended consequences which disadvantage the community, and further inequities occur. The situation will not be remedied quickly: while housing demand is large, and rising, then the operation of the property market (and including the influence of land prices) will cause fluctuations which local and national government will have great difficulty in controlling. Local authorities face particular problems. Housing is an emotive issue and one which also carries an almost overwhelming burden of past inequalities. Local authorities never catch up with demand and with changing economic forces and their attempts to behave with equity are severely hampered.

(ii) *The needs of special groups and areas*

Since the publication of the Plowden Report in 1967 and the beginning of the Urban Aid Programme in 1969 it has been increasingly accepted that positive discrimination in favour of the under-privileged is necessary. There are three problems in trying to fulfil this desirable aim. Local authorities must first define what is meant by 'need'. They must then find out how widespread and serious it is. Finally, in order to define need, they must collect information and data, and this is costly. They may, therefore, be tempted to solve the obvious and more 'visible' needs.

The problem of defining 'need' is illustrated by the Enquiry into Social Welfare for the Elderly, carried out by the Government Social Survey for the National Corporation for the Care of Old People. Local authorities varied widely in their provisions and it was clear that they were defining 'need' differently.[12] In fact there are very few absolute criteria and there is a strong tendency to define need in terms of what local authorities actually do, and then compare the best and worst among them. Need is often equated with demand, though the two are not identical, because this is a concrete and relatively easy practical solution.

Another solution is to divide people into different categories: the aged, those with bad housing conditions, and so on. And the needs of these different categories of people is again affected by what is already being done, both by local authorities and voluntary groups. Section 45 of the Health Services and Public Health Act 1968 for example, gave local authorities power to make arrangements – including using voluntary organisations as their agents – to promote the welfare of old people. These generalised and permissive powers resulted in widely differing views on what was needed and what could be provided. The involvement of voluntary groups also affected what was done.

How local authorities provide for the needs of special groups is also influenced by two further factors: administrative discretion, and existing rules and regulations. Administrative discretion is defended because it gives a more flexible and humane service. On the other side it can be argued that this discretion offends against the new democratic spirit which stresses the citizen's rights and the need to remove arbitrary authority. The outcome must be judged in terms of what happens to the poor, and there are still worries that discretion may not work well in certain services. This in turn leads to demands for more information for the poor to claim their rights. Neighbourhood law centres, where free advice can be gained, are rapidly being established in many poor areas. The other factor, the influence of rules and regulations, constrains definitions of need. Homelessness, for instance, has a legal, not a social, meaning. In some authorities there is still a problem of being officially declared homeless. Not to have a home is not enough; the family has to have been evicted in accordance with certain rules.

With the coming of the Social Services Act 1970, one local authority department now has the responsibility for identifying needs, ordering them into priority, and for assessing individual and area demands in their communities. But the operation of local authority Social Service departments since 1971 has shown that 'needs' far outweigh the present abilities of local authorities to meet them. Attempts to promote social justice by positive discrimination in favour of those in most need recedes under the pressures of past inequalities and of rising demands. And there is strong evidence of a 'cycle of deprivation' among the poor which makes inequality cumulative. The poor are deprived economically, socially and politically. Their children, already handicapped by poverty while still at home, benefit less from schooling. Bad housing reinforced family problems, and people are 'apathetic' and not involved in community life.

These problems are now seen in terms of whole areas, not just of individuals or their families. The idea that there were whole districts of our cities in need of a comprehensive approach comes originally from the Plowden Report of 1967 ('Children and their Primary School', *Report* of the Central Advisory Council for Education, HMSO, 1967). In the field of education this called for positive discrimination in favour of new 'Educational Priority Areas'. The Department of Education and Science agreed and allocated special funds for school building and other purposes in these EPAs. Five areas in major industrial areas were selected for a three-year positive discrimination programme, and a research study set up to analyse the effects. Subsequent criticism of the scheme suggests that the effects were piecemeal and inadequate. Nevertheless, the idea of 'positive discrimination' was established.

The Urban Aid programme of 1968 carried these ideas further. The Local Government (Special Need) Act of January 1969 allowed a new 75 per cent specific grant to be paid for urban projects. Some twenty-three areas in London and the Midlands with acute immigrant and other social problems were included in the scheme. The projects concentrated initially on nursery schools, day nurseries, children's homes and additional staff. Later, community projects, youth schemes, advice and play schemes were added. By the end of 1969 a further 89 local authorities were taking part (with some 500 projects involved). Also in the autumn of 1969 the government had announced the setting up of an action-research Community Development experiment based on local social services, voluntary groups and university research teams. The overwhelming need, the government felt, was to bring services together and help people to use them more constructively. These schemes would be eligible for help under the Urban Aid programme.

But there were criticisms of the Urban Aid programme. Money was always a difficulty, but the role of voluntary groups, and the nature of the collective approach, also caused conflicts. Hard-pressed local authorities needed the grants to support existing or desired services. Voluntary bodies found it hard to put their schemes forward since they were in fact competing with the local authority, through whom each project had to be submitted. This gave rise to bitterness on both sides. Others argued that it was unjust to concentrate aid in this way: it is difficult to identify 'deprived areas' and problems of poverty are found outside as well as inside them. A third problem is the lack of overall planning; as *The Times* leader caustically remarked: 'You can hardly have a coherent strategy for a lucky dip'.[13] The lesson that emerges is that social justice can be hampered, rather than furthered, by the defective overall planning of policy.

The Community Action projects were seen, by contrast, as more selective and more research-orientated. Research highlighted needs, there was feedback into local administration and policy, and an emphasis on citizen involvement. The projects stressed the need to get local people to feel concerned about their communities, more committed and less apathetic about themselves and their conditions. The projects were essentially an experiment, based on the American War on Poverty experience. Again, conflicts arose because, while the Community teams saw their areas in wide 'quality of life' terms, the local authority wanted to improve existing services. One town clerk saw the Community Development project as analogous to a management consultant firm helping to improve the local authority's social responses; the team, for its part, saw its role as improving social services and making social needs articulate.[14] Some councillors attacked the idea as revolutionary, while radicals dismissed it as an example of what Herbert Marcuse terms 'repressive tolerance', that is, allowing needs to be expressed but not providing fundamental changes.[15] The outcome of 'positive discrimination' must await future analysis. So far it remains an interesting experiment, not a cohesive policy. Special aid is no substitute for overall policy. There is still a need for clear objectives and reasonable consultative procedures for establishing priority among needs.

Criticism of local authority provision extends also to two other, almost intractable, difficulties. One is the plight of the homeless, the other is the question of race relations. Criticism is not always justified; rising demands, and the pressure of past problems, make it almost impossible for a local authority to provide for all needs. These pressures exist constantly and produce strong emotional and political responses.

The definition of 'homeless' is bounded by legalities. Local authorities' discretion in providing temporary accommodation has been severely criticised. It is said, for example, that some councils evade their responsibilities by offering to take the children into care – which then means they have no further duty to help the homeless parents. In some large cities the pressure for housing has resulted in the squatters' movement and the response of local councils shows how attitudes may change under social and political pressure. Squatting in empty houses is a civil, not a criminal, offence, but property owners have the right to expect that local authorities and the law will protect them. In inner London, however, the development of Squatters' Associations since 1968 has begun to receive active support from some councillors and social workers who argue that the balance of equity lies on the side of homeless families, not with private or council landlords who allow their property to stand empty for long periods.

The change of attitudes is reflected in court cases; in 1973 one county court judge granted a property company a possession order but made it clear he did so with reluctance. Subsequently the local council considered placing control orders on the houses to prevent further evictions. If the control order were imposed then the company would lose its rights to run the properties and could eventually be faced with a compulsory purchase order.[16] Other councils now collaborate with local groups to use empty council property for homeless families. The existence of many empty properties is becoming socially unacceptable. The traditional defence of property and the right of a local council to keep its property empty prior to redevelopment may have to give way to other considerations.

In one sense the homeless are a minority group which demands special treatment. Racial or cultural minorities, on the other hand, may suffer other kinds of inequalities. Attempts at 'positive discrimination' may be misunderstood. Even seemingly straightforward action, such as keeping separate statistics for employment, council housing or the extent of homelessness among young coloured people, can adversely affect community relationships. The government's expressed aims are equality of opportunity, and social peace, and this demands positive improvement of whole areas. The areas of stress need massive resources to help the poor of all races, not just for better 'community relations'. Mr Robert Carr, the Home Secretary, stated that the same social problems would be endemic to these areas even if the white population had remained and the migrants had never moved in.[17]

There is also evidence to suggest that a community's sense of identity affects attitudes towards coloured migrants and the need to balance what is provided for different groups. Some towns appear to possess a more coherent identity; they are stable and well-defined communities who accept large numbers of migrants without feeling threatened. This confidence is in turn reflected in political leadership.

The treatment of gypsies is less happy. The Caravan Sites Act 1968 requires local authorities to provide adequate permanent sites for gypsy families in their area and also empowers them to then prosecute those who park illegally by designating orders which must be approved by the Minister. This has worked oppressively since the number of families exceeds the number of pitches on authorised sites. The problem is, again, not merely the question of cost or the proper census of travelling gypsy families but that community fears and hostilities must be taken into account.

All these examples show how hard it is to balance the many and competing needs of the community. A further consequence has been the change of attitudes among voluntary groups, professional workers and councillors. Councillors and voluntary groups are considered in more detail in a later chapter. But here it should be noted that the changes among professional social workers pose further questions of justice and equality of consideration. Should the social worker be more of an advocate for the client's needs against 'the bureaucrats' at the Town Hall, or should they remain in their traditional, professionally 'neutral' role? They owe prime allegiance to their employer, the local authority, and to their immediate superior, the Director of Social Services. The theory of representative democracy demands this allegiance. But ideas of participatory democracy, stressing the right and power of individuals – including the poor – to take a direct part in activities which affect them personally, have stressed the newer, advocate role.

The social work professions are open to radical influences and to more overtly expressed commitment. They are under pressure to do so from neighbourhood and community action groups. But in doing so they risk their jobs; the solution to this must wait until community goals replace crisis work in social services.

(iii) *Equal citizen rights – planning*

We turn from considering the needs of particular groups to questions which affect everyone. Planning regulates and restricts individual rights. Since the implementation of the 1947 Town and Country Planning Act it must also preserve and promote a healthy and balanced community. Thus planning is concerned with moral values, since it deals with the distribution of scarce resources and with social justice. Planners are exhorted to provide an environment which will extend people's liberty, their effective choices and their access to everything that society can offer.

Planning interferes with the individual's freedom in a number of important ways: it controls the use of land and property, restrains development and the change of use of buildings, and promotes the use of land. A local authority, acting in a *bona fide* manner, is the sole judge of land use. A local authority can also acquire land for development or for other planning purposes by compulsion. These powers are safeguarded by the requirement that the Minister is satisfied that the land is needed and that development will take place within ten years. Similarly, where planning permission to develop land is granted by a local authority there is a condition that development begins within five years.

Control of individual freedom and the balance of competing resources implies that citizens are not equally powerful. As D. V. Donnison *et al.* remind us, democratic rights have a cash value where the use of land is concerned. The objector's democratic right to delay the implementation of a planning policy can itself sometimes be a crucial bargaining counter in negotiations.[18] Pressure of work is an additional factor; delays can cause 'wrong' solutions and frustrated and embittered applicants for planning permission. Similarly, appeals and public inquiries may be viewed by the citizen as nothing more than an opportunity to protest rather than a means of democratic consultation.

The individual may also be aggrieved because he has no say in what his neighbour proposes to do and little legal remedy against it, unless proposals are of an 'unneighbourly' character. Third parties are required, under this provision, to be informed beforehand but such development is very narrowly defined, and may still give rise to resentment. One source of grievance has been removed in recent years. Government departments now have to follow the same planning procedures as private developers, under the new code of practice laid down in Circular 80/71: 'Town and Country Planning Acts 1962-1968; Development by Government Departments' (Department of the Environment Circular 80/1971).

The modern concern with environment and amenity has highlighted the inherent dilemma of democratic planning in a dramatic way. Cars versus public transport, roads versus housing, jobs and homes versus 'environment', lead to difficult questions of choice and values. Conflict must be faced. How can people make choices and what is it that governs our values and our goals?

One attempt to answer this question is the development of the interdisciplinary approach to community planning. Since 1962, for example, planning legislation has stressed improvement areas, conservation areas, and comprehensive development areas. The necessity of this comprehensive approach has largely been the result of the pressure of urban traffic and slum clearance. The final touch was the announcement in 1972 by the Secretary of State for the Environment of a more total approach to urban problems. In six inner city areas urban study teams of Whitehall and local officers would tackle, with the aid of massive grants, problems of derelict land, house improvement, and slum clearance. At the same time, grants for environmental improvements in general improvement areas would be doubled.

These new ideas are also a response to changing attitudes to traffic and roads. The Department of the Environment now recognises that the protest against urban motorways is such that, if better compensation is not forthcoming, then the programme will have to be scaled down. This also reflects the growing call for discrimination against cars in favour of public transport. This is not a uniform protest; the other side argues that the individual and his mobility are being restricted and penalised by the failures of planners to provide adequate roads.

To establish the balance of advantage is formidable. The great cost of roadbuilding, especially in cities, must be weighed against tangible factors on the other side (the cost of subsidised public transport, and of freight and other business costs) and against questions of social amenity and convenience that do not as yet command universal acceptance among economists and the general public. The controversy seems a far cry from the Buchanan traffic management ideas of a decade earlier. Not only do fashions change but the great, and inevitable, delays in a mixed economy (the need for land accumulation at market prices and the democratic process of consultation and public inquiry) themselves tend to make the ideas outdated before they can be implemented.

Roads and housing always involve difficult choices. Attempts to arrive at coherent policy in the face of rising demands and changing values makes planning appear to lag behind desirable changes. Desirable changes, however, have to be arrived at by consultation. The current emphasis on two different kinds of activity – new houses and roads on the one hand, and conservation and amenity on the other – have made it harder to arrive at agreed solutions which can then be implemented within a reasonable time without causing blight or financial hardship.

Extreme housing problems call for drastic solutions. As well as slum clearance local authorities now have power, under Part II of the 1969 Housing Act, to designate general improvement areas. The aim is to halt decay and avert potential slum conditions and allow people to voice their views in the process itself. Commentators have seen the idea as having a twofold benefit. Homes are improved rather than demolished. And the opportunity for participation improves the general quality of local democracy. This sanguine view is not universal. Delays in agreeing that an area shall be treated in this way and getting residents (including landlords) to collaborate causes blight; poor and elderly tenants may be driven out if 'improved' properties are sold; and local people may in fact prefer to be rehoused rather than rehabilitated.

The desirable aims of preservation and conservation have similar potential inegalitarian effects. Clearly, preservation orders and the establishment of conservation areas under the 1967 Civil Amenities Act restrict the right of property owners to make the best financial use of their property and the site. This is necessary to preserve the county's heritage but conservation is always the art of the possible. In 'historic' cities the pressure of public opinion may prevail, while in other areas conflict over resources may tip the balance the other way.

Conservation means loss of profit to those who own property and so requires special public funds if it is to be pursued as a community goal. Conservation is increasingly regarded with favour; redevelopment is not. In some cases the rights of property developers are seen as contrary to those of citizens, residents and local council. Redevelopment and property developers are attacked – as indeed are planners and local authorities generally – from another point of view. The price of land, its use for housing, and its release by planners for development, causes controversy over the relative equity to different sections of the community.

In 1973 the government made further attempts to deal with housing problems. The White Paper 'Widening the Choice: the next steps in housing' (*Cmnd.* 5280, April 1973) was primarily an attempt to speed house-building. Expansion in the green belt would be allowed. New guidelines would encourage local authorities, in their handling of planning applications and appeals, to favour housing development. A new scheme would require developers to contribute to the cost of sewerage and other essential services on which development depended. This would distribute these costs more equitably between the community and the private sector. Finally, a new levy would be imposed on land hoarding. Land with permission to build must be developed within five years; after this developers would face an annual levy of 30 per cent of the full market value for each year they hoarded the land. This was more equitable than revoking the original planning permission.

In June 1973 a further White Paper, 'Better Homes – the next priorities' (*Cmnd.* 5339) on inner city stress areas, allowed local authorities to designate Housing Action Areas and compel landlords to improve their property. They would have stricter control over the sale of grant-aided improved houses and tenants who are displaced will have a statutory right to be rehoused by the council. Local authorities would also be able to rate empty properties, including office blocks, at full value. Critics still argue that this comes too late to stop private tenants facing increasing hardship and discriminatory treatment.

While the Conservatives continue to press for more land to be released for housing and for greater use of Housing Associations, Labour calls for a more vigorous support for land nationalisation and 'municipalisation' of rented property. Alternative measures, rather than land nationalisation, appear to be the immediate prospect. Clearly, however, values are changing and one difficulty is to measure and assess these changes. Planning inquiries, for example, only allow us to query the route of a road, not whether we need a road at all – or whether rail would be an alternative.

Planning inquiries, and the problem of blight and compensation, also illustrate the dilemmas inherent in democratic administration. The earlier doubts expressed about the equity of allowing routine appeal decisions to be decided by the inspector holding an inquiry under the Town and Country Planning Act 1968, Part III, now seem to have died down. Nor is delegation of routine planning applications to officers under s.64 of the 1968 Act a difficulty. Far more worrying is the cost (in time and money) of appealing against planning decisions and appearing at inquiries. These all work against the individual and the voluntary pressure group.

Equity demands that all who have a right to be heard, are heard. Information is, however, clearly unequal as between the citizen, on the one hand, and the bureaucracy on the other – marshalling the facts for your case will be costly and time-consuming; the expert can rely on the building up of data as part of his and his colleagues' work. This has now reached such proportions that there are suggestions for paying a kind of 'legal aid' to help people appeal against planning decisions.

There are also complaints that the planning inquiry procedure is too formal and legalistic, which deters ordinary people and prevents them from understanding what is being decided. Delays also cause harm, both to those wishing to maximise investment return and those needing housing. To alleviate this, the Minister has now removed the need for traditional public local inquiry into structure plans (though these are retained for local plans), and substitutes a public examination of the main issues, by s.3 of Town and Country Planning (Amendment) Act 1972. This is less formal, broader in scope, and should cut down blight by speeding up the planning process. Nevertheless, the increasing use of legal counsel at what were originally conceived as informal hearings may be making things worse, not better, for the individual. This is an ironic and regrettable outcome of the very procedure designed to protect his interests.

Planning can cause blight; that is, the market depreciation of properties which are, or are suspected of being, included in a scheme of development. This has led to new and more generous approaches to compensation. Under the 1969 Housing Act, market value rather than site value must be paid, the principle being that it is inequitable to inflict unnecessary hardship on individuals in the name of the public good. Compensation has also widened to include those injuriously affected by noise and other pollution (though their land is not taken) as, for example, in road building, as the White Paper of 1972, 'Development and Compensation – putting people first'

(*Cmnd.* 5124, October 1972, based on 'New Roads in Towns', *Report* of Urban Motorway Committee, HMSO, 1972) stated. Compensation is still based on market values but the 'well maintained' payments were doubled and a new 'home loss' sum would be paid to an owner or tenant of five years' standing.

Local authorities can now, under the Land Compensation Act 1973, buy in advance of requirements and owner-occupiers in clearance areas no longer have to wait for the lengthy process of compulsory purchase but are entitled to require local authorities to buy. In addition, owners and occupiers of residential and small business properties are compensated for loss of value of their property caused by nuisance from nearby works, even though their land is not taken. One result will be that the cost of urban road building may rise by as much as 15 to 20 per cent and thus have the further result of delaying or halting urban motorway proposals. It may well be, however, that this is a relatively small price to pay for alleviating individual hardship and also, by removing vociferous protest and costly inquiry delays, reducing community costs also.

THE NEED FOR AN OMBUDSMAN?

A generally accepted view of equitable local administration would be that outlined in a Court of Appeal decision in 1971. Lord Justice Phillimore stated that local decisions are best taken by local people but, if they were entirely free from checks, then justice and fair dealing would suffer. A council was entitled to agree on a policy provided they did not impose it inflexibly and they must keep an open mind and apply policy with regard to the facts of the case.[19]

These views command widespread support but in a complex society there will still be demands for a machinery of protest, appeal and restitution. It is this which has led to the development of a Parliamentary Commissioner for Administration as administrative discretion made legal remedies unavoidable or inappropriate. These same demands have now widened into areas previously excluded, such as the police and health services, and to local government.

Opinion has also changed within central, and local, government. Mr Wilson, the then Prime Minister, announced to the House of Commons in July 1969 that the government had accepted in principle the need for machinery to investigate complaints of maladministration by local authorities. A separate system was envisaged, not an extension of the powers of the existing Parliamentary Commissioner. This followed the general thinking advanced by the Report of

'Justice', under the chairmanship of Professor J. F. Garner, entitled 'The Citizen and his Council', published earlier that year (though not the idea that Ombudsmen might be on a functional or service basis).

The Conservative government of 1970 supported similar provisions. Local authority opinion gradually changed, but with the proviso that the machinery should be established by local government, who should also be responsible for its general administration and financing. The complaints claimed should go through local councillors. The Association of Municipal Corporations recognised that, since the public authorities were endowed with great powers to interfere with citizen rights this was almost invariably accompanied by the citizens' rights of appeal to the courts or to a Minister.[20]

If an individual has a complaint then he can bring this to a councillor who can raise it at council on notice of motion. The councillor can give some redress, by investigating complaints or channelling them to other committees or to members. But the councillor can only do this for a small number of problems and for relatively straightforward situations. He lacks supporting staff and resources and he has no power to require disclosures. Again it is difficult for councillors, who are in theory the ideal ombudsmen, to appear impartial since they are themselves a part of the administrative process. It is equally difficult for the town hall to act as judge in its own cause.

The Department of the Environment's Consultation document, 'Proposals for the creation of a Commission for Local Administration in England' (May 16, 1972) saw Local Commissioners assisting local councillors to protect their electors' rights. The Commission for Local Administration, an independent statutory body, would be appointed by the Crown and financed by local government. There would be nine or ten local Commissioners covering particular areas. The Commission would report to a body representative of local government.

The Commissioners' powers would be limited to maladministration and do not cover a local authority's discretionary powers, contractual or other commercial transactions, question of personnel, or the conduct, curriculum, internal organisation, management and discipline of any individual school or college. Complaints, in writing and within a time-limit, would be channelled through a councillor of the local authority complained of (unlike the Garner report which had called for complaints direct from the public to the Commissioner on the grounds that submission through a councillor might prejudice the appearance of impartiality). In certain circumstances (where one or more councillors refuse to forward complaints) the Commissioner may initiate investigations for himself. After investigation the Local Commissioner would report to the complainant, to the councillor who referred the case, to any person complained of, and to the local authority. The local authority would normally be required to make the report available to press and public.

Thus the provisions outlined in the consultation document do not in any sense allow a general questioning of a local authority's performance. It is a personal grievance machinery for cases where alternative remedies, through the court or appeal to a Minister, do not exist. The action complained of must, moreover, be such that the individual suffers a substantial disadvantage not suffered by other ratepayers.

The aim of the proposed procedure is to investigate maladministration so as to avoid injustice; it is not intended to institute legal proceedings against local authorities and their staff, and it will extend protection against action for defamation to both staff and authority. The work of a local ombudsman, if the system is eventually adopted, may be fairly routine, as that of the Parliamentary Commissioner has been. Similarly, a local complaints system might be, *vide* the national, a kind of 'audit'. Seen originally as a new and powerful ally of the citizen against the bureaucratic machine, the Parliamentary Commissioner has ended up carrying out what George Clark calls a kind of 'administrative audit'.[21] The main impact of the suggested new machinery might be its contribution to this auditing function and also its potential as an additional channel of consultation, complaint and information. If instances of maladministration are found, and removed, then the individual injustice would also be removed.

THE CONTINUED NEED FOR VIGILANCE

The concern for equal consideration of citizens, for equity and justice, embraces a wide range of current problems of local government. The democratic concern with equality has, over the last century or so, been influenced by two main streams of thought. First, there was the gradual development, as the franchise widened, of a broader conception of local government based on the idea of the citizen and the consumer of services as well as the ratepayer and property owner. In the period between the two World Wars this broadening outlook received a setback, under the impact of economic depression, so that 'municipal economy' predominated. Since 1945 new ideas and new demands have renewed the search for equal consideration and equality of opportunity. The second element in the democratic concern with equality is the recognition that it is only one element and must allow for, and compete with, what are seen as other desirable goals: individual liberty, the search for efficiency, the allocation of scarce resources to defined priorities, and a concern for majorities as well as minorities.

Local government has to tackle two other situations. One is the backlog of past inequalities, involving great expenditure on renewal and redevelopment of plant and services. The second situation arises also from this problem. The coincidence of multiple deprivation, which calls for positive discrimination in favour of certain groups and areas, has had a mixed outcome. The problems have been tackled with special schemes, research and money, but they remain piecemeal and may positively impede proper policy planning by individual local authorities.

The autonomy of local government, and its ability to treat its citizens of its own area equally and justly, according to local needs, is also a recurrent theme. One difficulty has been at what level certain fundamental decisions should be made. In a unitary society like Britain, equality may be thought of as best fulfilled by central governments promoting national legislation in response to national public opinion. But this still does not answer the question whether central decisions are more or less democratic than local ones. This difficulty, and other problems of central control and central-local relations, are dealt with in Chapter 8.

The central government's insistence on uniformity varies as public demands change. Local authorities are faced with this uncertainty and must learn to live with it. The extent to which they can resist government demands or central government can insist on uniform standards is also subject to changes in the political situation. The Conservatives have been the party of increased local freedom but, in housing for example, have had to resort to explicit legislation. Labour, for its part, tends to promote centralisation since its aims of social and economic justice and of equality of opportunity are based on uniform national standards. But the current situation is more mixed. Labour's 'social justice' philosophy has called for a large redistributive element and these have been particularly prominent in the social welfare field. In recent years critics of the party have argued that this ideal has been lost and equality of opportunity has replaced 'equality'.

On the other hand, the Conservatives emphasise increased private,

as opposed to public, provision. The result would be to shift the
greater part of the financial burden from the community as a whole
to the actual recipient or consumer. The definition – or perception –
of equality shifts accordingly. How far should the community provide for all, equally? How far should private provision prevail over
public provision? These questions have not been debated at the
purely local, as opposed to the national level, since the days of
'municipal socialism'. It looks now as though the 'public' versus
'private' debate will grow and affect the nature and extent of local
services.

The public is now more critical, less respectful of authority, and
more disillusioned with material benefits. These developments thrust
the argument back into the 'public' side of the debate. These contro-
versies operate at both local and national level and may well, in the
short term, lead to increased central control in the form of national
legislation, rather than less. Again, the inequalities of levels of
provision between local authorities may continue to be attacked as
indefensible anomalies, rather than democratic local variations.
Equality, from this point of view, can only be brought about by
national governments legislating for uniform policies and, through
inspection and supervision, making sure the policies are carried out.
And this reasoning leads to another, and damaging, criticism of local
government. If equality is thought of in this way, then equality and
fraternity are opposing forces. As was suggested in earlier chapters,
the Fabian and early socialist fight for equality and improved services
implied that this was so: to gain more equal treatment and consideration meant opposing other local forces, traditions and classes. Today,
fraternity in the local community may be a question of scale – it
operates best at the neighbourhood or parish level – but it can do
nothing about equality. That is a matter for national governments
and the search for equality may destroy, or ignore, fraternity. This
complex problem remains a difficult and disquieting area of democratic theory which will continue to influence the debate on the
status and powers of local authorities.

In all this the local authority is still responsible for the well-being
of the community as a whole and must govern: that is, it must work
out, in consultation with its experts as well as with its public, the
policies and priorities which it will pursue. How well it does this
depends not only on its administration, its definition of need and
provision of services, but also on the political process. The men and
women who take part, as elected representatives, members of local
parties and pressure groups, as voters and as individuals, form the

E

web of day-to-day local democratic life. It is to these questions of participation that we now turn.

NOTES

1. Hilary Rose, 'Rights, participation and conflict', *Poverty Pamphlet 5* (Child Poverty Action Group, 1971), p. 10.
2. S. I. Benn and R. S. Peters, *Social Principles and the Democratic State* (Allen & Unwin, 1959), p. 108.
3. John Rees, *Equality* (Macmillan/Pall Mall, 1971), p. 41.
4. Royal Commission on Local Government in England, *Research Study 5*, 'Local Authority Services and the Characteristics of Administrative Areas', paras. 9, 21 and 22.
5. F. R. Oliver and J. S. Stanyer, 'Some Aspects of the Financial Behaviour of County Boroughs', *Public Administration*, Vol. 47 (Summer 1969), pp. 182-3.
6. James E. Alt, 'Some Social and Political Correlates of County Borough Expenditure', *British Journal of Political Science*, Vol. I, No. 1 (January 1971), pp. 57-62.
7. Noal Boaden and Robert R. Alford, 'Sources of Diversity in English Local Government Decisions', *Public Administration*, Vol. 47 (Summer 1969), p. 203.
8. Noal Boaden, *Urban Policy-Making* (Cambridge University Press, 1971), p. 15.
9. Cf. Bleddyn Davies, Andrew Barton and Ian Macmillan, *Variations Among Children's Services Among British Urban Authorities* (George Bell & Sons, 1972).
10. Stuart Weir, 'Guide to the Housing Finance Act – Rent Rebates and Allowance – I', *CRO Paper* (Citizens' Rights Office (Child Poverty Group), 1972), p. 11.
11. Housing Finance Act 1972, Schedule 4.
12. Amelia I. Harris, *Social Welfare for the Elderly* (HMSO, 1962), p. 2.
13. 'Help For Decaying City Centres', *The Times* (14 April 1971).
14. Martin Walker, 'The Battle is Just Beginning', *The Guardian* (8 February 1972).
15. Herbert Marcuse, 'Repressive Tolerance' *in* Robert Paul Wolff, Barrington Moore Jr. and Herbert Marcuse, *A Critique of Pure Tolerance* (Beacon Press, 1965), pp. 81-117.
16. 'Council May Act to Stop Eviction of Squatters', *The Times* (19 January 1973).
17. 'Mr Carr Defends Race Relations Policies', *The Times* (15 February 1973).
18. D. V. Donnison, Valerie Chapman, Michael Meacher, Angela Sears and Kenneth Unwin, *Social Policy and Social Administration* (Allen & Unwin, 1965), p. 148.
19. 'Policy decisions of local authorities and the law', *Sagnata Investments Ltd. v. Norwich Corporation, The Times Law Report* (11 May 1971), *The Times* (12 May 1971).
20. 'Complaints of Maladministration', General Purposes Committee, Appendix B, *Municipal Review Supplement*, p. 76.
21. George Clark, 'The Case for Strengthening the Ombudsman's Hand' *The Times* (26 January 1971).

Chapter VI

PARTICIPATION

THE NINETEENTH CENTURY LEGACY

J. S. Mill called on all men to take a full part in local affairs. But, in practice, the good government of the community lay in the hands of a propertied élite. The result was a restrictive view of local democracy, with limited means of participation and communication. People took part mainly as councillors, officials and voters.

These attitudes arose from the problems facing Victorian society. The prime need was to tackle urban squalor in a speedy, efficient and economical manner. To do this, responsible local government had to be established, and order brought to the chaos of areas, rates and elected and non-elected bodies. At the same time there was a growing demand for the extension of political rights to men as inhabitants of local communities. It was argued that, if men could be given the vote in national elections, and could stand for parliament, then why could they not do so locally? More responsible and responsive local government would help the fight against corruption and inefficiency. Corrupt local oligarchies should give way to representative local institutions.

The result was a democracy of ratepayers. Until 1880 council membership was based on a property qualification. The removal of this restriction, so that any person on the Burgess roll became eligible for election to the council, still meant ratepaying householders only. In the countryside the landed classes and the gentry governed as appointed Justices of the Peace in Quarter Sessions until 1888. Some representative bodies existed, the Poor Law Guardians for example, but they too were drawn from among the prosperous ratepayers. In the 1880s an exclusively ratepayers' democracy was challenged by the widening franchise and by the fact that taxes, as well as rates, were used to finance local services. If all contributed, then all should have the right to take part.

The legislation of 1888 and 1894 produced two different kinds of local government. In the towns and in the parishes, there was some kind of community identity. In the towns there were more contested elections and ordinary people could take part without having to travel great distances. The parishes could claim to be closely knit communities with common interests. In the counties the reverse was true; few people could afford time and money to take part and there was no readily identifiable common interest. There were fewer contested elections than in the towns (and so more virtually 'co-opted' members) and a weak sense of community identity. Working men took little part and the traditional rule of squire and magistrate continued. Socialists and Fabians attacked the oligarchic nature of local government and urged working men to take part and to use their majority power to extend services. In the Webb's view the exclusion of the working class had led to the rule of shopkeepers, builders, publicans and some professional men.[1] The working class must challenge the claims of these people to be considered the natural leaders of the community.

After the extension of the franchise in 1867 the Liberal and Conservative parties established local organisations to get out the vote for municipal and school board elections. This broadened the base of participation as more candidates fought local elections. The intense interest in school board elections had its roots in religious differences. It was the town councils which offered a broader base for party activity since the local council was a stronger unit of participation which reflected the interests of the whole community. But it was not until the rise of the Labour Party after 1900, and particularly after 1918 when individual membership was possible and local parties formed, that party made its greatest impact.

Working-class candidates first appeared in local elections in the contests for the new School Boards set up after the 1870 Education Act. They were normally connected with trades councils or with local radical Working Men's Associations. To a very much lesser extent, they also stood for Boards of Guardians and occasionally for borough councils. The creation of the Labour Representation Committee in 1900 had little immediate effect, but the numbers of working-class councillors grew steadily and after 1918, when local Labour parties were set up, there were sweeping Labour gains. This increased working-class participation fell back in the 1930s but grew again after 1945.

In the 1930s the national Labour party recommended, but did not enforce, a set of model Standing Orders for local Labour groups. Conservatives and others argued that this altered the nature of the individual's participation as a councillor. It tied him to the wishes of the local Labour Party and so undermined his accountability to his constituents. This argument faded after 1945 when local Conservative parties, under pressure from the centre, also stood for the council as party candidates. By the early 1950s, J. H. Warren concluded, the party system was found in about 90 per cent of the counties and large towns, half the urban districts and about a quarter of the rural districts.[2]

Throughout these developments, however, the theory and practice of local government remained unchanged. The widening of the franchise, the rise of the working class to positions of power, the extension of the party system, did not result in new kinds of participation. Between the wars, the Webbs, Laski and Cole suggested different kinds of functional representation, consumer participation and neighbourhood government. But by the 1940s radical opinion was no longer so receptive to changes in local participation and power. The growing success of Labour moved the struggle to parliament and Whitehall and superceded calls for new forms of local democracy.

THE ELECTORAL AND PARTY SYSTEMS

Participation depends on the electoral and party systems: both are based on locality. In the towns, prior to 1973, the individual wards returned three members, each serving a three-year term. One councillor from each ward retired each year. Thus there were annual elections, with one-third of the councillors retiring at any one election. Annual elections, it was argued, helped to remind people of council affairs and gave them an opportunity to influence their local councillor. But the drawback was that retirement by thirds slowed down political change. The existence of aldermen, who were not directly elected, served for six years, and formed one quarter of the council, also slowed down the rate of change.

In the counties each electoral division returned one councillor. Councillors served for three years and all retired together. Although aldermen still distorted electoral response to some extent, it was possible for power to change hands at a county election. But this rarely happened. Many areas returned the same party for long periods and there were many uncontested elections. This reduced democratic accountability. A council of sixty to a hundred members is not like a public board or a new town corporation; the work is different and councillors are accountable to the local community, who can remove them at the next election, not to a Minister. Thus where there are no contested elections then the principle of accountability fails.

In the previous county system the bias was towards area rather than individuals, with councillors speaking as representatives of communities. Now, under the 1972 Act, the old over-representation of rural, compared with urban, inhabitants has been removed; far greater attention is paid to arithmetic to give more standardised councillor/elector ratios. The aldermanic system is also abolished.

The 1972 Act lays down that, for all councillors outside Greater London, the term of office is four years. Previously, county, county borough and district elections had been based on a three-year cycle. In London, a three-year cycle of elections was retained but s.7 provided that the Minister may, by Order, modify this to bring London elections into line with the rest and it is anticipated that this will be done. Counties are based on single member electoral divisions. In metropolitan districts wards must return a total number of councillors divisible by three. In the non-metropolitan districts there is no such division; the district council may negotiate with the Boundary Commission on the number of councillors for each ward and this is then authorised by Order of the Secretary of State.

In the first elections of 1973 non-metropolitan districts (who had largely retained their ward or divisional structure with some amalgamations) returned a varying number of councillors from a mixture of single and multi-member wards or divisions. The criteria was the councillor/elector ratio. But the districts will be affected by the Act's provisions for annual elections. Section 7(9)(c) of the 1972 Act lays down that where a district wishes to have annual elections (with one third of the councillors coming up for election in each of three successive years, the fourth year being left free as the county election year) then 'one third of the whole number of councillors in each ward returning a number of councillors which is divisible by three and, as nearly as may be, one third of the whole number of councillors in other wards' shall be those who retire in that year.

By the next elections in 1976, therefore, the districts will be forced to establish, for each ward or division, three or a multiple of three councillors. This will be contentious, since it reduces the original flexibility of the system. Only if they opt for elections every fourth year instead of annually, will these local authorities be able to return a varying number of members for each ward.

Under the 1972 legislation, mixed urban/rural districts can have mixed electoral systems: annual elections with three-member wards for the urban areas and single member wards with elections every fourth year for sparsely populated areas. No doubt the electoral system will become familiar in time. But this insistence on annual elections rejects the opportunity for the clarity and focus that triennial elections and single member constituencies would have given.

From 1974 onwards the participation of ordinary people as elected representatives differs in two main ways from the previous system. First, the overall number of councillors has fallen dramatically (from the former figure of 40,000 to some 24,000 not including parish councillors). Second, since the new county councils range in size from 54 to 107 members and the average electorate varies from around 5,000 per councillor to over 10,000, there is an increased problem of remoteness.

A continuing grievance under the new system is eligibility for candidature. Local authority employees, of which perhaps school teachers are a significant group, are disqualified from membership of the local council which employs them. They may serve for neighbouring authorities (if they are qualified by reason of residence) but the increase in size of areas after local government re-organisation makes this more difficult. Labour has argued that this is particularly inequitable since candidates with sectional interests – estate agents, property developers – can legally and properly be elected to local councils and become chairmen of housing and planning committees.

Qualification for council membership, unlike that for the vote, remains at twenty-one years. Citizens of the Irish Republic resident in this country are also eligible. The Local Authorities (Qualification of Members) Act 1971 revoked the 1969 Representation of the People Act's disqualification of those with a property but not a residential qualification. The 1972 Local Government Act reaffirms this and also continues to allow parish or community council candidates to reside in the area or within three miles of it.

After April 1974 poll cards will be distributed by counties and districts. This will be a valuable aid to electoral contests. The Home Secretary did not press this for the first elections in 1973, although some authorities used their discretionary power to do so. Candidates will not, however, enjoy the free distribution of literature available to parliamentary candidates. But they will benefit from the Representation of the People Act, 1969, which allows the description of a candidate (including party affiliation) on the ballot paper. This will, it is argued, encourage a truer reflection of people's real intentions.

If people do not bother to take even a minimum part in local government, by voting, then this may be the fault of the parties. They fail to excite interest, maintain close contact (through councillor 'surgeries' for example), or get out the vote adequately. The counter-argument stresses that this would have little real effect. National fortunes affect a party's local support and this cannot be counter-acted by increased efficiency of the party's organisation. But in opposition to this it can be claimed that the electorate's 'apathy' is not a response to irrelevant party politics, and there is reason to believe that party contests actually increase electoral turnout. The intervention of parties means more contested seats and so more opportunity to participate. Recent research also suggests that local organisation, and the closeness of party competition – the battle over marginal wards – will also draw more people to the poll. K. Newton shows how the parties concentrate on these wards, rather than their 'safe' seats and people have a greater opportunity to influence the result. In fact it seems that social class, not party organisation or effort, determines how a ward will vote and whether its people will be 'apathetic' or not.[3]

Parties remain, nevertheless, the main influence on electoral participation. Since 1945 national party labels have become almost universal. There are fewer Independents, but, in some areas, purely 'local' parties still reflect community individuality and vigour. This party activity is crucial to recruitment of councillors, since for some groups in the population (manual workers, younger people, women) the parties are indispensable as a vital avenue of recruitment to the council.

But local government is not a straightjacket of party conformity. J. G. Bulpitt shows how important are environment, tradition and historical accident.[4] Even Labour party activity varies from place to place. In large cities Labour may behave as a 'strong government', taking all chairmanships and controlling all patronage when in power, but this is not necessarily universal. And fears of 'Tammany Hall' politics, controlled by the party outside the council chamber, largely disappeared after 1945, since the experience of working together produced informal conventions and procedures which regulated potential controversy. This, of course, does not reduce the force of the argument that, in homogeneous one party areas real democracy takes place *within* the party, in the selection of candidates.

It is held that, since polls are low (around the 40 per cent level in urban areas and even lower in rural areas) then elections will still not provide democratic local government even under the reformed system. Low polls, and uncontested seats, reinforce the councillor's already existing belief in 'strong government', that is, to govern as he thinks best with little attempt to draw ordinary citizens into the process. Councillors can also safely discount local opinion since people are really voting for national, not local reasons. The safety of his seat depends, therefore, on the fortunes of his party at national level.

The counter-argument stresses that a councillor must, even if polls are low, anticipate local reactions to council policy. Roy Gregory suggests that the effect of this 'Rule of Anticipated Reactions' is exaggerated. Councillors overestimate their own relevance in the voter's eyes and underestimate the importance of national party fortunes.[5]

REPRESENTATION AND REPRESENTATIVES

How councillors see themselves and the voters depends in the first place on their role as representatives. Representation includes such ideas as standing for, accountability to those represented, acting as a symbol of, representing sectional interests, and representing political interests. Controversy surrounds almost all of these ideas.[6] One such problem is the idea that the representative should 'mirror', in his social characteristics, those he represents. The Maud Report *Management of Local Government*, and other writings, however, show that this is more ideal than real. Councillors differ from the general population in several important respects. They tend to be older, more middle class and retired. Few women, manual workers and younger people sit on local councils. This is important because, as I have suggested elsewhere, there is a need for balance in community life. That is, though councils need not be an exact replica of the general population they should reflect significant sections of it. Currently, they fail to do this, particularly in terms of younger members and women.[7] Nor does representation mean just a passive reflection of the public (however accurate) since the representative must be capable of taking action, of governing.

As a result there will always be controversy over the question of what representatives actually do and what they ought to do. The former idea sees representatives as relatively independent: performing their duty on the basis of knowledge, good faith, trust, and obligation. The latter argument emphasises the need for more truly 'representative' members, tied to specific mandates from their publics, and more open to recall and dismissal.

These ideas reflect the traditions of local government. In the 1830s reformers were agreed that the new Municipal Corporations needed men of status, wealth and intelligence to manage town affairs. By the 1850s, however, there were already doubts that men of substance would come forward. Gradually, however, new fears were heard.

The men of substance, the large ratepayers, had no qualms about raising rates to finance the capital works (paving, sewerage schemes) demanded by improved public health standards. The small shop-keepers and businessmen protested at the heavy rate burden and the councils passed into the hands of these 'economisers'.

There was no belief, however, that representatives had to be a true 'cross section' of the community. Elected members represented their constituents politically, not socially. That is, the representation of people's interests was a political skill, based on what the councillor could achieve in office, not on who he was. At this period of a narrow franchise, of course, the elected member was also the virtual representative also, since elected and electors came from the same social groups. And the most desirable characteristic of the representative was his skill in managing the town's affairs.

After 1880 this was challenged by the demand for greater working class representation and for councils which reflected more closely the social characteristics of their area. The extension of local services brought different demands: that councillors should represent a cross-section of the consumers of these services. The growth of Labour representation after the turn of the century had for a time, a more sinister aspect: Labour councillors spoke up for the specific interests of council workmen and their wages. This died down after the spread of national negotiating machinery after the First World War.

The question of the calibre of councillors was still vigorously debated and the call for men of leadership and administrative skills predominated. E. P. Hennock shows how these demands for differing kinds of skills and representation has, in our own time, given rise to a wide spectrum of views on the quality of councillors. What characteristics they should possess depends on what job they are expected to perform. And this, given the increasing importance of official expertise, is ambiguous. The local authority is now more of a consumer council, on which councillors represent the cross-section of inhabitants' needs, rather than a board of directors which makes policy.[8]

Today the idea of the representative covers a very broad spectrum, from a board of directors to watchdogs, and with demands for intellectual abilities, managerial skills or the right to speak for social classes or special interests. Certain qualities (the ability to take decisions and exercise political judgement) may be aided by the executive experience gained in certain occupations and these, L. J. Sharpe claims, are relevant to council work.[9] G. W. Jones argues, equally validly, that council work demands committee skills which many Labour members learn from their party or trade union work. This may be a better source of relevant skills than executive occupations.[10]

The characteristics of local councillors are now well known. Councillors are, on average, older, better educated and more middle class with the professions (law, education) playing a major role. And, as in Parliament, white-collar workers may be replacing more traditional manual or skilled occupations. The political parties reflect these characteristics to differing degrees, with the Labour party recruiting more working class candidates. Even so, Labour councillors are still more middle class than the community as a whole, a fact which Barry Hindess suggests is part of the reason why working-class support is turning away from the Labour party in large urban areas.[11]

The signs to which Hindess points are important. Since the time of J. S. Mill it has been considered a virtue of English local government that it gave opportunities for everyone, whatever their class,to take part. But local government is particularly important to working-class people since, without it, they would be largely confined to the role of followers in national political life. The Labour party has profoundly affected local politics in bringing working- and lower middle-class people into prominence and into relations of political equality with other classes. If, as Hindess suggests, local Labour parties are increasingly dominated by the middle classes then this will add to the already deterrent effects of the new larger authorities in potentially reducing working class participation.

The fact that local councils are unrepresentative, in their social characteristics, must be kept in perspective. Local appointed bodies, and voluntary organisations, are even more socially unrepresentative than local councils.

The local community is not a self-contained unit, and councillors' values reflect those of society as a whole and, in particular, its class and party divisions. These values are also shaped by local factors such as the industrial and social life of the area, the personal background of councillors and the way they see the community and their own part in it. The modern representative faces a challenge. He must play not one but many roles: as spokesman for his party, as the representative of his constituents and in defence of the public interest as he sees it. He must be a leader and a mediator.

In practice there is no such thing as 'the elected member' and the representativeness of modern democratic government depends on many varying interpretations. In local government this is well known: councillors have been variously described as policy leaders, public persons, ward representatives, interest group spokesmen, parochials, party men, backbenchers, tribunes of their people and so on.

COUNCILLORS, CONSTITUENTS AND PRESSURE GROUPS

The local council is a local élite which differs significantly from those whom it represents and serves. As we have seen, councillors are not a representative cross-section of their community. Their attitudes and motivations towards council affairs also differ: they are more committed, and more partisan, than the majority of their constituents.

Councillors see themselves as representatives of a party and its philosophy as well as of individual constituents. These attitudes are reinforced, particularly on the Labour side, by the expectation that aspiring candidates will take an active part in the ward, to serve a kind of party apprenticeship, before being considered for inclusion on the panel of candidates. For both Labour and Conservative councillors, work on the council reinforces party ties. This comes about in two main ways. Where the council is run on strong party lines then the caucus group, committee life and general council atmosphere all establish rules of the game for the individual member. In addition, the member will normally have ties with the party in the borough or the constituency.

For many councillors the ward committee of the party is often the only body which draws attention to local problems, brings councillors in touch with individual electors, and raises long-term issues. But this may be changing, so that more and more of this attention to wider problems is being taken over by groups and interests outside the main party channels. It is still true to say, however, that it is parties and pressure groups which make representation a reality. The parties produce candidates and thus representatives and leaders. They enable representatives to be held to account. Interest groups, by means of informal contacts or more direct links, also influence the attitudes and behaviour of councillors.

The main concern of recent years is not the influence of party but the impact of the growing complexity of council work. As services become more complex, then, Heinz Eulau suggests, the individual is no longer a delegate from his constituents but a trustee of public affairs who must use his own judgement after following the advice of professional officers.[12] Recent research suggests that the majority of councillors may agree that they are 'trustees' rather than 'delegates'. But a substantial minority of younger, newer councillors still believe in their role as delegates from their constituents. A smaller number see themselves as 'politicos', combining both delegate and trustee roles – representing constituents and judging issues in the light of their knowledge and experience.[13]

As the councillor's length of service increases, so he tends to specialise and to become more interested in policy. But, as policy-making becomes more sophisticated and complex, so many councillors retreat from policy into a mass of technicalities and spend a lot of time in committee and in considering reports. They also tend to concentrate on personal 'casework' for individuals. These features were highlighted by the Maud Committee findings. The average amount of contact between councillors and individual constituents is small but a minority, notably Labour members in working class wards, spend a very great deal of time on individual problems.

H. Hugh Heclo believes that the councillor, particularly in poor wards, is increasingly being called upon to be a 'welfare officer'. Though this may contradict classical ideas of political representation, it is here to stay.[14] This, of course, varies according to the ward. The welfare councillor is usually found in the poorer areas, while councillors who see themselves as 'delegates' are normally found in marginal seats, particularly as they are new to the job and building up a reputation as a local spokesman. Councillors in safe seats, and senior members and chairmen, are freer to develop as trustees – policy-makers using their own judgement – or as politicos trying to combine the two roles.

Both Hill and Newton conclude that there is a developmental process, from young members who act as delegates through the mid-career men in politico roles to the long-serving members relying primarily on their judgement and position of responsibility. But even the experienced councillors do not lose touch with the ward and its needs completely, and committee chairmen in particular must guard against charges of remoteness by members of their own party.

The skills which today's councillors need are formidable. They range from sensitive interpersonal skills within the ward, bargaining abilities as party men, and the critical judgement of the committee member. All of these are possible within one local council and within one party or group. But it must be recognised that, in the new larger authorities, this will call for very skilled political leadership. If councillor roles are diverging as much as current research suggests, then the 'welfare state representatives' may find themselves in conflict with council leaders. As a result they may be tempted to join forces with outside groups who seek more direct solutions than those offered by the traditional avenues of committees and council departments.

For most councillors, however, the main justification of their work is that it helps the community and the individuals within it. Councillors stress community and public service reasons for taking up council work. Some want to help to solve individual problems, or take up the cause of a group, but the majority see themselves as working for the good of the community as a whole. The nature of council and committee work compels them to have opinions, take stands on issues, and to evaluate what is being done. As a result, councillors defend themselves from sectional pressures to a greater extent than do M.P.s. Central government accepts pressure groups as part of democratic life. Local councils, by contrast, are more reluctant to encourage what they may see as an infringement of their right to govern. Similarly, calls for wider participation may be welcomed as a sign of a more sympathetic electorate or disliked because they threaten efficiency and smooth administration. Councillors refuse to surrender any power to more 'popular' systems of consultation. The same is true of officers. They are already accountable to elected members and do not want to explain their work directly to individuals and groups.

Councillors welcome local voluntary organisations – but as helpmates or handmaidens, filling gaps in local authority services or drawing attention to (soluble) problems. Another feature is that councillors view local associations in rather a restricted way. Many councillors, when they speak of local pressure groups, are referring to branches of large national organisations such as the Civic Trust. These, and the traditional welfare organisations, are the groups which are seen as legitimate and trustworthy. The newer, more vociferous groups may be viewed with suspicion as irresponsible and unhelpful. To some extent these varied attitudes are paradoxical since councillors are themselves members of a large number of local organisations. Indeed, as Maud showed, they belong to more associations (outside their council duties) than the ordinary citizen. The paradox is partly explained by the fact that, for most councillors. associational membership is part of their general public life which extends, but does not challenge, their council work. A substantial minority of councillors do maintain active links with particular groups but others, once they reach senior positions on the council, have more nominal and honorific contacts.

The contacts which ordinary people have with voluntary associations is equally varied. It has often been observed that participation is a cumulative phenomena. Some people are 'joiners', taking part in more than one kind of organisation so that there is a considerable degree of overlapping membership. This varies between the classes, and between the parties, with the working class and Labour supporters and councillors least likely to have this rich associational life. The middle class are most involved in voluntary organisation, but the type of involvement also varies with age. The younger, white collar and professional people are more likely, in recent years, to be found in the newer radical groups and the older and more traditional middle class in the well-established groups. The upper classes, by contrast, are the most traditional: Roger V. Clements states that they see voluntary work as a worthwhile alternative to council member-ship, which is disliked for its party politics.[15] This does not mean that they lack contacts with the council or have no influence on what it does. On the contrary, they have a close and continuous connection with council decision-making because of their property and business interests. They are 'insiders', linking the political system with the economic and social systems.

By contrast, most voluntary organisations are more 'distanced' from the council. The majority of councillors take a favourable view of their activities but do not think of them as equal partners in com-munity affairs. Councillors judge groups according to whether they are more or less worthy, reliable and helpful and prefer those whose demands and methods of working are closest to council thinking. As a result, the favoured groups become domesticated: they do not need to resort to pressure tactics and are reluctant to make 'unacceptable' demands or use 'inappropriate' procedures.[16] Most groups recognise that they will be most successful if they behave in the traditional manner; this calls for a professional and responsible organisation and the acceptance in the eyes of officials as reliable spokesmen, fact-gatherers and co-workers.

THE INFLUENCE OF PLANNING

Local planning authorities, while reluctant to accept direct participa-tion in the making of plans, have always recognised the need to consult interested parties. But the main source of participation in the past has been the individual's right to appear at planning inquiries. The democratic process requires that those who are affected have the right to be told what is planned, to put their objection forward, and to have it considered (by the local authority, the Ministry Inspectorate, and the Minister). This necessarily slows down decision-making. But there are other difficulties. These are: cost (in time and money); the form of the proceedings; and excessive delays. One outcome has been the suggestion that 'legal aid' should be available for planning appeals, or that voluntary groups should receive public money to help them to be represented at enquiries. As well as the cost factor, objectors are also at a disadvantage because they have no right of access to documents prepared by officials and others.

The appeals procedure is quasi-judicial: the Minister, through his Inspector, hears all sides of the case and then adjudicates. Planning enquiries may now be too legalistic. Professional advocates argue in the style of the courtroom and technical experts also adopt a formal stance. As a result the individual is deterred from appearing. The formal atmosphere may also cause attitudes to harden and produce a confrontation situation.

In future, the traditional right to participate by objecting will continue to operate at local plan level but for structure plans a new form of public examination will replace the public enquiry. This will allow for a general examination of policy, for which the normal enquiry procedure is unsuited, and it will be more informal and less cumbersome. The Town and Country Planning (Amendment) Act 1972, s.3, enables such a public examination to be held and for participants invited by the Minister to take part in a shorter, informal debate of key issues. Individuals and groups will still have the right to submit written objections, and these will be considered before the key issues, and who is to take part, is decided.

The new procedures are welcome but there are still doubts whether the public will get a chance to consider real alternatives. The public examination comes at the end of the process and thus, claims Ian Lyon, misses the original advantages of Professor Self's suggestions for a statutory conference at the half-way stage which would have given the planning authority an opportunity to rethink its proposals.[17]

Participation in planning is not confined to public inquiries. It is argued that people should be able to make their views known at a much earlier stage. Currently, there is an additional concern for improvements in the system as planning is redefined to embrace wider social and economic problems and local authorities use a battery of techniques to assess needs and determine priorities. The main concern is still, however, to improve plans and to make them more acceptable. If people knew more about planning, and were able to make their views known at an earlier stage then, it is argued, there would be less criticism and opposition. This in turn would help to reduce the ever-increasing burden of public inquiries and central supervision. Planning would be easier and quicker.

The 1968 Town and Country Planning Act, which devised a new and hopefully speedier method of plan-making, gives the individual the right to take part in the making of both structure and local plans for the first time. At the same time the Skeffington Committee called for more public involvement. The Skeffington Committee, appointed in 1968 to advise on how participation in plan-making could be fostered, reported in 1969. It defined participation as 'the act of sharing in the formulation of policies and proposals'.[18] This meant more than the statutory right of objection to plans and called for a close relation between councillors and public in all aspects of local services, not just planning. Skeffington's suggestions for a community forum (to promote discussion between and among local groups and the council) and the community development officer (to promote and seek the opinions of non-joiners and the passive majority) have unfortunately met with little response. Local authorities preferred more informal methods.

But the spirit of Skeffington has influenced legislation. S.8 and s.12 of the Town and Country Planning Act of 1971 lay down that authorities are to take steps to secure adequate publicity and to make sure that people who want to make representations are made aware of their rights and are given an adequate opportunity to make representations. And the Ministry circular 52/72 on publicity and participation in planning calls on local authorities to foster contacts with the press and other media, to publish a timetable of participation, and warns against the problems of blight.[19]

The Skeffington call for informed participation – for adequate publicity, information and use of the press and other media at definite stages or pauses in the process – is welcome. But its proposals are little more than exhortatory. Skeffington has also been criticised for its naivety in implying that increased understanding and involvement lessens conflict and makes planning more acceptable. This ignores the genuine clash of interests involved.

The Report also ignored the political world of the council and the relations between members and officers. The Committee's broad definition of participation could equally well serve as a definition of democracy. Democratic local government has always depended on people taking part: as members, officers, voters and local inhabitants. Instead of trying to devise new methods, the Committee could well have tried to tackle how this worked and suggest remedies based on what councillors, committees and officers actually do. Skeffington also ignored another vital aspect of democratic participation. People should be able to discuss the reasoning behind planning – why should an area be developed, not merely how this could be done – and this implies a political debate.

The alleged divorce between planners and planned is not just a question of delay and conflict of interests but arises from the secrecy surrounding plan making. The effect of planning on land values means that secrecy has to be maintained but in the past this has been too marked. It is now being relaxed to some extent, as alternative proposals are offered in the structure plan process, and because of the more generous compensation for blight.

An equally serious factor is to be quite clear when people's views and demands are needed and when the question is more one of public relations. Participation may not be necessary for new shops in the suburbs but it is essential for the development of a twilight residential area, and this distinction is at the heart of democratic government in urban industrial society.

The need to make a proper distinction between the two distinct kinds of citizen involvement in planning – participation and public relations – is well illustrated, argues Derek Senior, by both the Skeffington Report and the 1968 Act.[20] Skeffington was wrong to suggest that participation has its main part to play at the late stage of the planners' 'preferred proposals' and not at the earlier, more crucial stage of identifying the choices available. Admittedly, the public needs guidance. It must await the considered assessments of the experts; but then it has the right to comment on these available choices which it is the planners' duty to put forward in lucid and intelligible forms. The Skeffington assertion that policy choices can offer no place for major public involvement is particularly unfortunate in local, as opposed to strategic, planning. It is at this stage that people have the right to learn about the choices which immediately affect their own interests.

The new system of planning under the 1968 Act is slowly proceeding. Structure plans have been under way in several parts of the country (as designated by the Minister; other areas are proceeding with the old development plan machinery) and draft reports for some of them were appearing by the beginning of 1973. They had all made positive efforts to encourage participation, mainly from interest groups and their 'umbrella' organisations. Even so, the response from the public has been very low and the majority, in spite of publicity, random surveys, intensive press coverage and public meetings, remains passive. The planners must produce a structure plan which is economically feasible and has a reasonable political chance of being implemented. The public, by contrast, is only interested in the structure plan insofar as it touches their broad concern with their environment and its conservation. More local and direct intervention can be expected when the next stage of local plan-making begins.

Planners are ambivalent towards public participation. They are sensitive to outside criticism – including the charge that they advocate more participation to improve their own image and make their work acceptable – while recognising the need for genuine consultation. One severe criticism of planners is that they become committed to their decisions and that once the process is set in motion it cannot be diverted or halted.

Other critics have suggested that planners, by virtue of their training and their day-to-day work, are committed to an ideology of faith in the future, of the truth of their professional assertions, and the need to make people see this truth as they do. They are, to use John Gower Davies' term, 'evangelistic bureaucrats', impatient with the resistance of ordinary people – for example, of local residents to the redevelopment of their area.[21] And in many cases, people respond to this; many accept the planners' belief that protest is harmful and that participation means behaving 'reasonably'. Only when residents realise that they have little chance of changing the planners' views, and that their future is threatened by the uncertainty of the plan-making, do they become impatient and hostile.

The most telling criticism, however, is one which applies not to the planning profession but to the groups who criticise them. Change can only come about through political (not necessarily party political) organisation. This means more than expertise, appeals to self-evident truths or to the good of the community. The civic amenity groups, for example, have tended to think of planning as a politically neutral activity in which problems are self-evident. This is not true: indeed, their own success shows how important are political skills: ability to marshall the evidence and use a variety of tactics to press their point effectively.

Some pressure groups, especially those made up of younger, professional people, recognise this and consciously aim to influence planning decisions. John Ferris shows that in some cases they, rather than the council, decide what the problems are as well as the appropriate solutions.[22] This is a very powerful political weapon: amenity groups have an ideology (what the good life consists of and how it may be preserved) through which to judge the council. The political action of most groups is still, however, defensive and negative. It arises out of opposition and has little or no initiatory role.

The new ideas on participatory democracy have affected the outlook of planners and some have adopted a radically critical attitude to what they regard as the sham of participation. Sherry Arnstein's 'ladder of citizen participation', for example, begins with Manipulation, Information and Consultation and climbs up to Partnership, Delegated Power and Citizen Control.[23] In this country participation is largely confined to what Arnstein calls the 'tokenism' of limited involvement – information and consultation. Nowhere do we see, in planning or other areas, a significant degree of partnership, delegated power from authority to neighbourhood or group, or citizen control. Our theory and practice of local government virtually excludes this. Nor do we see any evidence of widespread acceptance of Paul Davidoff's 'advocacy planners': people employed by neighbourhood groups to fight city hall and control their own plans.[24] These ideas have had only a limited impact here, but some of the younger planners do see themselves in less professionally neutral terms. They want to help the poor to take part in the issues they understand – housing and urban renewal – but there is little hope of this unless money is forthcoming to develop it.

We have examined planning in some detail because planners have had a large and formative involvement in the participation issue. They have dominated the debate when, as Brian J. Styles suggests, it might have been better to see participation as an issue of government – the shaping and sharing of power – and not of planning at all.[25] The public concentration on planning has had a further unfortunate effect. It has made people's views more widely known but has not necessarily made planners or councillors more responsive. And it is responsiveness which is the great problem.

THE INDIVIDUAL AND THE COUNCIL

The definition and nature of participation varies, depending on who is involved and whether or not they are part of the official local government machine. Much participation is consultation and the sounding of opinion. Some would argue that it is mere public relations and propaganda. It is an adjunct to good administration, a necessary part of a politician's contact with constituents, and a normal feature of democratic life. Unless officers and councillors can get people to participate by making their views known then their work will be that much harder. For example, over controversial issues such as planning or housing policy, consultation may help – though it cannot solve – some of the questions of priority.

But participation in actual decision-making is limited. Actual involvement of outsiders in council work is confined to a handful of people. The 1972 Local Government Act and various other statutes allow outside members to be co-opted to council committees. But local authorities do not use this power extensively. The majority of people have, in fact, only limited, informal and spasmodic contacts with council affairs.

It is often said that ordinary people do not want to participate in local government. Most people want fair and impartial services, not an opportunity to take part. Only about a third of the electorate bothers to go to the poll and although there is a general belief in democracy the ordinary man knows or cares little about what his council does. The individual's main interest, as Jean Bonner showed twenty years ago, lies in the effectiveness of local services and if he wants help he goes to officers. He is not disinterested, but pragmatic; and low polls do not, therefore, mean he is 'apathetic'.[26] Most individuals have a limited, sectional interest and do not want to take part in 'local government'. The Redcliffe-Maud research found that those with higher status and education were more interested and more knowledgable.[27] But this may equally be a sectional, not a 'local government' interest, since these people live in areas with better local services, and so they have a direct interest in maintaining their quality.

The majority of people, especially working-class citizens, also have an undemanding acceptance of authority. In addition, people's views and actions are remarkably stable. Lester W. Milbrath typecasts individuals as 'apathetics', 'spectators' and 'gladiators'; it takes real effort, or the shock of specific events, before people change their behaviour from one kind of role to another.[28] In fact, as Gabriel A. Almond and Sidney Verba demonstrated, Britain has a remarkably 'participant' culture: 70 per cent of the sample believed they ought to be active in local affairs and 78 per cent felt that, if necessary, they could do something to make a local council change a policy which was unfair or unjust.[29] This shows approval or acceptance, not necessarily the desire to take part. Undoubtedly, for the majority of people, services are accepted and unquestioned. But we now recognise that community life is much richer than had previously been thought.

People get involved, not just to get things done, but to gain the personal satisfaction of helping others or feeling part of important events. This satisfaction is an important ingredient in the democratic process. It binds people to each other and to their government and is part of what we mean by citizenship. These views, and the experience of involvement, including tolerance for other viewpoints, are important. Participation does not come naturally, it has to be learned and the best training is actually taking part. Participation, including protest, is also important as a symbol. Councillors and officers argue that it should be kept within reasoned – and reasoning – grounds; protest and direct action are unjustified. But this ignores the symbolism of much protest. It is a necessary, not a threatening feature, of open societies.

In English local government, however, the reformist approach is still the most important. Most people take part to protect their interests, improve conditions and change what is done. Even in areas of controversy the idea of consensus is strongly entrenched, with the normal pattern being to get people to sit down and argue out their problems. Such attitudes are reinforced by the way local government works. It is far easier to take part in the implementation stage of decision-making – in social work and in the use of voluntary associations as the agents of the council – than in the policy formation stage. And, in order for participation to be effective, people have to see that they are being consulted at an early enough stage for their views to be taken seriously. This is still a stumbling block. Nor can participation be a mere sham. If people see that the political structure does not respond to their demands then they are realistic to be apathetic and take no part in it.

PARTICIPATION: THE NEED FOR NEW MACHINERY?

The last decade has seen a new challenge to accepted ways of doing things. Participation, protest and direct action have not overthrown representative government. They have, however, been instrumental in changing – not always for the better – attitudes and procedures. The dominating problem has been to encourage participation within a largely unchanged framework of local decision-making. In 1968 the Skeffington Report on People and Planning and the Seebohm Report on The Personal Social Services suggested a variety of publicity, opinion-seeking and consultative procedures. The reform of local government, for its part, encourages traditional forms of involvement but little that is new in the way of neighbourhood or community action.

Local government reform will be a mixed blessing. Larger units, with fewer elected members may be more remote. But there may be more contested elections, and a higher level of voting. Increased party interest may encourage a more lively grass-roots within the parties themselves. Finally, the new, larger authorities might stimulate more powerful and effective pressure-group activity. Others argue that local government reform will leave such grass roots opinion unheard. New machinery of community action will be more, not less, important.

It is argued that a new framework is needed because modern society is technically complex and dominated by bureaucratic institutions. This makes it difficult for ordinary people to make their voice heard through traditional channels. It is even harder for the poor who, as ever, are often outside the established procedures of representative democracy. They, and many other groups, can only be helped by new kinds of involvement. Some of this activity in community groups, tenants' associations and squatters groups, now takes place to a considerable extent outside the existing political partners and, in particular, the local council.

The new groups challenge conventional local council decision-making and *fait accompli* decisions. Often their demands are populist – give people the right to voice their demands and make their decisions directly on each local issue rather than trusting their representatives sitting in council committees. For some, community action is the new non-political politics. Others argue that desirable social change will not come about unless present methods of working are challenged and power redistributed and the poor less deprived.

Most groups demand less than this but do want to extend the ways in which they take part and to have their right to suggest new schemes taken seriously. They do not see themselves as 'helping the poor' so much as encouraging people to make their own demands and solve their own problems. If people participate in the services set up to help then, it is argued, things will be done in a more democratic and more humane way. Services will also be improved because they are based on better information.

The new ideas of participation also challenge the old beliefs about the justification of such involvement. The argument is about power and its distribution, not just about consultation. The nineteenth-century debate about basic participation – giving men the vote – was an argument about power as well as about public opinion. Now it is claimed that there is a need to revive this kind of concern since present-day participation is manifestly sectional and unequal. The socially and economically powerful, or those who have some emotional leverage because of the nature of the issue (such as housing), will dominate the rest. This makes it harder, not easier, to set priorities and reflect the public good.

These demands for more participation are reflected in modern legislation. The Seebohm Report explicitly calls for more involvement of those affected by social services in defining and discovering need and in helping to formulate remedies and carry them out.[30] But it is still an extension of existing co-operation between the council and voluntary welfare groups.

Participatory democracy, by contrast, calls for more dramatic changes, mostly in the field of community development and community action work with the poor. Similarly, tenants' movements call for more direct involvement in the management of council estates. Tenant participation has little chance of immediate acceptance; the involvement of parents in schools may be more successful. The demands of parents for a greater say in educational matters is on the increase. Plowden urged that Parent/Teacher Associations should play a larger part in school affairs but they are still not a statutory requirement and local authorities and teachers are reluctant to face what they see as possible interference. In some areas there are now positive attempts to reform governing bodies to include staff, pupils and parents. Currently, there are legal snags over the age of appointment which hampers the use of pupil governors. But the real problem is more basic. The political parties, while agreeing to the reduction in purely political appointees to governing bodies, are reluctant to take the first step, particularly as these posts also give them important patronage powers.

Tenant involvement in housing management, and parent participation in the schools, are both examples of the involvement in a service by the people who benefit from it. One danger is that the result may be selfish and sectional; people are only interested in their own needs and have little concern for others. The public interest, and the accountability of elected representatives, is then lost sight of.

The danger of selfishness could, it is argued, be overcome by a new body – the neighbourhood council – which has succeeded in establishing itself in some inner city areas. As with community action, the idea comes largely from American experience.[31] The American neighbourhood council idea is based on citizen participation and the decentralisation of authority. In England the neighbourhood council is an additional means of representation – particularly of minority and interest groups – and a valuable sounding board of opinion. As such it complements, not contradicts, the local authority. It can also help, as parish councils have traditionally done, to put pressure on other authorities in a reasoned and accepted manner.

Michael Young and others have shown that people do see their 'home area' as a real and potentially viable setting for mutual help.[32] But actual neighbourhood government as opposed to consultation or pressure, depends on having money to hire staff, control funds and formulate policy. And this is normally lacking. An important substitute activity may then turn out to be the demand that local people, not middle-class outsiders, should control local voluntary action.

The 1972 Act, in spite of the Redcliffe-Maud Report recommendations and the development of an organised movement (The Association of Neighbourhood Councils) makes no provision for statutory neighbourhood councils for parts of towns. Parish councils are retained for rural areas (including rural boroughs) and only in Wales can statutory community councils be established for boroughs, urban districts or for parts of urban areas. But there is virtually no difference between English parishes and Welsh communities since a community cannot be established within an 'excepted borough' and these are the six biggest towns in Wales in which urban 'neighbourhood councils' might be valuable.

Some 69 boroughs and 200 districts in England will also be able to set up their own town councils and town mayors when they are incorporated into the new, large districts in 1974. These existing 269 authorities are successor parishes under the 1972 Act and are essentially urban parishes which perpetuate the identity of existing small towns. They will have parish powers; but they may in time become a means of presenting the communities' wishes to the new county and district councils. There are signs that future governments may reconsider this position; Labour supports elected neighbourhood councils, and the Liberals fight vigorously for 'community politics'.

There are fears that local neighbourhood councils would be a cumbersome and ineffective machinery. In large cities they would be so numerous as to present a burden of consultation out of all proportion to their benefit. This is to assume, probably erroneously, that there would be a desire for them in all areas. A more serious criticism is that the prosperous suburbs, not the deprived areas, would benefit most. The middle-class suburban neighbourhood council might achieve many gains, particularly in consultation over planning matters. This leads to a second difficulty. The existence of neighbourhood councils, unless they are merely sounding boards of opinion, may again fragment overall policy-making.

Councillors, who spend their time in committees dealing with definite problems – however minute or detailed – are frequently irritated by the feeling that while community action may be urgent, it is also notoriously vague. The spokesmen for neighbourhood self-help are happy with this vagueness which they see as flexibility, humaneness and spontaneity. Local authorities, for their part, believe that there must be accepted political means for establishing priorities. Both of these attitudes are a necessary part of local affairs. The danger to guard against is that of deceiving people, under the guise of community action, into believing that local government is going to change overnight into neighbourhood self-governing communities. It is not; the local authority is the legitimate government and the contribution of community action movements will potentially enrich it but will not overthrow it.

The new ideas may be resented by local authorities whose services operate in a framework of consensus in which council, committee and social worker are seeking the same ends. The new approaches, by contrast, bring conflict: the client is encouraged to demand his rights and the social worker is a fighter for justice, not just a 'helper' of the poor.

A word of caution is needed. Community action and community development have different meanings. Community action concerns change and thus, potentially, conflict. Community development, by contrast, is concerned with building up local groups and institutions and stresses co-operation and collaboration. Community action has been influenced by American ideas. But, even before the cutbacks in the U.S. War on Poverty in the 1970s, there was evidence that its impact was marginal. The poor had little influence. Local self-help did not replace the need for national solutions to national problems. These were social and economic problems, not just 'participation' ones. Radical action could offer little by way of alternative programmes and policies. This reinforces the theme of this book: frameworks and institutions shape democratic processes, but no more. Policies have to be deliberately sought, evaluated and made effective. And this needs political will and the recognition that participation, like equality and justice, is a matter of conflict and compromise over scarce resources.

The main value of community action may turn out to be its impact on the secretive nature of English local government. But this is a delicate task. As with more traditional forms of participation, there are dangers of failure and of increased suspicion of local bureaucracies. Instead of being progressive, this can make things worse: the political parties themselves become hostile and more, not less, local authority decisions are taken in secret. From the other side, demands for more participation give rise to disquiet. The new movements draw in the poor (or their spokesmen) but most effective participation continues to be a middle-class preserve. Effective involvement takes time, knowledge, motivation and resources. Two potentially harmful results may follow. One is that the ordinary man with none of these benefits will be ignored. The other is that, even where money and skills produce effective involvement, the end result may still be frustration and alienation. One of the byproducts of this participatory age is that some people, particularly those who normally take little interest in council affairs, learn only too well the real cost of being involved. Disillusionment and defeat are just as real as the costs of money and time.

PARTICIPATION AND POWER

Territorial democracy, says J. G. Bulpitt, rests on the 'Traditional Orthodoxy' of community, participation, local government, decentralisation and democracy. But this traditional orthodoxy is ambiguous about how power is actually to be shared between people.[33] The traditional ideal of local people attached to their community and involved in its affairs is quite compatible, in theory and practice, with government by a local élite. Nor is it clear to what extent the citizen is expected to take part beyond the act of voting.

Other writers claim that the individual's participation in politics has little real meaning if society itself offers few real choices. Democracy is imperfect because most people do not have the opportunity to take part in decisions at work, in the schools and in their local areas. In addition, there is evidence to show a positive correlation between participation and the sense of political competence – and these reinforce each other.

The idea of participation is not a new one. The debate about government has always included arguments about who should take part, and on what terms, in political life. The extension of the franchise brought a recognition that participation did not depend solely on civil and political liberty. In order to take their full part, individuals had to have a minimum competence: some education, freedom from the extremes of poverty, disease and disorder, and a means of expressing their demands while recognising those of their neighbours.

Representative institutions fulfilled these demands in an orderly way. They allowed for the expression of opinion and control of representatives. The vote, and the widening circle of candidates, drew more people into the political process. Elected councillors were accountable to their constituents and in close touch with local opinion. Political parties encouraged ordinary people to stand for their local council. Representative government was also flexible. As society and government became more complex it came to terms with interest groups. Government had always consulted opinion; now this was developed more widely through many formal and informal groups.

In recent years, however, representative government has been criticised as remote and bureaucratic and the question of participation has been re-examined. It is alleged that the traditional forms of representative government restrict rather than encourage citizen involvement. One international survey says that English local councils are secretive; content to consult the citizen only when required to do so by statute or Ministerial direction. They have not gone out of their way to promote citizen involvement.[34] And it is a widely held view in this country that the public, for its part, is ignorant and apathetic and shows little interest in representative local government.

Traditional means of participation are also unable to cope with rising demands and rising protest. Representative institutions find it hard, in the planned economy and the welfare state, to meet all the demands made upon them. Local government brings positive services and interferes with individual freedom. It is increasingly difficult, in this situation, to make governors accountable or check what they do. People are then tempted to turn away from the accepted channels.

The search for remedies gives rise to new pressure groups, who are more willing to become politically involved. They do not shun controversy. And they may also support demands for 'direct action': confrontation with officials and elected representatives and attempts to change decisions not through the vote, but by immediate protest.

In both traditional and new debates on participation the idea of 'taking part' implies an active citizenship. Unless a high proportion of people take some part, participation has little meaning and even representative government is a sham. There has been, over the last decade, a lengthy debate on this point. Participation is both the instrumental and effective. That is, people take part both to achieve real goals and to satisfy their need for esteem and self-achievement.

The wide-ranging arguments of recent years reflect the vitality of community life. They are a welcome addition to the local debate and will enliven rather than hamper local government. But there are dangers that political will and direction may be lost. As Derek Senior reminds us, disinterested reformers too must organise, to fortify the failing will of central and local government to make the necessary changes which no interest group wants, and to oppose those pressures which no single group can effectively counteract.[35]

There is also the problem that, as consultation widens and elements of participatory democracy encourage greater citizen participation, the role of opposition is potentially weakened. Representative democracy depends on the marshalling of opinion and on accountability and responsiveness. It also depends, in this country, on both governing and opposition roles as legitimate expressions of power. The role of opposition in local government has often been weak because it faces a monolithic and immovable majority in large cities or country areas. This may change in the new local government system. But, by then, the new features of involvement and intervention may have pre-empted some of the functions which reinvigorated opposition should fulfil.

The argument for greater citizen participation is an argument about power. Power is the crucial issue; who is to decide local policy and where control is to lie, are central. The danger is of rule by liberal veto. That is, councils propose policies but find that (in housing or welfare for example) these cannot be carried out unless organised groups in the community can be marshalled in support. These groups may have undue influence so that what is done is subject to their veto. This kind of destructive influence can only be prevented by vigorous government and opposition within the council chamber itself rather than outside it.

NOTES

1. Sidney and Beatrice Webb, The Development of *English Local Government 1689-1835* (Oxford University Press, Home University Library, 1963), p. 179.
2. J. H. Warren, 'The British Party System', *Parliamentary Affairs*, Vol. V, No. 1 (Winter 1951), p. 180.
3. K. Newton, 'Turnout and Marginality in Local Elections', *British Journal of Political Science*, Vol. 2, No. 2 (1972), p. 255.
4. J. G. Bulpitt, *Party Politics in English Local Government* (Longmans, 1967), p. 118.
5. Roy Gregory, 'Local Elections and the "Rule of Anticipated Reactions" ', *Political Studies*, Vol. XVII, No. 1 (March 1969), p. 46.
6. Cf. Hanna F. Pitkin, *The Concept of Representation* (University of California Press, 1967).

7. Dilys M. Hill, *Participation in Local Affairs* (Penguin, 1970), pp. 96-8.
8. E. P. Hennock, *Fit and Proper Persons* (Edward Arnold, 1973), p. 336 and pp. 342-4.
9. L. J. Sharpe, 'Elected Representatives in Local Government', *British Journal of Sociology*, Vol. XIII (1962), p. 204.
10. G. W. Jones, *Borough Politics* (Macmillan, 1969), pp. 152-3.
11. Barry Hindess, *The Decline of Working-Class Politics* (McGibbon and Kee 1971), p. 120.
12. Heinz Eulau, 'The Legislator as Representative: representational roles' *in* John C. Wahlke, Heinz Eulau, William Buchanan and LeRoy C. Ferguson, *The Legislative System* (John Wiley & Sons, 1962), pp. 285-6.
13. K. Newton, 'The Roles of Elected Representatives in Local Politics', *Discussion Papers Series F*, No. 14 (University of Birmingham, Faculty of Commerce and Social Science, January 1972), p. 9.
14. H. Hugh Heclo, 'The Councillor's Job', *Public Administration*, Vol. 47 (Summer 1969), p. 191.
15. Roger V. Clements, *Local Notables and the City Council* (Macmillan, 1969), pp. 60-1.
16. John Dearlove, 'Councillors and Interest Groups in Kensington and Chelsea', *British Journal of Political Science*, Vol. 1, No. 2 (April 1971), pp. 3-5 and pp. 150-1.
17. Ian Lyon, 'A New Form of Public Inquiry', *Town and Country Planning*, Vol. 39, No. 7-8 (July/August 1971), p. 349.
18. 'People and Planning', *Report* of the Committee on Public Participation in Planning (HMSO, 1969), p. 1.
19. 'Town and Country Planning Act 1971: Part 11 Development Plan Proposals: Publicity and Public Participation', *Circular 52/72* (Department of the Environment, 1972).
20. Derek Senior, 'Public Involvement in Planning' *in* William A. Robson and Bernard Crick (eds), *The Future of the Social Services* (Penguin, 1970), p. 94.
21. John Gower Davies, *The Evangelistic Bureaucrat* (Tavistock Publications, 1972), pp. 109-12.
22. John Ferris, *Participation in Urban Planning: the Barnsbury case* (G. Bell & Sons, 1972), p. 71.
23. Sherry R. Arnstein, 'Eight Rungs on the Ladder of Citizen Participation', *reprinted in* Edgar S. Cahn and Barry A. Passett (eds), *Citizen Participation: effecting community change* (Praeger, 1971), pp. 69-70.
24. Paul Davidoff, 'Advocacy and Pluralism in Planning', *Journal of the American Institute of Planners*, Vol. 31, No. 4 (1965), p. 333.
25. Brian J. Styles, 'Public Participation – a reconsideration', *Journal of the Town Planning Institute*, Vol. 57, No. 4 (April 1971), p. 163.
26. Jean Bonner, 'Public Interest in Local Government', *Public Administration*, Vol. 32 (Winter 1954), p. 427.
27. Royal Commission on Local Government in England, *Research Study 9*, 'Community Attitudes Survey', p. 92.
28. Lester W. Milbrath, *Political Participation* (Rand McNally, 1965), p. 20.
29. Gabriel A. Almond and Sidney Verba, *The Civic Culture* (Princeton University Press, 1963), pp. 127 and 142.
30. Committee on Personal and Allied Services, *Report* (1968), paras. 491-5.
31. Cf. Thomas D. Lynch (ed.), 'Neighbourhoods and Citizen Involvement: a symposium', *Public Administration Review*, Vol. 32, No. 3 (1972), pp. 189-231.

32. Michael Young, *The Hornsey Plan* (Association for Neighbourhood Councils, 1970), pp. 15-16.
33. J. G. Bulpitt, 'Participation and Local Government' *in* Geraint Parry (ed.), *Participation in Politics* (Manchester University Press, 1972), pp. 285-7.
34. 'Participation', *Studies in Comparative Local Government*, Vol. 5, No. 2 (International Union of Local Authorities, The Hague, 1971), p. 27.
35. Derek Senior, *op. cit.*, p. 102.

Chapter VII

COMMUNICATION

COMMUNICATION AND DEMOCRATIC SOCIETY

Democratic government is impossible without an informed public opinion. At local level this sometimes seems a difficult requirement; people are relatively ill-informed and local politicians, and the local press, play a less active part than their national counterparts. This is hard to justify, since one of the defences of local government is that it offers a close and unique contact between councillors and citizens. People need clear and accurate information not because they want to take a continuous interest but in order to keep community life under surveillance. Part of this surveillance is to probe possible corruption. But the main criteria of adequate communication is that people can, if they need, get information quickly and accurately – and in a form they can understand.

The public's right to know has a respected place in the struggle for civil and political liberties. J. S. Mill stated that if men are required to fight for their country, pay its taxes and obey its laws then they should be told what for. Their consent should be sought and their opinion counted at its worth – though no more, since all have the same right.[1] As the franchise widened, voters needed information in order to hold their representatives accountable. This applied to government at all levels. In the twentieth century the political parties, and the mass media, have greatly enriched the flow of information but, it is argued, more at national than local level.

Democratic society needs a variety of responses from its citizens. A minority of people will take a fairly continuous interest but the majority will be only intermittently concerned in public issues, except at critical times, particularly in elections. The electorate needs to observe what is happening with accuracy, discuss it, and evaluate it rationally in the light of their own interest and that of the community. Democratic theory also demands that the elected representatives take decisions on the basis of full and accurate information.

The ways in which political messages are transmitted in the local community are determined by the structure of local government, the attitudes of members and officers, and by the 'rules of the game'. Councillors, political parties and community leaders must be able, therefore, to lead opinion and interpret it. Councillors in particular, must be aggregators of demand: that is, they must bring together the various strands of opinion and transmit them into their work on the council and in the party.

In practice, democracy does not live up to these varied ideals. Information is imperfect. Both voters and elected representatives select and filter what they see and hear. People do not observe what is available, they ignore information or are indifferent to it. Some of this indifference is explained by the fact that the individual does not feel that it is worth going to the trouble to obtain information. Local government works much as usual, whether he votes or not, and if he has little effective influence then the search for information will be a wasteful activity. Research shows that only a small minority of people discuss political issues and that, when they do, it is with their family, friends and workmates whose opinions already correspond to a large degree with their own. Finally many people do not want to be informed; they may see much of what official bodies say as propaganda or as a form of entertainment. The mass media may agree with them so that politicians are presented as entertainers, rather than as informed leaders.

In local government there is also an additional weakness which does not apply at national level. This is the difficulty of effective opposition where one-party control in urban areas, and the permanent non-party, conservative administration in the countryside, has been the norm for long periods. Democracy must, as Richard R. Fagan emphasises, provide adequate means of communication for various kinds of 'oppositions'.[2] But this is hard to achieve at local level. One-party rule weakens vigorous opposition; there are fewer outlets, through the local press, than in national politics; and there is a lower level of interest in community affairs.

In local government it is hard for opposing voices, especially from outside the council, to get accurate information on which to mount a case. On controversial issues this may be overcome by sympathetic 'insiders' and by a probing press. But most individuals and groups lack those sustained means of expressing a point of view which the 1949 Royal Commission on the Press said was necessary in a democracy.[3]

Communication has both a horizontal and a vertical dimension. The horizontal dimension consists of communications between members, committees, officers, departments and voluntary associations.

F

This is the group of community rulers, as it were, talking among themselves. Vertical communication is that between council and public. The citizen is a subordinate and passive receiver of information and publicity. His active role is largely confined to expressing his opinion by his vote. Further than this, he can contact councillors and departmental officers for advice and help with individual problems.

Communication is also concerned with the question of who has access to information and who controls it. The main issue here is how the different classes and groups in the community use the information available to them and how they prevail on elected members and officers to take heed of them. Political power and the effective control of communication go together: the more influential sections of the community are the more middle-class, more educated and more organised members. The language in which discourse is conducted also reinforces the power of middle-class educated opinion.

LOCAL AUTHORITY PUBLICITY AND PUBLIC RELATIONS

Local authorities are required by statute to publish certain information. The rate demand note must show how money is spent on services. The minutes of council meetings, and the Abstract of Accounts, must be open for inspection. But minutes and accounts make dull and often unintelligible reading. They call for little positive initiative by the local authority and the public does not look to them as major sources of information.

All local authorities want to project a favourable image, to increase the public's interest in the work of the council, and to maintain good relations with the public, They recognise the need for public relations but are limited in what they can do by the criticism that it is wrong to spend ratepayers' money on what appears to be advertising. In practice, little in the way of formal public relations are carried out. Only a minority of local authorities, in the large towns and in London, employ full-time public relations or information officers. By contrast, central government publishes a vast amount of information and publicity.

The difference may in part be explained by the argument that, since local authorities carry out services already laid down by national legislation, additional publicity is mere propaganda for the party currently controlling council affairs. The councillor considers that he, as the representative of his constituents, is the major link with the council. Public relations is unnecessary except to promote local services in a favourable way.

These traditional attitudes are now responding to wider pressures. Local authorities are reappraising their attitudes to the press and to local broadcasting and also reacting to the demands for more open conduct of their business from community action groups and others. But they still jealously guard their right to judge what is best for the local community. They have never responded, to any great degree, to the continual barrage of good advice on publicity and public relations offered by central governments or political parties.

In the immediate post-war period it seemed, for a time, that this might change. The reconstruction programmes of the political parties and NALGO pointed to the public's desire for more information and involvement. In 1947 the Minister of Health (then responsible for local government) set up a Consultative Committee on Publicity for Local Government. Its Interim Report (now out of print) said that publicity would aid local democracy and encourage people to take part as councillors and as officers. The 1948 Local Government Act gave local authorities the power to provide information centres, courses on municipal affairs and grants to voluntary bodies. The enthusiasm was halted by the financial crisis of 1949. The Consultative Committee was disbanded in 1950, and local authorities cut back on their publicity activities.

The political parties and the local authority Associations have continued to urge local authorities to maintain better contacts with the public and provide more information and publicity. In 1962 the four local authority Associations set up the Local Government Information Office. This has provided advice and practical help to individual local authorities with particular emphasis on encouraging a higher level of turnout in local elections. In 1970 the LGIO and the Institute of Journalists issued joint recommendations to local councils, the press, radio and television, suggesting that councils should have a definite policy on press relations and promote better contacts, and newspaper editors should encourage senior staff to specialise since local government affairs are becoming more complex.

Local officers, like councillors, see the need for good communication to promote co-operation from local people and sustain their interest in the work of council departments. In the ten years from the mid-1950s NALGO encouraged more publicity by local authorities. NALGO saw this as a way to promote both the image of local government and of their own status and earning powers. After 1967, with the adverse financial situation and the prices and incomes policy, NALGO's position changed. In 1968 public relations activity turned almost exclusively to trade union and economic matters.

In 1972, with the move towards the new local government system, the Bains Report supported the need for local authority public relations. Local authorities have a firm duty to inform the community and should put forward their views on matters of concern.[4] Bains suggested that the large local authorities should set up full-time public relations and information units. But, above all, local authorities should adopt 'an outgoing and positive attitude' to their inhabitants.

Today, public relations plays a minor, if necessary, part in local government. The real arteries of political communication are, at both national and local level, the political parties, the pressure groups and the mass media. And it is the media that cause most controversy. Political communication is an exercise of power since the way political messages are sent, not just their content, influences their effectiveness. This power lies with the communicators – in the parties, the pressure groups and the mass media. In the local community this works imperfectly; councillors put over their messages in a less forceful and skilled manner than national politicians. The mass media – the local press – is also less effective because it does not act as a probing or informing media to the same extent as its national counterparts.

The attitudes of councillors and officers are not the only impediment to better communication. The structure of the committee system, and the nature of its working, is crucial. It is difficult for the public to locate responsibility for particular decisions, to seek information and get a positive response. It is also difficult to assign responsibility for publicity and information. Normally, the Clerk and his department will be responsible for these functions but departmentalism may cause jealousies and suspicion. Chief officers and committee members may want to control what is published and they resent the central dissemination of information. As a result, no one may take responsibility; the problem is dealt with by informal methods to avoid trespassing on the sensitivities of committees and departments.

The working of the committee system means that a planning committee, for example, will only rarely have to face debate and questioning in open council. The opportunity for public scrutiny may thus be lost. This is unfortunate, says R. J. Buxton, since debate on planning applications concerns policy issues about how the community as a whole should develop and citizens are entitled to know who is responsible and what their attitudes are.

There is a second reason why this is particularly true of planning. R. J. Buxton states that a planning committee may often have to decide in a matter where the council itself has a direct or indirect interest – for example, a request to develop shops which may compete with a local authority city centre development – and these problems should be faced in public.[5] Local authorities may, on the other hand, suffer because they have no means of putting over issues of principle (for example in education) to local people in a meaningful way. When this happens the danger is that 'informed local opinion' turns out to be vested interests. This is now more important than ever. In order to assess needs accurately local authorities must seek out views, not just wait for them to appear. The growth of local pressure groups increases the danger that what local authorities hear is what is shouted loudest by particular interests. As a result, the most needy will go unheard. It is the job of local councils, a Fabian Group has argued, to employ community development officers to remedy this situation.[6]

People must learn of the council's plans, and make their own views known, when priorities are being determined. At later stages the process becomes one of publicity and propaganda for what has been decided. And this must be a genuine two-way flow of information; if the public merely learns of matters at an early stage but never influences final decisions then dissatisfaction and frustration follow.

It is the timing, and openness, of the two-way flow of information that lies at the heart of much dissatisfaction with local government secrecy. The difficulties of secrecy, and of local councils putting their case effectively, could arguably be overcome by opening local council committees to the public and the press. This is dealt with below (see pp. 174-175).

COUNCILLORS, PARTIES AND CITIZENS

The ordinary man spends little time or effort in getting information. This is a reasonable attitude, given the limited influence which he has. Referenda or opinion polls cannot, and do not, improve this situation which, in theory at least, depends more on the relation between councillors and their ward constituents. In the local community information and opinion come from many sources, including the council, the political parties, newspapers and other mass media, local associations and individuals. The flow of information depends on the political structure – the council, its members and officers.

There are generally thought to be, as a result, three main defects of local communication. First there is an overriding belief that governors must govern and that the contacts of councillors with their constituents are an adequate and sufficient means of gathering local opinion. Second, local communication is defective because the local press does not effectively challenge the secrecy surrounding council affairs. It has been suggested that given alternative sources of reporting – radio and television – this situation would change as competition challenged the complacency of monopoly.

The third defect of local communication is that, as part-time councillors struggle to cope with the increasing complexity of council work, so people turn to officers for help. In this situation the important factors are the beliefs and attitudes of officers. Councillors, for their part, believe that they are best placed to bring local knowledge and local opinion into council deliberations. There is no need to widen local communication by consulting pressure groups, co-opting individuals on to council committees or setting up community forums to elicit their views.

These attitudes and actions are understandable in the light of the conventions of local government. It is argued that a main advantage of territorial democracy – government of small areas close to the people – is that the ward gives reality to the ideal. Councillors and people live close to each other and meet frequently, not merely through common membership of party or other organisations, but in ordinary daily life. As a result, councillors do not merely act as transmission belts – passing information down, and opinion back up, to the council – but aggregate demand. Councillors play a positive role in explaining and justifying what is done in the name of local citizens. They also shape and mould public opinion. They are more than 'brokers', explaining one side to the other without intruding their views. They have views – and positively believe in their right to have them – and these play a large part in how people communicate with each other.

These ideals may not always work in practice. Not all councillors are actively 'ward councillors'. Some spend much of their time, if they are leading council members and chairmen of committees, with officers and in policy-making. In addition, not all councillors live in the ward they represent or have the close contact with constituents that tradition or myth suggest. The research findings of the Maud Committee on Management of Local Government showed that both councillors and electors feel that ordinary people do not know enough to make full use of services or to form a balanced picture of what the council is doing.[7] Councillors were fairly pessimistic about raising the level of public interest but about one third thought that public relations, publicity and more press and television coverage would help and some 12 per cent thought councillors themselves should organise more publicity. But even Maud recognised that, given the amount of information available through the local press, it still does not seem to make much impression on most of the electorate exposed to it.

Councillors feel that the public has a favourable view of them, though not of the council itself. Councillors see public ignorance as due to lack of interest rather than lack of information. Electors, for their part, claimed the local newspaper as their main source of news but only about one in four of them had heard of any council activity in the previous month.

The Maud Committee research showed that informal, personal contact is more important, in the eyes of most councillors, than the more formal links of parties or pressure groups. In large urban areas, however, parties and pressure groups do play a larger part though councillors still see themselves as the centre of the communication network. The electorate takes a different view. To them, main contacts are with the town hall and its officers. Councillors themselves also look to the town hall, i.e. to officers and to committees, for their main information. Their contact with constituents, according to Kenneth Newton's findings, seems to be a response to demands for individual help with personal problems rather than a means of monitoring public opinion on particular issues.[8] The councillors' views of public opinion are instinctive. They act according to a 'law of anticipated reactions'; that is, they carry out policy in anticipation of how the public will react at election time, not on the basis of detailed personal knowledge of local opinion.

Nor do elected representatives, or the political parties, use voluntary organisations as the major source of local opinion. Most of the contact between voluntary groups and the council is through local officials. D. S. Morris and K. Newton believe that councillors and parties are not, as democratic theory suggests, the main means of drawing together the variety of informed opinion in their area. Local officials and departments are the real key to the collection of local opinion.[9]

Informal, personal contacts between councillors and electors are, nevertheless, still of value. Where councillors have extensive contacts of this kind they are potentially an important means of bringing local opinion into council work. And many younger, campaigning councillors do take this view. In addition, we now have a more informed lay public in the voluntary associations. They, rather than political parties, may offer councillors and public an arena of debate.

LOCAL OFFICERS AND THE LOCAL PUBLIC

Local government officers, unlike civil servants, are close to those they serve, both in the course of their work and in everyday life. The amount and kind of communication which results depends on three factors. First, there is the position of the officer as the official, the spokesman of the council and department. Second, the officer is a professional who has particular expertise. Finally, there are the expectations of the individual or group. Many officers, for their part, still adhere to what A. J. A. Morris calls the Old Whig view of public opinion as a checking but not initiating force.[10]

The Maud, Redcliffe-Maud and other research shows that, for most people, the normal approach to the local council is through the town hall. Citizens take the sensible view that when they need information then this is to help with a particular problem or issue rather than in the abstract. Similarly, when a local voluntary group wants information, or to put its point of view, it too will seek out the experts. Political parties are rarely seen as appropriate channels, except by groups which already have some contact with the parties, such as trade unions.

It can be argued that, if people see the officers as a main source of help, then this should be encouraged by setting up community forums in which officials, voluntary workers and local people can meet each other regularly. In addition, the public should be invited more readily into schools and other institutions and wider informal contacts promoted. Josephine P. Reynolds has even suggested that a new, auxiliary system of communication is needed, to link professionals and public directly, and bypassing elected representatives. In planning, this would help to bring lay ideas into the process.[11] The Skeffington Report (see Chapter 6) stressed the need for local council information and publicity. In this, officers would play a prime part as the full-time, expert participants.

These developments must be seen in perspective. On the one hand, what officers do depends on councillors' attitudes to them and the freedom that they have to seek out and promote local opinion. This varies from one place to another and is affected by political and other local traditions. On the other hand, the communication between officers and local people depends on how information is controlled and how the public's views are relayed back into the system. Officers may, for example, control what is decided by successfully confining contacts to the 'proper channels'.

From the citizen's point of view the officers' control of information, though not always obvious, has serious implications. Norman Dennis has shown how in a redevelopment area, the planning department and its officers controlled information, not the planning committee.[12] A further problem was that officers were too ready to see criticism as an attack on their professional competence. Councillors, for their part, were too willing to let officers get away with this defence. The local residents suffered also, says Dennis, not because officers gave them no information, or misinformed them, but rather because they received only partial information. This was confusing, and impeded their potential influence on what the planners did.

Dennis concluded that local communication is defective in two ways. The quantity and timing of information is unsatisfactory. The individual learns too little, and too late, about council problems and issues. The other defect is that the two sides have different expectations. For example, Dennis shows that the local residents in the redevelopment area differed profoundly from the planners on what information meant. The residents wanted reassurances about the social structure of the area and their personal future in it. The planners, on the other hand, stressed the need for 'rational' communication, based on 'facts' about the state of the houses, the time-table for renewal, and so on.[13]

The relations of local groups with officials depends also on the nature of the group and its standing in the community. The long-established welfare and amenity groups are respected as trustworthy and non-political. Because they are 'non-controversial' they will be able to maintain links with officers who are likely to avoid contacts with more controversial groups.

The officer's insistence on 'relevant knowledge', and the correct technical language to be used, is now challenged by newer, radical groups. So too is the professional's control over the timing and extent of communication. Examples can be found in the urban and community development movements, where social workers try to widen the consultation networks, especially in the deprived neighbourhood. This then contrasts markedly with professional officers controlling information in the traditional vertical chain of communication.

COMMUNICATION AND SELF-INTEREST:
THE CITIZEN'S RIGHT TO KNOW

In planning and other local services the individual's interest in knowing what is done arises in two main ways. First, a minority of people take a general interest in the community and its services. For such people the normal way to get information would be through a special local group.

Second, there is practical self-interest. Individuals want to know more about services which affect them directly – as ratepayers, owner-occupiers, tenants, parents or residents of a particular area or road. There is no one public or public opinion; there are a variety of publics which shift, change and overlap. Thus the search for knowledge is sectional, limited and intermittent. As a result people who need information, and to put their point of view back to councillors and officers, are often at a considerable disadvantage, since they lack continuous contact with those who are knowledgeable.

Individuals need news quickly, in an understandable form, and before decisions are finally taken. This is hard to achieve. Similarly, to be effective, citizens must be able to put their views in a way which can be understood by officers as well as councillors. To do this they need political skills which they often lack and are inexperienced in handling.

In recent years more positive attempts have been made to improve council information in sensitive or controversial areas such as planning, transportation and the social services. At the same time local councils have tried to improve their data collection and assessment of needs, in order to ensure smooth administration. The Skeffington report suggested a number of ways in which this could be improved and individuals given more help to air their views. The community forum would bring together councillors, officers and various community groups. Councils of Social Services would help in this process (although the right of consultation is not given to them or to any other local group). The Skeffington proposals relate primarily to the preparation of plans, at the structure and local plan level. The community forum has not developed, and, though there are improvements, information is still difficult to get. Another criticism is that the new planning process, like the old, does not really provide more information but more publicity for the local authority's – predetermined – point of view.

It is also difficult for people to see what developments are taking place. The Town and Country Planning Act 1971 requires local authorities to keep a register of planning applications which must be available for public inspection. Similarly, plans are normally available for inspection at the council's offices. But this does not always mean that the public sees them. The copyright is the architect's, and if he or the developer want to avoid publicising their plans then he can refuse to allow anyone to copy the plans or to publish them. Marcus Binney states that this happens far too often.[14]

Communication in the planning field is also defective in three other areas. These are: public inquiries, road proposals, and slum clearance and redevelopment. Chapter 6 showed the impediments to participation that arise from the over-formal, legalistic atmosphere of public inquiries and the effect this has on costs and on the individual's rights. There are other problems. Most of these arise in cases of refusal of planning permission. The manner and language in which planners present their case can be an obstacle; objectors have great difficulty in seeing the detailed official case which they must fight; and the 'professionalisation' of the procedure bewilders the ordinary man.

The problem of road proposals is rather different. Major roads, particularly motorways, involve the Ministry and its regional offices as well as county and district authorities. The main problem is that of announcing draft road alignments because of the blighting effect this has on buildings and the inflationary effect on land. There has been, as a result, an outcry about secrecy; the Waltham Holy Cross case, for example, has attracted considerable attention. The Department of the Environment, through its regional construction unit, warned the urban district council over disclosure of a secret motorway plan. This then leaked to the press and there was a lengthy correspondence in *The Times*. The council, defiant, said they would continue to give the public the information it should have. Now, however, the Department is allowing alternatives to be put to the public for discussion.[15] But the new consultation procedures are still being used in a limited way. Local authorities still feel caught between their own constituents and the Ministry.

The same problems of alignment and blight apply to all road schemes. The Department of the Environment circular 52/72 says that local authorities should give publicity only to those road schemes 'which investigation has shown to be soundly based in terms of effectiveness and economy'. In the case of trunk roads, the Regional Controllers must be consulted; this also applies to proposals for principal roads if the local authority wishes to claim grant in respect of blighted properties.[16] This degree of secrecy would be justified, as a *Times* leader pointed out, if it did prevent unnecessary anxiety. But in fact it merely mitigates, not eliminates, blight. It would be better to accept the consequences of blight and publish the results of surveys and alternatives as soon as they are completed.[17]

The third area of controversy in planning is over the quantity and quality of information in urban redevelopment. There are a number of disquieting factors. First, those most affected are likely to be the poor and the elderly, who lack the necessary skills to get information and use it. If they are helped to organise, by voluntary workers or others, this may lead to confrontation between the council and the residents and to a breakdown in communication.

Second, the language in which communication takes place only reinforces the gap between the two sides: the planners use 'jargon', the residents make unthinking, repetitive assertions. Third, the dialogue is misleading because, understandably, no one wishes to have to tell residents that in fact they may lose anyway. In the long run the area will be redeveloped; local residents cannot all be rehoused together as a community; and most will have to accept flats instead of houses.

The fourth factor – the slow procedure of notification, survey and inspection, compulsory purchase and inquiry – makes communication protracted, wearisome and frustrating. Local authorities do give information on their reasons for making a Compulsory Purchase Order and what its effect will be if it is confirmed. But this is a late stage. Local people have little chance in the early stages of the preliminary thinking, either to argue about principles (why redevelop at all?) or to get accurate details about how the process will affect them – or when. Nor do these groups have the veto power of more middle-class pressure groups. They may also feel that, although their councillors will transmit their views and help with individual aspects, they too are committed to the planning ethos of the bureaucrats.

As a result of these problems there have been the now familiar suggestions for special help in potential redevelopment areas. Community and other workers can actively marshall local views and also interpret officials to residents. Similar suggestions are made for the social services. Seebohm stressed the need for adequate information, particularly about housing. This is a familiar theme in the general field of welfare: people need to know their rights and how to get help. In this area a variety of old and new methods, including the CABS, welfare rights stalls, neighbourhood law centres, and the personal help of community workers, are being tried.

Bryan Glastonbury *et al.* assert that, in the social services, the extent of the public's ignorance suggests that there are fundamental communication problems.[18] There is a gap between the professionals on the one hand and consumers on the other. The former doubt the wisdom of conducting a dialogue about people's 'real needs' since professional standards might then be undermined. They also have difficulty in drawing on reliable and broad spectrums of opinion. The consumers, for their part, are ignorant about social work, misinformed about their rights and confused by professional jargon.

These findings pose a paradox. The need for information is glaring, but it is by itself not enough. What is missing is the picture of the councillors as the spokesmen for the needs of an area and its people. Social and community workers can only do this to a limited extent. There still remains a need to bring these different, narrow needs together into one whole. If this is not clearly recognised, then local government is in danger of dissolving into separate, limited areas of concern. The heaviest users of the social services will then be in a very weak position, considered as citizens as well as welfare recipients.

LOCAL AUTHORITIES AND THE LOCAL PRESS

There is evidence that provincial press coverage, in terms of the number of independent local papers and the space they gave to council affairs, has steadily declined from its heyday in the last quarter of the nineteenth century.[19] G. W. Jones has shown how, in one large town at the turn of the century, the daily evening paper devoted a large amount of space to local politics and council and committee affairs. With the shortage of newsprint in the First World War and the increasing 'centralisation' of party politics, coverage declined.[20]

The 1949 Royal Commission on the Press said that democratic society needed a clear and truthful report of events, a forum of debate and a means of transmitting people's views and their arguments for particular causes.[21] Rudolf Klein maintains that although lip service is paid to the importance of the press and other media there are virtually no clear and specific descriptions of what they actually do, or ought, to contribute.[22] At the same time the press have their own problems. They have their own views of what is newsworthy. Staffing and space problems may restrict their efforts. Whatever they do they are likely to be accused of trivialisation or sensationalism. There is also the fiction that the citizen will take trouble to get information. As Anthony Downs shows, however, the individual operates on an informal cost-benefit system. He only incurs the cost of seeking information if this contributes to making a decision, over which he has some control.[23]

In local government, councillors see the press as the main channel of communication with the public, although they have reservations about the ways in which local newspapers report the news. The electorate, as I have argued elsewhere, also sees the press as the main source of local news though this does not necessarily mean that it aids or encourages their knowledge and interest about council affairs.[24]

The provincial press is financially healthy, with an increasing revenue from the growth of classified advertising in the last decade. Although the local newspapers are mainly in the hands of a small number of organisations, this concentrated ownership leaves editors free to pursue their own policies (although it may make for a bland, non-controversial editorial approach) and they feel it their duty to present local council affairs in their papers. Often, they claim, they print more council news than their readership demands; they are keeping democracy alive, not suppressing a more lively debate.

Newspapers fill a variety of needs – entertainment, news, features and advertisements – and there is no evidence that individuals are stimulated into a greater interest in local government merely by reading local newspapers. Ordinary people are content with this situation: they express a generalised wish to be better informed but they believe that if they need to know more then they can find it out easily through the town hall, family, friends and councillors.

Readers of the local paper are both generalists and specialists. As voters, they have a general (if circumscribed) need for political information at election times. As specialists – members of particular groups and interests – they want information and news about certain issues in a more detailed way. One local paper cannot always meet these needs and additional means – community newspapers, broadsheets, the use of multiple television channels – may be a better solution than trying to change the existing mass media themselves.

The local press has been, until recently, the only organ of news and opinion and it has been hampered in its job by many difficulties. These problems include the concentration of ownership into large financial holdings; inadequate resources of staff, space and money; hostile or unhelpful attitudes in the town hall; legal restrictions on council and committee reporting or informal embargoes, and the very late release of news. For their part, local authorities argue that newspapers, since they are commercial enterprises competing with other media, do not really care about council affairs. They sensationalise issues, prefer to concentrate on personalities and controversy rather than report news in depth or give background information, and rely on young and inexperienced reporters.

Local authorities also deny that this situation could be improved by opening all committees to the press because this risks premature disclosure involving financial and land transactions, and may introduce unnecessary party politics into committee. The counter-argument suggests these fears are exaggerated and must give way to the public's right to know. In national government, we do not expect the Cabinet and its Committees to be open to the public or the press. Why, then, should local council committees be treated differently? The answer lies in three features of central, as opposed to local, government. First, parliamentary debate is extensively reported. Second, there is a wide range of contacts between government, politicians and newsmen. The final factor is the diversity of the media itself. There are many outlets for news and these also vary in their style, coverage, interest and potential audience.

None of these features can be found to the same degree at local level. Councillors have a more cautious attitude, opposition parties have fewer outlets, and there is a relatively restricted coverage by the media. There is far less investigatory journalism than in the national press and broadcasting. There may be, therefore, a good case for opening council committees to the public, especially as they deal mainly with day-to-day administration rather than high level policy.

The 1972 Local Government Act agreed; it made committees open, and the government, in spite of local authority reservations, insisted that resolutions to hold proceedings in camera must be made at each meeting, rather than in advance for periods of up to twelve months *en bloc*.

The situation is governed by the 1960 Public Bodies (Admission to Meetings) Act which enjoins local authorities to provide agenda and minutes for those meetings which were open; the 1972 Act does not apply these provisions to all the committees which are now open and it remains to be seen what co-operation will be forthcoming. This co-operation depends above all on the attitudes of councillors and editors and the way they accommodate to each other.

The history of previous legislation illustrates this clearly. The 1882 Municipal Corporations Act, like its 1835 predecessor, laid down the rules governing council meetings but said nothing about the admission of the public or the press. In 1908 the Local Authority (Admission of the Press to Meetings) Act admitted the press to council meetings, the meetings of joint committees and joint boards exercising delegated powers and the meetings of education committees. The press could be excluded if, in the opinion of the majority of members (expressed by resolution), this was in the public interest.

In the period after 1945 there was growing dissatisfaction with this position. Many councils used their powers to exclude the press excessively. The matter came to a head with the provincial newspaper dispute of 1959. In this dispute, the exclusion of reporters from council meetings, particularly in the large cities, became a matter of general controversy and was debated in parliament. Mrs Thatcher, a backbench member, introduced a Bill to try to establish 'a minimum legislative code of practice'. This became the 1960 Public Bodies (Admission to Meetings) Act. In practice, the Act was ambiguous and councils could and did evade its purposes. The Act applied to the full council meeting, to the Education Committee (a largely formal body since much work is done in subcommittees) and to all committees on which all members of the council sat. It was thus relatively easy to rearrange committees to include less than all the members, to divide agendas, and to operate informal embargoes. The problem of confidentiality remained unsolved. The public and press could be excluded 'whenever publicity would be prejudicial to the public interest', and this enabled councils to continue much as before.

The relationship between councils and the press depends on trust and confidence rather than on legislation. Gradually the situation is changing under the pressure of events. In certain fields, particularly planning, transportation, conservation and social problems, there is a demand for more information. Many newspapers and reporters would like to pursue this growing interest. They recognise the need for confidentiality in some council matters but do not think this justifies blanket exclusion from committees, if they have the time, staff and space to use these opportunities. The attitudes of some councils is also changing, and more authorities are experimenting with open committees.

In December 1970 the LGIO and the Institute of Journalists produced recommendations to local councils, press, radio and television stressing that local authorities should have a definite policy on press information, including the use of PROs and the early release of information. Editors, for their part, should encourage their senior staff to specialise. This informal code was endorsed by the Local Authority Associations and the Guild of British Newspaper Editors circulated it to all its members for information.

In spite of these developments, the majority of councils have not changed their policy. It has been estimated that only 10 per cent of local authorities in England and Wales allow free access of the press to all their main committee meetings, though another 40 per cent open some main committees; these are normally the larger authorities.[25] A somewhat similar situation was discovered in a 1971 survey of councils with a population over 80,000. More than half held the majority of their committees in private.[26]

The press has no special privilege to obtain information and must not publish defamatory matter. The qualified privilege of councillors means that, unless there is malice, they are protected from liability for defamation. Qualified privilege also applies to agendas and other documents supplied to newspapers for those meetings which are open to them. Similarly, fair and accurate newspaper reports of meetings are covered by qualified privilege but, to retain this, newspapers must insert contradictions and explanations if requested.

The local press, outside London, is characterised by its monopoly position and by the concentration of ownership. Most towns and cities have only one local newspaper and the 'big five' (the Westminster Press, Associated Newspapers, the International Publishing Corporation, the Thompson Organisation and United Newspapers) now control nearly half the provincial press. Chain ownership may not mean that proprietors dictate editorial policy but rather that the need for large circulation to sustain advertising revenue puts excessive stress on profitability so that hard news gives way to entertainment. The group ownership also means the syndicating of editorial and feature material (so that the same items appear in different 'local' newspapers). This is a disturbing feature, because if the individual papers in a group are virtually the same paper under a different name for each area, then there is a suspicion of uniformity and a lack of a true community outlook.

What is reported is also influenced by the frequency of publication and the area covered. The large evening papers, with their city-centre base, provide national and local political news and feature material. Weekly papers, in the small towns, suburbs and rural areas, are more parochial in scope and limited in coverage. Both kinds of paper, however, may be guilty of trivialisation. Cox and Morgan argue that the manner of presentation is fairly uniform: 'snippets' of news and little background detail on the big controversial issues. As a result, Harvey Cox and David Morgan believe, the reader is offered a diverting mélange which may create a bewildering and dull image of council affairs.[27]

Some three-quarters of the provincial press' revenue comes from advertising. The amount of space available for news, including local news, depends on the amount of advertising, not on newspaper policy. This does not matter unless additional commercial pressures – for example, regional and local television and radio – threaten the advertising revenue of the press. Up to now, the reverse has been the case: more revenue, and more pages, have been a feature of provincial publications in the last five to ten years.

Editors, their sub-editors, news editors and reporters, are not neutral transmitters. Their opinions – and prejudices – are crucial to their position as 'gatekeepers' or mediators of news and opinion. They transmit news from public bodies to their readers but they also 'mediate', process and colour what is printed, though of course this is governed by the normal laws of libel and the conventions of news reporting.

Editors see their audience as a family readership: they also believe that council news is only a minority interest (which they provide to a greater extent than is demanded) and which must be put over in a lively manner to have any impact. Editorial views are also affected by the attitudes of councillors and by the influence of local pressure groups and the demand that grievances be aired by the local paper. For example, where planning is a local issue then the paper has great potential influence. Councillors are overwhelmed by the complexities of their task, and in the large cities no longer act as gatherers of public opinion. Pressure groups, claims Simon Jenkins, then turn to the local newspaper. They, and journalists, seek out the planning department and its chief officers for information and influence. The officials, similarly, look to the press for sympathy and publicity. Jenkins argues that this new relationship between press, public and planners is radically altering the constitutional structure of local government.[28]

The result of this kind of press influence is that power shifts from the inner world of the council and the party to the public arena of press, planners and pressure groups. Although this can be beneficial to those involved it is inevitably sectional and, as ever, the poorer areas are not heard in the general middle-class clamour. We should, therefore, look to means of improving the councillor's position rather than encouraging a mere proliferation of pressure groups, with its danger of the 'liberal veto'.

It is not necessarily the case, however, that more formal contacts – the use of press officers, systematic press conferences and so on – would alter the relations of councils and the press. Very few local authorities have such arrangements, preferring to leave the initiative to the local paper. The press also prefers this situation, which prevents the local authority, in their eyes, from relying on prepared statements and allows them to probe and to pursue their own contacts.

Currently, the local press, for all its defects, has a strong watchdog function. This will be all the more necessary in the new larger local councils and will call for more sophisticated, more informed and more experienced reporters which, given the increased costs it implies, may be difficult to achieve.

John Delane's famous adage, as editor of *The Times* in the 1850s, that the press lives by disclosure, does not seem to apply at local level – since rivalry does not exist. The scoop is important, but this is rather different: to be first, but to be safe, might be a more appropriate adage.

ADDITIONAL SOURCES OF NEWS AND INFORMATION: RADIO AND TELEVISION

It is argued that new advances in broadcasting – local radio, and television outlets which encourage amateur, community recordings – will improve democratic communication. The newspapers' monopoly of news would be broken, and this would stimulate more competitive and investigatory journalism. There is little evidence that these aims can as yet be met. Newspapers continue to be the main avenue of local communication, and citizens seem as contented – or indifferent – as before. Clearly, a multiplicity of sources of information does not by itself increase people's awareness and interest.

The new media, however, do exist and more will come. They cannot be ignored or dismissed. They also suggest that the local community is still an appropriate setting for information – a view which the BBC re-organisation of its radio services might be thought to uphold. In the mid-1960s the BBC networks were re-organised, the regional programmes were gradually phased out, and local radio stations were established. Cynics argued that, although those involved in the introduction of local broadcasting had stressed democratic ideals, they were mainly motivated by the need to tap the mass audience for popular music, which the 'pop pirates' were successfully exploiting.

About 92 per cent of the adult population are radio listeners, but only a minority tune in to local stations. In the period up to autumn 1972 (when the audience was limited to those with VHF sets) under 20 per cent of the total adult population listened regularly to their local radio station. This will now increase with the extension to medium wave.

The audience for local radio is largely confined to those already interested in local affairs, who have strong local ties, are active in local organisations and heavy readers of the local newspaper. This is still a minority of citizens. One survey estimates only a very small minority of people are really aware of local radio and virtually none envisaged giving up their newspaper readership in favour of an alternative, radio source of local news and current affairs.[29]

The Pilkington Committee (The Royal Commission on Broadcasting, 1961-2) welcomed the possibility of local sound broadcasting and saw it providing local material of particular interest to its community. Both Conservative and Labour governments agreed and an experimental service was introduced by the Labour Government in 1967. The first local BBC radio station, at Leicester, opened in November 1967. There are now twenty in operation, covering some 70 per cent of the population of England. The local radio station managers have complete editorial control and decide how and when to broadcast local material and when to take programmes from any one of the BBC's four national networks.

The stations originate between five and ten hours of local material each day. They are autonomous in making and transmitting programmes and there is no central control, although there is the strong influence of BBC professionalism. All the stations believe in audience participation and encourage listeners to 'phone in and comment and to take part in a variety of discussion programmes. The relationship between the local station and the local council varies. In some areas BBC reporters have the same facilities as the press to attend committee and council meetings, but may not directly record proceedings. In others an edited version of council meetings is broadcast, concentrating on the central debate.

Each station has a local broadcasting council made up of local people. Since June 1971 this has been appointed by the BBC Board of Governors and not, as originally, by the Minister – which means potentially an even greater say by the local manager. The local advisory committees include local councillors who sit as individuals, not as representatives of the local authority.

The advisory councils do not have editorial or executive powers but do comment on programme schedules and content. There are similar provisions for the commercial stations. The 1972 Sound Broadcasting Act amends the 1964 Television Act to require the Independent Broadcasting Authority to appoint local advisory committees to cover each radio station locality or a combination of localities. The people appointed must reflect, as far as possible, the range of tastes

and interests of local residents. Local authorities, separately or
jointly, must be invited to nominate to the advisory committee, one
third of which must be made up from these nominations. These may
not, however, be very influential bodies.

The local authority Associations supported the introduction of
local BBC radio but subsequently felt they could not comment on
commercial radio.[30] Commercial radio, however, need not mean
music interspersed with news items. In America there is a great
variety of news, music, educational and community radio. In this
country some attempts at community radio on the American model
may eventually be possible.

A total of sixty commercial stations is proposed; but the need for
commercial viability suggests a smaller number and the individual
stations will cover much larger regional areas than originally
envisaged. In 1971 the Minister of Posts and Telecommunications
defended the regional nature of the first commercial stations on the
grounds that frequencies were scarce and also that the important
factor was the area of natural community, not its actual size or
population.[31]

But it must be recognised that commercial and technical pressures –
including the fact that it is in the interests of the IBA for its transmitters to be powerful enough to cover conurbations so that
advertisers have wide catchment areas – are inevitably working for
regional, not local, community, radio. There are also fears that
commercial radio will eventually be a national network service with
local 'opt-out' programmes rather than true local broadcasting.

The commercial radio stations will be governed by a set of rules
designed to prevent concentrated ownership by either television or
newspaper interests. But there will inevitably be some concentration.
Local newspapers with a circulation which is significant in relation
to the population of the station's transmission area have the right to
acquire an interest in the station. This is in order to protect the
paper's commercial viability. But a local paper with a local monopoly
cannot acquire a controlling interest.

Local broadcasting is, potentially, an additional source of news.
But there are a number of queries. There is the suspicion that
commercial radio, for example, will not be able to afford the news
service provided by local BBC stations. News service accounts for a
large share of each BBC station's budget and staffing; the station is
also backed by the substantial support of the headquarters organisation and by its access to the network programmes. It is unlikely that
local commercial stations will enjoy the same resources and

news-gathering as the BBC and will be dependent on news agency sources, local reporters and the London news station service.

Another problem is the source of local news. The 1972 Sound Broadcasting Act does not require that the local commercial radio news service must be provided independently of any newspaper source, though the IBA will not accept a news service wholly supplied from the local paper. The original requirement of the Sound Broadcasting Bill that news should be collected by 'suitably qualified journalists' and be 'independent' of the local paper, was successfully deleted by the Government at the Report stage of the Bill.

The London news station, which started transmission in the autumn of 1973, has a large news staff, co-operates with Independent Television News and supplies a news service for its own area and to the whole commercial network. The news bulletins are interspersed with music, features and advertisements. This will inevitably loom large in the network. It is probably unrealistic to expect a multiplicity of journalistic sources at the community level, but the danger of news concentration is a worrying feature of the new system.

In the future, new forms of television communication, as well as local radio may be used. American and Canadian experience, and some experiments in this country, show the possibilities of community broadcasting, i.e. programmes produced by people who have no special training but who wish to explore their community. This is made possible by the development of lightweight equipment, such as portable video cameras producing video tapes which can be played back in the individual's own home, in hired halls, or – if he can get access – on the local station network.

These possibilities may be aided by another development: the more extensive use of cable, whereby television programmes are transmitted into people's homes by cable (or 'wire'). The advantages of the cable system is that a great many more items – radio and television, telephone, educational programmes and many others – can be transmitted over a single cable. Cable can carry messages in two directions, so that, potentially, viewers can communicate with the broadcasters.

In 1972 the government sanctioned an experiment by relay companies in five areas in England, who were already providing television by cable, to include local programmes. The programmes, which are transmitted for one to two hours in the early evening, carry no advertising. The experiment will run for a number of years. The Government also announced, early in 1973, that the BBC charter and the 1964 Television Act, both due for renewal in 1976, were to run until 1981; by then there will be a considerable experience of these local experiments and of the potential expansion of cable television as such. This could well be the major form of transmission in the late 1980s and offer a wide variety of potential uses.

The use of portable video equipment by amateurs, and the possible developments of cable television, highlights the problem of how these programmes will reach the community and who will have the power to promote, or prevent, them. Access and control remain the central political questions of communication. They are particularly important in the area of television since this, not radio, has the major listening audience.

In this country, unlike the American and Canadian experience, the question of control of the companies, the granting of licences, and the relation between local and central bodies would be resolved in favour of the centre. The question of central influence and control looms large in all aspects of local affairs, including BBC radio, commercial broadcasting, and no doubt in any new developments. The danger is that the alleged diversification of the media at the regional and local level may in practice reinforce centralisation. Resources are scarce and the temptation to amalgamate into one network is strong.

The information situation is potentially uniform in another sense. It is possible for written information to be displayed on television screens, by means of a simple adaptation to a conventional set. It is also possible to provide a facsimile print-off of a newspaper in every home and customers could dial in to a central organisation for prints. These experiments are being actively pursued by both the BBC and the commercial companies.

The widespread use of these developments lies in the future and their threat to the press is still an open question. Other ideas may not be so far in the future. The use of portable video recorders for filming community affairs, for example, has been extensively examined in the course of the Community Development projects promoted by the Home Office.

'Community broadcasting' is ambiguous and does not necessarily offer better two-way information. The broadcasters seem able and eager to encourage local programming, but on their own terms. Councillors and officers remain, for the most part, as cautious as before. In this situation the broadcasters are very powerful. They stress 'balance' (in political and other terms), clarity and order. Many groups in the community, eager to put their point of view, find they are at a disadvantage since they do not have the skills which the media demand. The programme producers then have a profound effect on how opinion is found and promoted.

COMMUNICATION – THE TRIUMPH OF TRADITION?

Communication is a vital part of democratic accountability and control. In English local government the existing patterns of communication reinforce the concentration of power in the hands of councillors and officers in a traditional, hierarchical manner. Political parties do relatively little to diversify these patterns, and do not forcefully combine public opinion and demands as democratic theory assumes that they should. Voluntary organisations are beginning to change this situation, but their contacts are mainly with officials and departments, not with political decision-makers.

The press remains the main source of local news, but the way in which it contributes to democratic government, while important, is less investigatory and opinion-forming than national journalism. Radio is now diversifying the range of local communication, although it has not, as yet, profoundly altered what local councils do – or how they do it. Future developments in the mass media may help ordinary people, especially less articulate and less well-educated people, to 'talk back' to local councils. But none of these developments necessarily means an upsurge of interest and involvement. Local people are as contented – or unconcerned – as before.

These attitudes are to be expected. Information is necessary for those who want to help or want to do things and, although there are defects and delays, this is still possible in a great variety of ways. What is of concern, in an age of reform of all kinds, is the need for councillors and officers to act positively in the system: they must collect facts speedily and accurately; anticipate new needs; aggregate demands for the community as a whole not just sections of it, and be close to their constituents, clients, consumers and voters.

These tasks do not get any easier as local government areas are increased in size; services become more complex and management innovation increases centralisation inside the town hall. It is to the impact of reforms that we now turn.

NOTES

1. John Stuart Mill, *Considerations on Representative Government* (Longmans, 1861), p. 167.
2. Richard R. Fagan, *Politics and Communication* (Little Brown, 1966), p. 67.
3. Royal Commission on the Press, *Report*, Cmd. 7700 (1949), p. 101.

4. 'The New Local Authorities: management and structure', Department of the Environment/Local Authority Associations Study Group *Report* (1972), p. 86.
5. R. J. Buxton, *Local Government* (Penguin, 1970), pp. 182-3.
6. A Fabian Group, 'People, Participation and Government', *Fabian Research Series*, 293 (1971), p. 11.
7. 'The Local Government Councillor', Committee on Management of Local Government, Vol. II (1967), p. 11.
8. Kenneth Newton, 'Links Between Leaders and Citizens in a Local Political System', *Policy and Politics*, Vol. 1, No. 4 (June 1973), p. 296.
9. D. S. Morris and K. Newton, 'Onymous Empire: voluntary organisations in Birmingham politics', University of Birmingham Faculty of Commerce and Social Science, *Discussion Papers*, Series F, No. 10 (1970), p. 29.
10. A. J. A. Morris, 'Local Authority Relations with the Local Press', *Public Law* (1969), p. 295.
11. Josephine P. Reynolds, 'Public Participation in Planning', *Town Planning Review*, Vol. 40, No. 2 (1969), p. 146.
12. Norman Dennis, *Public Participation and Planning Blight* (Allen & Unwin, 1972), p. 176.
13. *Ibid.*, pp. 130-2.
14. Marcus Binney, letter to *The Times* (11 August 1972).
15. 'Participation in Road Planning', *Consultation Paper*, Department of the Environment (1973).
16. 'Town and Country Planning Act 1971: Part II, Development Plan Proposals: publicity and public participation', Department of the Environment, *Circular 52/72* (1972), para. 15.
17. 'Public Highways From The Start', *The Times* (27 November 1972).
18. Bryan Glastonbury, Margaret Burdett and Rita Austin, 'Community Perceptions of Social Work', *Policy and Politics*, Vol. I, No. 3 (March 1973), p. 206.
19. Ian Jackson, *The Provincial Press and the Community* (Manchester University Press, 1971), pp. 9-11.
20. G. W. Jones, *Borough Politics* (Macmillan, 1969), pp. 13-15.
21. Royal Commission on the Press, *Report*, Cmd. 7700 (1949), para. 362.
22. Rudolf Klein, 'The Powers of the Press', *Political Quarterly*, Vol. 44, No. 1 (January-March 1973), p. 33.
23. Anthony Downs, *An Economic Theory of Democracy* (Harper, 1957), pp. 215-16.
24. Dilys M. Hill, *Participating in Local Affairs* (Penguin, 1970), pp. 111-14.
25. 'Local Government Administration in England and Wales', Committee on Management of Local Government, Vol. 5, pp. 427-8.
26. 'The Public's Right to Know', *Municipal Journal*, Vol. 79, No. 39 (24 September 1971), p. 1305.
27. Harvey Cox and David Morgan, *City Politics and the Press* (Cambridge University Press, 1973), p. 72.
28. Simon Jenkins, 'The Press as Politician in Local Planning', *Political Quarterly*, Vol. 44, No. 1 (January-March 1973), pp. 50-3.
29. '7m. May Hear Commercial Radio', *The Guardian* (2 February 1972).
30. Local Commercial Radio', General Purposes Committee, Appendix B, *Municipal Review Supplement* (December 1970), p. 271.
31. Christopher Chataway, House of Commons Debates *Standing Committee F* (9 December 1971), cols 212 and 214.

Chapter VIII

DEMOCRACY AND THE REFORM OF LOCAL GOVERNMENT

THE TWENTIETH-CENTURY DEBATE ON REFORM

The nineteenth-century legacy of local government is largely one of good administration enriched by the ideal of voluntary public service. Victorian reforms had a definite aim: administrative and financial efficiency on the one hand and the extension of popular democratic control on the other. Up to 1870 three features predominated. First, there was the tendency to create *ad hoc* bodies for particular services. Second, as the century wore on, the trend was to transfer power from smaller to larger units. Third, and the main influence on how popular control ought to be exercised, was the dominance of the borough and the principles of the reformed municipal corporations.

The creation of the Poor Law Union was the only occasion on which areas were looked at in terms of principle: that of administrative convenience. But this had no effect on the historic boundaries of the counties or the primacy of the boroughs. The extension of the franchise in the 1860s, and the public health advances in the 1870s, might have provided the opportunity for radical recasting of areas and powers. But they did not. The public health legislation of 1872 and 1875 distinguished between urban and rural areas. This, and the Local Government Acts of 1888 and 1894, divided town from country. In the twentieth century this developed into a conflict of interests – over catchment areas, rateable values and overspill.

The hopes of the reformed system were soon lost. Two sets of factors emerged together. One was the division of town and country, and their subsequent rivalry, established by the legislation itself. The other factor was the revolution in transport – and in social and intellectual horizons – which outgrew the old boundaries. The idea and ideal of community altered its scale and its nature. The 'final nature' of the new local government system was also weakened by the fact that the great Victorian reforms were the end of an era rather than the beginning of a new one. Yesterday's problems were solved, largely with yesterday's means.

The twentieth century brought new problems and a great increase in government intervention. But no alteration took place in local government powers or boundaries, its constitutional status or its financial base. There was an attempt at review of the system in the post-First World War period. But, although the poor law was finally abolished and important public health measures consolidated, little else was achieved. The Royal Commission on Local Government of 1923-9 (the Onslow Commission) was an ameliorative device. And although the Local Government Acts of 1929 and 1933 formed the basis of the system until the 1972 Act, they were largely administrative and consolidating measures. They did not change the existing dual organisation of town and country, or the ways in which local authorities provided for the needs of their areas (although some increase in the size of units was effected by the amalgamation of authorities in the county areas).

Once again war gave rise to a mood that favoured change. The post-war Labour government established a Local Government Boundary Commission. Its 1947 Report made suggestions for reform of areas but stated firmly that in spite of its terms of reference it could do little unless it considered powers and functions as well. The Commission was disbanded in 1949 by Aneurin Bevan, the then Minister of Health, and local government areas remained as before. The Labour government, impatient to bring in sweeping new economic and social changes, could not wait for a reformed system of local government and used the public corporation, the area board and the *ad hoc* body instead.

The post-war debate subsided until, in 1954, the Minister of Housing and Local Government urged the Local Authority Associations, in spite of their differences, to submit views on possible reforms. Then in 1957 the Government issued three White Papers – on Areas and Status, on Finance, and on the Functions of County Councils. The first of these, 'Areas and Status of Local Authorities in England and Wales, 1955-56' (*Cmnd*. 9831) called for larger areas but was again essentially ameliorative. The old town versus country conflict remained.

From the late 1950s onwards there was also a renewed interest in the internal organisation of local authorities. By the early 1970s the reform of the structure of local government was accompanied by substantial changes in management and internal re-organisation. The fifties also saw a revived interest in the staffing of local authorities and in the quality of elected representation. Post-war legislation had changed the nature, as well as the scope, of many local services. The relation between officers and councillors was also changing, as the need for expertise increased and committee work became more demanding. At the same time, central influence and control affected the internal organisation of local authorities by standardising their procedures. The finance system also changed its balance, so that more revenue came from central grants than local rates.

There was a growing call for reform in all these areas – in organisation, in the work of officers and councillors, and in central/local relations – which paralleled the debate about areas. There was also a call for the revitalisation of local democracy as such, though this was more muted, perhaps because low polls and 'apathy' was seen as more intractable – and as less threatening – than the other difficulties.

In the event, the 1958 Local Government Act set up two Commissions, one for England and one for Wales, to investigate local government. London had a separate Royal Commission (the Herbert Commission), set up in 1957, whose report was largely accepted by the government and implemented in the 1963 Local Government Act. This gave a two-tier metropolitan system. The Greater London Council was responsible for strategic planning, major roads, fire and ambulance and concurrent powers with the boroughs in housing. Thirty-two London boroughs, with responsibilities for personal social services (and sharing powers with the GLC in housing and planning) were established, together with the Corporation of the City of London. The outer London boroughs control their own education service but in the area of the twelve inner boroughs education is provided by a separate body, the Inner London Education Authority. This is a special committee of the GLC and is made up of councillors from both the GLC and the twelve inner boroughs.

These reforms came into full operation in April 1965 but, even so, they do not meet all the problems. The GLC is smaller than the regional catchment area of London and much smaller than the South East Economic Planning Region set up in 1964. Its constitutional form was virtually unchanged and the committee and aldermanic systems continued.

The fate of the other two Commissions was unhappy and few changes were made. The English Commission, like its predecessors, was constrained by its terms of reference. Outside the Special Review Areas of the main conurbations (where alone it could make recommendations about functions) it was largely confined to suggesting amalgamations of existing units. The Commissions were given the elusive and contradictory twin criteria of 'effectiveness' and 'convenience' of local government as their terms of reference. There were no established and agreed measures by which these could be judged, given the variety of factors which they had to keep in mind. The lack of formal guidance – or research – allowed the vested local interests full reign.

These problems, however, lapsed with the demise of the Commission in 1965. In February 1966 Mr Crossman, the Minister of Housing and Local Government, set up two Royal Commissions, one for England and one for Scotland. The situation looked hopeful since the government, while acknowledging the potential conflict between the need for large-scale administrative areas and accessible democratic communities, seemed determined to find solutions. The Royal Commission had wider terms of reference, including the regional dimension, though difficulties over 'effective and convenient' local democracy still remained.

The English Royal Commission's (the Redcliffe-Maud Commission) deliberations were aided by the work of its predecessors, and by research facilities. It could commission analyses of important problems – on size and efficiency, community attitudes, socio-geographical problems, experiences of reform in London – as well as gather opinion. But its work was impeded by the establishment in 1959 of the Royal Commission on the Constitution (the Crowther Commission). This meant that radical changes of function, including the return of powers from *ad hoc* bodies to regional authorities and of reduced central governmental control, could not be effectively dealt with. This, together with the restriction on its deliberations on finance, circumscribed the Royal Commission's findings.

The Redcliffe-Maud Royal Commission proposed sixty-one new areas for England covering town and country together. In fifty-eight of these areas unitary authorities would be responsible for all services. In three areas – Birmingham, Liverpool and Manchester – there would be a two-tier structure comprising a metropolitan authority and metropolitan districts. The sixty-one areas, together with Greater London, would be grouped together into eight provinces. The provincial councils, with strategic powers, would be indirectly elected from among their constituent local authorities, plus some co-opted members.

The Royal Commission also stressed the need for equally vital changes in central/local relations, so that control could be diminished. On administrative arrangements the Commission followed the broad lines of the previous Maud report on management, although it replaced the management board with a policy committee. It recommended that the main authority should be limited to seventy-five elected members and the aldermanic system should be abolished. The Commission also suggested that there should be a wider local tax base, although rates were likely to remain the main tax.

Mr Derek Senior's dissent from the main proposals was on the grounds that the Report ignored the facts of social geography. His 'city regions' incorporated urban centres and their commuting hinterlands and his alternative proposals were for five provinces, thirty-five city regional authorities, and 148 district authorities. Common Councils would give, in parishes or within the towns, a neighbourhood community forum.

The Report succinctly analysed four key factors. First, boundaries rendered obsolete by mobility made for authorities which were ineffective as comprehensive planning bodies. Second, 'effective' could be defined as efficient, merely workable or as meeting popular (not necessarily right) demands. Third, the definition of 'viable' also depended on whose point of view was taken and what degree of popular control was thought necessary or desirable. Finally, criteria such as effective and viable could not be thought of in relation to any one service; they had to embrace all services and consider local authority work as a collectivity.

Jane Moreton claims that, in practice, the Commission stressed functions, particularly planning, and interpreted effectiveness in terms of efficiency and minimum population. Democratic viability was a temporing, not a prime, factor.[1] By contrast, the Wheatley Commission on Local Government Reform in Scotland concentrated on the right to exercise power and took the interdependence of town and country, and the importance of planning, for granted. The Wheatley suggestions, for seven main regional authorities, thirty-seven districts and county councils, aimed at enabling democratic local authorities to bring government to the people.

The main doubt about the Royal Commission approach was that too much weight was given to the search for an optimum area for planning and transportation. There was then a temptation to fit other services into this pattern. But the Commission failed to stress the potentially democratic value of their approach. The unifying unitary local authority which encompassed and reconciled conflicting interests did potentially offer its citizens the opportunity to view all services as a whole. The Commission neglected this point and so laid itself open to the criticism that it favoured efficiency above democracy.

The Commission felt that, although the research did not show a clear relation between size and efficiency, the large unitary authorities were justified on a number of grounds. The first was their belief in linking services together. The second was the virtual unanimity, among the various Ministry and professional witnesses, that around a quarter of a million population was a minimum (and optimal) size for 'their' particular service.

The general principles of local government which emerged were that town and country were interdependent; all-purpose authorities should link services; authorities must be of a minimum size to command sufficient specialist staff and resources; and that authorities must not be above a maximum size (around 1 million population) or management would be hampered, popular control lessened and apathy made more likely. The provincial council, unitary authority and local council met all these principles.

A further general principle may be noted. The Royal Commission, in its majority report and Senior's memorandum of dissent, focused on the city, the urban area and its hinterland, rather than on the economic region. Its principles were firmly rooted in local government in the traditional sense. They were traditional in another sense in seeing their task as providing a uniform system of local government.

Uniformity was seen as essential in order to make the reform acceptable to governments and to those officers and councillors who would have to run the new system. This traditionalism was markedly reinforced by the Commission's assumption that, broadly speaking, councillors' and officers' roles would continue as before. There were no proposals for a directly elected Mayor or other chief executive or for a small full-time paid executive board. Voluntary, part-time, unpaid public service remained the bedrock of the system (although, interestingly, the Wheatley Commission had recommended paid councillors in Scotland). In this respect the Commission did not distinguish between representative, accountable democracy and popular, responsive, consultative democracy. It stressed, in fact, the traditional strength of English democracy which combined representative and popular democracy into one councillor role.

The reforms of 1972 were seen by many as a backward step since they split local and regional responsibilities between four bodies: the two tiers of local government, the water authorities and the health service. The Labour Party's White Paper, 'Reform of Local Government in England' (*Cmnd.* 4276, February 1970), had broadly accepted the Redcliffe-Maud proposals. It differed, however, on the need for a provincial level, which it dropped to await Crowther's deliberations. The number of metropolitan counties was increased from three to five, to include West Yorkshire and South Hampshire, and education was given the top-tier level rather than the metropolitan districts. Finally, Labour's White Paper rejected the idea that local councils should share in main services in favour of an advisory kind of community forum. Unitary authorities should also decentralise administration to district committees on which local council members would sit.

The Conservative opposition, however, pledged an alternative two-tier system of local government. This reflected the relative support for the two parties in town and county and their governing experience: Labour as the party controlling, in normal times, the large urban centres, Conservatives as the party of the countryside and small towns. In the late 1960s the Conservatives were also stressing the need for more local autonomy; they feared that the unitary authorities would swamp the countryside with local Labour-controlled councils.

The Conservative government, in their White Paper, 'Local Government in England' (*Cmnd.* 4584, February 1971) and in the Bill, established a two-tier system of counties and county districts for most of England. The metropolitan pattern was broadly similar to Labour's except that the number was increased from five to six (South Yorkshire and Tyne/Wear were added and South Hampshire dropped) and the education function given back to the metropolitan districts. Most functions in the metropolitan area went to the districts, with the exception of strategic planning and transport which, together with the Passenger Transport functions, went to the county. In the rest of the country this division of functions was reversed, with the districts retaining only housing and some planning powers as their major tasks. The counties, not the districts, were the social services authority. In Wales, a system of eight counties with thirty-six (later, thirty-seven) county districts would be established, while in Scotland the broad principles of the Wheatley Commission for a region/district were accepted.

The Conservative White Paper on English Reform also stressed that power should be returned to the people and decisions should be taken as locally as possible. J. A. G. Griffith believed that, as ever, the proposals had a strong flavour of that conventional wisdom typical of all government pronouncements on reform, which could be summed up by the four words: 'democracy', 'efficiency', 'flexible' and 'realistic'.[2] But this was misleading since local government reform was not primarily about local democracy as such but about raising the standard of living of those with serious housing and other problems.

The background to the Redcliffe-Maud Commission was wider, however, than a concern to speed up the previous attempts at boundary changes. The 1960s was a period of debate about the need for change in many areas of public life. Many of these problems touched local authorities directly. The Maud and Mallaby Reports of 1967 proposed a streamlining of local authority management; the Seebohm Report of 1968 called for unified social services departments; and proposals for the national health service stressed more effective use of resources and better management (which threatened to deprive local authorities of their health functions). The search for efficiency was pervasive – as were fears of 'remoteness' and diminishing local autonomy.

Dissension arose when reformers tried to solve these many problems and set priorities among the various objectives. More or less participation, more efficient services, the nature of unpaid public service, and the need for new managerial structures all highlighted the conflict implicit in the 1956 debate: 'The test of any system of local government in this country should be whether it provides a stable structure capable of discharging efficiently the functions entrusted to it, while at the same time maintaining its democratic character.'[3]

In one sense, reform is never finalised and if the debate ceased, then this would indicate a dangerous complacency. But the formula expressed by the 1956 White Paper – that functions should be exercised at the lowest level consistent with efficiency and economy – does not take us very far. It is a sentiment which has been reiterated by both Labour and Conservative governments since 1956 but reform has, in the last analysis, crystallised around two political and historical traditions. One is the 'big city' or county borough pattern, associated broadly with the Redcliff-Maud Report and in modified form with the then Labour Government. The other is the two-tier, county tradition which, again in broad terms, is associated with the Conservatives and their 1972 reforms.

Missing from both traditions, in any really meaningful sense, is the wider question of decentralisation in a developed, complex industrial society – representative regional institutions and effective community or neighbourhood bodies for urban as well as rural areas. One reason for this is that decentralisation of central government departments, and administrative devolution, may both retard local government reform and reduce the need for it.

Decentralisation through a variety of regional bodies and government departments is potentially more flexible than local government changes, where many political problems stand in the way of reform. Central government can devolve powers and responsibilities to different public bodies and to groupings of civil servants. The ways in which this is done – the setting up of the Regional Economic Planning Councils as nominated not elected bodies for example – affect the scope and operation of local government itself. Local government and central government's field administration are intricately related; the relationship depends on overlapping memberships (of local councils and various boards and agencies) and informal contacts between officials, councillors and interest groups.

In recent years the question of devolution and decentralisation – and the principles behind the changes and reforms, if principles there are – has seen the introduction of yet a further form. This is 'regionalisation from below' and is exemplified by the Regional Passenger Transport Authorities. These bodies were set up under the 1968 Transport Act and cover the major conurbations of the West Midlands, West Riding, Merseyside and Tyneside. The PTA Board is made up of persons nominated from among the constituent local councils and the administrative organ – the Passenger Transport Executive – is composed of full-time officials. These bodies are, as it were, the familiar joint boards or joint committees of local government writ large. They co-ordinate the running of a service over a wider area than the individual local authority. With the reform of local government they will pass under the jurisdiction of the new metropolitan counties.

It can be argued, however, that we are still looking at reform in the same way as the Victorians: struggling to solve past problems rather than making a fresh start. Even the advent of the Crowther Commission on the Constitution is unlikely to make changes that would radically alter either the map of local government or the constitutional position of local authorities in the state.

THE RELATION BETWEEN SIZE AND FUNCTION

In the period since 1958 there has been increasing interest in the correlation between the functions of local authorities and their size and area. The criteria of size alone is an unsatisfactory and ambiguous guide to performance *per se*, but it is clear that different services have differing needs. Superficially, this is not a barrier to rational reform; personal services need to be administered close to those they serve while more planning and other technical services call for large-scale operation. But this simple solution has not been easily available since the administrative criteria of 'span of control', and use of scarce professional skills, has led to calls for the planning of all services over wider areas than the immediate locality.

These difficulties have been resolved, in practice, by seeing one or two services (and their criteria of effectiveness) as paramount. In England this has led to a preoccupation with planning and, it can be argued, to a system where reform was in fact debated in terms of the size and area of the local authority to carry out the planning function. Ironically, one of the effects of the reform is to split the planning function between the two tiers of the new county system.

The research and the deliberations of the years leading up to reform have not, and probably cannot, solve the question of optimality. Even the belief that it is possible to have at least a criteria of minimum size (since the 1972 Act, 40,000 population is the formal minimum size for a district authority) is illusory. Agency arrangements will diversify the size, area and mode of actual administration in some services. We are thus no further than before in defining or evaluating an optimal size for a particular service.

In the period after 1945, local authorities of equal status were treated equally, in spite of variations in size and resources, when powers were conferred on them. To this extent, legal status was the important criteria, not size or area. As a result, variations between local authorities had to be recognised. This had two consequences. First, functions were allocated to the top tier on grounds of efficiency. Second, anomalies were mitigated by the distribution of government grants to bring the poorer areas 'up to' an average standard.

The treatment of equal status authorities equally, and the conferment of powers on the counties and county boroughs, had a further important consequence for the division of powers. Functions were given to local authorities according to category, but once given they could not be subdivided. For example, counties and county boroughs were made the local education authorities by the 1944 Education Act; this conferred the whole range of public education provision upon them. In the counties, however, the need to consult the various district councils, and to administer services on an area basis, meant that the principle was soon eroded.

In the post-war period delegation to district councils, or devolution to area committees (which remained sub-committees of the full county council committee), brought local and county councillors into the day-to-day administration of education, children's and planning services. The system operated under a greater or lesser degree of county control, and the schemes also varied between services and between different parts of the country.

The district councils demanded more opportunities to take a greater part in these services. In response, the Local Government Act 1958 (which added health and welfare to the services which could be delegated) allowed councils of a population of 60,000 or more to claim delegated powers as of right. Thus equal status and the principle that functions should not be subdivided gave way to a complex pattern of administration. Under the 1972 Act powers were not divided in this way. The major functions were firmly allocated to the counties, or in the metropolitan areas, to the districts and the counties.

The agency provisions allow district councils to carry out certain functions, mainly in the fields of town development, libraries, consumer protection, roads, transport and traffic management, and refuse disposal. Social services, education and police are excluded from agency arrangements. The system does not involve delegation to local district committees of county and local councillors since this would replicate, it was felt, the old features of delegation under the previous county council system.

The agency arrangements stressed that districts take part as the agents of the county, not as bodies to which powers are delegated as of right. This is a real distinction, not just a semantic one. Cooperation may operate eventually much as delegation did but power lies with the county and it has the legal responsibility for executing the functions in question.

In the metropolitan districts the emphasis is reversed; the need is to safeguard the overall strategic role of the metropolitan county, particularly in transportation and planning. The metropolitan districts control education, social services and libraries and the great need will be for the districts to pass full and reliable information up to the county level rather than, as in the case of the non-metropolitan counties, the reverse.

The discussion of the 1972 reform has been most critical of the division of the planning functions. The division split up existing teams of planners and, it was claimed, weakened a county's comprehensive strategies by divorcing development control from overall policy. The opposing argument was that district councils had a democratic right to know what was planned for their area and to propose solutions. They could best do this by being the responsible local planning body. Development applications should also go to them in the first instance.

The debate reflects the interests of the two kinds of authority. There is no reason why the planning function (or indeed all functions) should not be divided rather than letting districts share in delegated powers. But two doubts remain. One is that the planning arrangements were decided on political grounds, i.e. that it would give to the districts a significant power which logically reinforced their housing functions and mitigated against the loss of other services. The other doubt is potentially more worrying. Before 1947 planning was split between many authorities. The 1947 Town and Country Planning Act reduced these to about 140 (the County and County Borough Councils). The 1972 reformed system more than trebled the number of authorities concerned with planning in England and Wales (to around 420). The fear is that, as a result, overall planning will suffer. Local plans will be more difficult to harmonise with county strategy and there will be less effective control of the amenity and conservation aspects of planning.

CENTRAL CONTROL

The areas, size and functions of local government units are also affected by the increasing centralisation of the modern state. The demand for uniform standards, for equality of social and economic opportunity, and for a high level of provision which can only be financed from a national tax base, have all made increased dominance inevitable. Owen A. Hartley outlines the two views of central/local relations, both of which have their roots in the nineteenth century. On the one hand there is the Chadwick view of the relationship as one of principal and agent. On the other hand there is the Toulmin Smith belief in partnership: local self-governing bodies equal to parliament.[4]

Elements of both views persist to our own day. The Local Government Manpower Committee, in its First Report of 1950, saw local authorities exercising their powers in their own right, not as agents. The Redcliffe-Maud Royal Commission of 1969 laments the subsidiary position of local authorities but, while stressing the ideal of partnership, in fact settles for agency status. This paradox is reflected in the White Paper, 'Local Government in England' (*Cmnd.* 4584, 1971) which talks both of the need to return power to local people and of the need for national policies. Hartley's own work also suggests, interestingly, that it is easier for the centre to control an innovatory local authority than bring an inactive one up to standard.[5]

A continuing question for democratic theorists is the 'correct' level at which democratic majority decisions should be taken. In a unitary state such as Britain the accepted position has generally been that the centre must overrule the localities. As Peter G. Richards has put it, if democracy means majority rule and majority opinion then 'it would seem to be as democratic to follow the will of the Minister who represents the national majority as it is to follow the wishes of those who represent but a local majority'.[6] But there are difficulties. One is the accepted 'democratic centralism' of the unitary state itself. The debate about regionalism and nationalism has called the state's overriding 'democratic majority' into question, and more freedom for regional and local divergencies are now demanded.

A second difficulty is, of course, that democratic theory and practice are concerned with a diversity of aims, including majority opinion as expressed in elections, the protection of minorities, individual rights and duties. The localities hold elections, are representative bodies, and are responsible to local opinion. Again, as Peter G. Richards notes, if democracy is defined as having regard to local opinion, then the local units, including the very smallest, have moral rights over the larger – whether it is the parish against the county or the locality against the centre.[7]

The problem is not solved by assuming that, since local authorities operate within national legislation, the central majority must prevail. Since local administration is carried out through local elected bodies then local opinion must play a part or the system is a sham. Increasingly, the dilemma has been met by the sheer bulk of legislation and the response of the national electorate to national party policies and electioneering. The public reaction to government action, and the volume of statutory powers which local authorities must operate, combine to reduce the debate about the appropriate level of democratic decision – until political controversy becomes particularly heated.

The general arguments about central control are familiar. Governments manage the economy and in so doing must control investment, promote growth and curb inflation, and plan the orderly development of services. Local authorities must fit into this national pattern although, since needs and resources vary from area to area, they will be helped, to differing degrees, to bring their services up to standard.

The public has a right to expect equality of treatment and this means central guidance and surveillance. Although this is accepted, there are fears that this has gone too far. Financial control, and detailed administrative supervision, are the main complaints. Central government now meets more than half the total amount of local expenditure and inevitably exercises control over local policy and priorities. Similarly, control over loan sanction has severely curtailed local autonomy. Control by individual Whitehall departments – over plans, data collation and standards – is too detailed. The former system of District Audit, and the powers of surcharge, made local authorities over-cautious and obsessed by details. The new 1972 Local Government Act relaxes these provisions but it will take much longer for attitudes to change.

Increased central power also arises from the imperatives of modern business and investment operations. Economies of scale have been as important in the investment sphere as in the use of plant, materials and staff. Centralisation does not mean, however, the end of local government. On the contrary, local units become more important, since they must carry out the services which governments determine. As government departments become more overburdened, then pressure to decentralise to field agencies, or devolve more functions to local authorities, increases. Co-ordination between services in the field becomes even more necessary; traditionally, this is a prime function and justification of local government.

But again this co-ordination, from the central government's point of view, calls for increased size (and financial strength) of local units. Governments also view local services in the light of effective performance of governmental aims and have increasingly controlled the areas to receive particular treatment. In the Urban Aid programme, for example, the government selected the authorities and even determined the districts within their areas, and the particular projects, to be supported. Similarly, unacceptable inequalities of provision may result in greater government control rather than a rethinking of the way services are provided. Governments are also tempted to direct local authorities' efforts – more houses or more schools – in order to fulfil their own promises. Finally, central departments are increasingly turning to new techniques such as output budgeting which reduces local authority discretion still further.

These arguments are likely to outlive the reform of local government, part of whose justification has always been the need for larger areas to 'stand up' to Westminster and Whitehall. They are important, however, since the nature and extent of local powers and the relation with central government affects the local democratic process. Citizens deserve equal consideration and so, for example, wide variations in services which do not match widely differing circumstances, are not justified. More uniformity, more control from the centre, must remedy these defects, particularly in housing.

Local citizens are also national voters and have a right to expect that government policies will be implemented, not flouted, by local authorities. Principles of equity have also justified control through the courts to make local authorities perform their duties and to make them behave justly. But democratic administration demands local decision-making. Local councillors, and their constituents, all have a right (and a duty) to take part in democratic society, including helping to make decisions and carry them out. Local councils cannot do this if they are mere puppets. Nor can they treat citizens, consumers and clients with due and equal consideration if their freedom to do so is rigidly controlled.

Another difficulty is not so much rigid control as changing economic fortunes. This can have serious consequences. At times of national financial crisis – or even changing priorities of governments – a local authority may find it almost impossible to plan coherently, especially for its capital programme. For example, Elizabeth Layton states that in the late 1950s local authorities had become so discouraged by changes of levels of expenditure, interest rates, loan sanctions and so on, that they had largely ceased to try to co-ordinate their capital building programmes.[8]

In the 1970s the question of local powers was widened. Certain problems became more contentious – council rents and housing finance was one example. Education also gave rise to controversy over comprehensive secondary schooling and the question of subsidised school meals and milk. But we must be careful not to over-dramatise. The arguments could be seen as part of a general party political battle which happened to involve the local level, rather than an argument about local initiative. With this in mind, what were the problems in these contentious areas?

One worry has been the default powers of the Housing Finance Act 1972: the Ministry could send in a Housing Commissioner if the authority refused to carry out the legislation. Councillors could be surcharged, and standardised rent scales implemented. Schedule 1 of the Act also requires local authorities to set up a Housing Revenue Account, and lays down strict rules for its operation. Here was detailed control with a vengeance. Local authorities are debarred from using the housing revenue account either to reduce rents or for general town purposes. Any balance must be credited to the account for the next year, or be treated as a surplus. Such a surplus must be paid to the Secretary of State and, after certain adjustments, half will be returned (although again it cannot be used to subsidise rents). This is a serious change in the power of local authorities to determine their own rent levels on their own views of equity and justice.

By contrast, the furore over the government's restrictions on local authority provision of school meals and milk seems to raise less basic issues, even if it was politically contentious. The Education (Milk) Act of 1971 was based on the Conservative Government's White Paper, 'New Policies on Public Spending' (*Cmnd.* 4515, 1970). The Act provided for free milk for all school children up to the age of seven years (instead of to twelve years) but those over seven with a medical need would continue to receive it free. A saving of £9 million a year would result.

Local authorities were upset by the lack of prior consultation. They would have preferred the government to ask for net savings, leaving the details to be worked out in consultation with local authorities (who might have preferred, for example, to make cuts in other services). Several local authorities ignored the law or sought to evade it by a series of technicalities, but by the beginning of 1972, the local protest was over. The government's attempts to reduce public expenditure had produced a disquieting feeling that prior consultation might have avoided this emotional reaction.

The whole of education shows the influence of government but in recent years arguments have been mainly about the policy of comprehensive schooling. Accusations were made, according to which party was in power, of either dogmatic central control or of local intransigence undermining national policy. In practice, schemes have varied widely, and the slow implementation of schemes does not appear to imply excessive central control. Policy in this area is always subject to national political argument.

Political arguments also surround the policy over local authority directly employed labour. This has always been controversial, with Labour Councils favouring the use of a municipal labour force for maintenance and minor works (and in a few cases, quite large-scale schemes) and Conservative councils, on grounds of principle and cost, opposed. In 1972 the Secretary of State for the Environment announced a limit of £40,000 (total cost excluding land) for road works, above which direct labour could not be used, unless the work was won in competition with contractors. For trunk road work, evidence on tenders would be required by the appropriate Regional Controller (Roads and Transportation). The government circular 90/72 stressed that this was to test efficiency by competition, not to place an arbitrary limit on the use of direct labour.[9] The question is again one of differing concepts of public and private provision, which continues to divide the parties, but it is not necessarily true that it needs to be decided by central government rather than the local community.

A different problem is illustrated by the new social services legislation. One disappointment is the government's continued insistence on the statutory establishment of a specific committee, and the scrutiny of the choice of the new directors of social services departments. The other is the regionalisation of local authorities children's homes. The regionalisation of local authority planning for residential care is an interesting example of compulsory collaboration. The Children's and Young Persons Act 1969 provided for the setting up of eleven English, and one Welsh, children's regional planning committees to establish a comprehensive and integrated system of local authority and voluntary homes. These are purely planning bodies, and local authorities and voluntary organisations still have executive power. It is an interesting example of government compelling authorities to share facilities on a regional basis. Because of the nature and sensitivity of the service (with juvenile delinquency rates rising), the Government felt it should not be left to voluntary co-operation.

In other areas, widening forms of intervention have been less welcome. One such problem is the investigatory activities of Select Committees of the House of Commons. In 1969 the Select Committee on Education and Science included local education authority colleges in their general inquiries about university and college students, arranged visits to local authority establishments, and took evidence at public hearings. Similar visits were arranged by the Select Committee on Race Relations. Select Committees should not, in J. A. G. Griffith's view, seek to probe individual local authorities in this way.[10] Members of Parliament may also help to increase government intervention because of their constituency work. G. W. Jones has argued that the MP, while defending local interests, is also responsible for increasing central control from both departments and from Parliament.[11] This comes about because the MP passes local complaints and grievances to Ministers and Departments – thus drawing them into local affairs – rather than referring them to the local authority.

Membership of the EEC will also affect some areas of local authority autonomy and mean further standardisation of certain services. The main impact will come from the Common Market objectives of free movement of labour and capital, and the detailed regulations over such matters as vehicle construction and safety, and weights and measures. The free movement of labour requires that migrant workers shall have the same rights of access to housing as nationals – which clearly has implications for local policies.

The directives on public works contracts also affects local authorities. Public works contracts above a certain level must now be open to non-nationals and follow standardised procedures on advertising, specifications, time limits and acceptance of tenders. There will also be parallel provisions for the supply of goods and materials, which will apply to all contracts over the value of £25,000. A further worry is that, as Ron Rhodes points out, it is not clear what exactly 'public enterprise' is for EEC purposes and whether such matters as rate subsidies to municipal services would contravene community legislation.[12] Regional policies of the EEC will also, in time, affect Britain's own policy and if this should increase the regional aid received from the Community then it will also increase the scrutiny from Brussels.

It is finance, however, which continues to be the dominant source of central control. K. J. Davey has argued that local autonomy is primarily a question of responsibilities, resources and discretion.[13] To this end, elasticity of income is vital. That is, the tax base should expand naturally, as the economy grows, and so should keep in step with the rate of inflation and with demands for expenditure. The early 1970s have, unfortunately, completely overturned Davey's conditions for local autonomy. Inflation, and rising demands, have outpaced the growth of the tax base. By 1973 revaluation of rateable property, rising costs, and the pressing needs of the big cities, combined to make for a crisis situation and government was called upon for additional rate relief.

The degree of dependence on central financial support does not, of itself, determine the degree of control of its direction. The whole range of relationships – advice and data gathering, submission of plans and the distribution of ministerial circulars, the role of audit and surcharge, and the influence of leading authorities, officers and Associations on central government – must be taken into account. The crucial financial point is that, as Davey states, whether revenues are independent or not they should nevertheless be sufficiently elastic to give a margin for discretion and innovation.[14]

Central grants then, are not necessarily undermining initiative; the question is rather how grants and loan sanctions operate. The operation of central governments grants has swung between two different forms and aims since the 1880s. On the one hand, there have been specific grants for special needs. On the other, block grants

– the allocation of money without specific ties – has been used to allow authorities to allocate the money according to local needs. Both schemes have defects. Specific grants can encourage waste, since local authorities expect their spending to be matched by appropriate grants. Block grants can prove more illusion than reality given the necessity to spend so large a part of the budget on statutory services.

The two types of grant system tend to go in a cycle, with periodic 'fresh starts' of block grants (as under the 1958 Local Government Act). As time goes on, additional money, on a specific basis, is made available – normally for new, expanding or hard-pressed services. At any one time, therefore, the two kinds of grant system are generally intertwined (particularly since specific grants are traditionally used for the police, probation and fire services).

The system currently in use is that of the Rate Support Grant. Under the Local Government Act of 1966, grants were based on three factors – the 'needs element', the 'resources element' and the 'domestic element'. Even so, specific grants (for development and redevelopment, for reclamation of derelict land, for special provision for immigrants) remained. Rate Support Grant orders were made in advance for two-year or more periods.

The Rate Support Grant negotiations depended on the total revenue Whitehall accepted as reasonable, the percentage they were prepared to pay as grant, and the amount of relief to domestic rate-payers. But inflation made for uncertainties. In the autumn of 1970, the Conservative Government's White Paper, 'New Policies for Public Spending' (*Cmnd.* 4515) cut the original annual growth of the RSG from 1 per cent to $\frac{1}{2}$ per cent by halving the increases in domestic rate relief. This element had originally been introduced to mitigate the harshness of rising rate demands. The White Paper said that it was unhealthy for local democracy for domestic ratepayers to be insulated from the costs of the services they were demanding.

From April 1971 the government also relaxed its control over local councils' capital expenditure. Projects are divided into three types. First, 'key sector' expenditure, including education, housing, principal roads, police, social services, water supply and sewerage disposal. These schemes still need departmental approval but, after that, a local authority would be free to borrow to purchase land for these projects.

Second, 'locally determined' expenditure would include such projects as libraries, parks, baths, town centre development and minor roads. For these there is a block allocation within which authorities are free to determine their own programmes. Third, there are capital schemes financed from revenue and from certain special funds, and local authorities are free to determine their own spending in this area.

The provisions still leave considerable control in the hands of central departments: over individual items in the 'key sector', and over standards and limits in the 'locally determined' sector. In the counties a single block allocation for locally determined projects had to be divided between county and district authorities, and this was contentious.

The new developments relaxed control but were a somewhat hollow victory. Since some 60 per cent of capital expenditure fell into the key sector, 'freedom' depended on how much was left over for 'own choice' spending. The Secretary of the Institute of Municipal Treasurers and Accountants viewed the change as financial and administrative tidying up, since control by loan sanction had already become redundant in the 'key sector' areas. But the sum allocated for the whole area of a county, to be divided by agreement, was an admission by Whitehall that it could not devise a formula for distributing capital funds among authorities who varied in size, in capital programmes, and over time.[15] The reformed two-tier local government system may perpetuate this difficulty and Whitehall might then reimpose direct control.

Central control over financial expenditure continues to be a problem. So too is the rating valuation base of local taxation. New rating valuation lists came into force in April 1973. They showed an average assessment of 2·56 times the previous rateable values. Inflation prevented this from being neutralised by a corresponding decrease in the rate poundage levied. The government increased the relief for domestic ratepayers in the Rate Support Grant of 1973-4. But in some areas, with high revaluation, even domestic ratepayers faced high extra demands. And the large conurbations faced both revaluation problems and inflation.

The government announced, in its 'Control of Inflation: Monitoring of Rates' (Circular 21/73) that it would monitor rate increases. Local authorities have a traditional freedom to set their rate level within the overall framework of grant and capital expenditure limits. Rate monitoring, even in a period of heavy inflation, was seen as an added interference. Circular 21/73 made it clear that rate-fixing is the local council's responsibility but the Department, after discussions with local representatives, could ask them to reconsider and, if necessary, lower their rates.

There were renewed calls for the complete recasting of the rate support grant and even for a complete change in the finance system. The government, in its Green Paper 'The Future Shape of Local Government Finance' (*Cmnd.* 4741, 1972) and in its Consultation Paper 'Local Government Finance in England and Wales' of June 1973, still favoured, with limited modifications, the existing system. Rates would be the main tax, with some improvements – for example, the full rating of empty properties and more frequent revaluation (although not the rating of site values), together with an improved rate rebate scheme.

The Green Paper did not examine the financial aspects of local democracy from first principles and rejected a local income tax on the grounds of the cost of administration and the problems of local assessment and variations. But although the present situation thus seems likely to continue, there is more widespread support for new ideas than ever before. Local income tax, sales tax, motor taxes – even lotteries – are all familiar and much debated ideas. But they now receive support from the IMTA and from the local authority Associations.

Local authorities fear ever-increasing central control in both revenue and capital expenditure. This had been in train since the late 1950s, when the Radcliffe Committee on the working of the monetary system (*Cmnd.* 827, 1959) led to restrictions on short-term borrowing by local authorities. It had been continued by the Plowden Committee on the control of public expenditure (*Cmnd.* 1432, 1961) and subsequent White Papers on investment and expenditure. As a result, one leading spokesman feared that the definition of capital expenditure would increasingly widen and be more subject to central control.[16]

The current situation offers little hope that there will be sufficient elasticity of resources in the near future to enable that local autonomy of which K. J. Davey speaks. Changes in attitude, as well as dramatic changes in tax raising and allocation, are needed. Genuine reform would entail a political decision to devolve substantial powers to local authorities and less standardisation of services. There seems to be little evidence that this would command widespread public support or government backing. Another factor which militates against relaxation of central supervision is a combination of political expediency and political inertia. Governments are praised, and blamed, for 'their' housing programmes or whatever. Governments and political parties are not necessarily, therefore, very enthusiastic about genuine local autonomy. It follows, *The Times* concluded, that the difficulties inherent in drastic financial reform were hardly justified if the political will to make autonomy a reality was lacking.[17] From their side, the local authorities have also appeared cautious. There has been a fear, for example, that if *ultra vires* is relaxed and superseded by a general competence principle then a more general control of local authority spending might follow. Even if they were granted a general competence a government grant system would still be necessary and loan sanction would still apply. Local autonomy has been, then, a muted theme in the reform debate.

REGIONALISM

England is one of the few countries with no intermediate level of government between the localities and the centre. In recent years this situation has given cause for concern. Central government has become over-burdened, has lacked co-ordination in the field and has increasingly taken the view that larger local government units were imperative. The economic planning machinery, together with more *de facto* administrative devolution within departments are, however, preferred to a radical recasting of central and local government.

The need for some form of regional machinery has been recognised since the beginning of this century, when the main interest lay in the need to reorganise local government into larger units. In the inter-war period, however, regionalism was considered as an aid to central government organisation on the one hand and the distribution of industry on the other. The Royal Commission on the Distribution of the Industrial Population (the Barlow Report, 1940) suggested that a system of regionalism would help to promote more effective national policies. Two other reports, from the Scott and Uthwatt committees, were concerned with land use planning rather than industrial policies, but pointed in the same direction. These inquiries were concerned with economic problems and with administrative machinery. Political inquiry was largely absent and the long-standing reluctance to contemplate a regional level of government was exacerbated by the wartime appointment of Regional Commissioners. They did not, in the event, have to use their emergency powers, but were regarded uneasily by local authorities and the system was dismantled at the end of the war.

Government departments were, from 1945 onwards, decentralised into nine standard English regions (together with Wales and Scotland). The 'standard regions' brought together staff from different Whitehall departments but did not match the administrative areas of the nationalised industries or other bodies. In the 1950s some Ministries, of which Housing and Local Government was one, virtually dismantled their regional organisation. In 1965, the setting up of the eight Economic Planning Regions in England (plus Scotland and Wales) effectively replaced the standard regions. Now the whole forms a managerial and advisory, rather than a political, system.

Regional areas are forms of decentralisation based on administrative convenience and economic needs as these are defined by the centre, not by the localities. In this country three factors are currently part of the regional debate: economic versus urban models of government and the – intermittent – intervention of cultural and economic nationalism. The economic model depends on such factors as levels of employment, industrial configuration and on previous attempts to aid 'depressed areas'. It must look at the centre and the regions together, if it is to bring rich and poor areas into one system. This has been the goal, if not the reality, since the establishment of the Economic Planning Regions in 1964.

The urban model of regionalism, by contrast, looks at the influence of certain major towns and cities on the economic and social life of their surrounding towns and countryside. In the last decade students of government argued that this urban regionalism should be recognised in the reform of local government. Mr Senior's Memorandum of Dissent to the Royal Commission report, for example, emphasised this point. The third factor, Scottish and Welsh nationalism, emerged with the success of nationalist political parties at local and national elections in the mid-1960s and the demands for greater economic, political and linguistic autonomy.

In British political life there have been, L. J. Sharpe argues, two regionalisms.[18] One, regionalism from below, stems from local government. Regionalism from below is concerned with economies of scale for local services and in the particular problems of the conurbations or metropolitan areas. The main aim is to strengthen local government. By contrast, regionalism from above has been mainly concerned with making central government effective and strengthening its ability to manage the economy. This means keeping the regional bodies firmly within their advisory framework. The aims of the two regionalisms are distinct and it may be tempting, therefore, to suggest that local government should be considered separately from central government aid, unhampered by economic concerns. This is, however, impossible since economic and land-use planning are now recognised as inextricably related. On the other hand this does not necessarily call for a single, omnibus authority to meet these distinct but related aims. The main task, given the government's view of the role of the economic planning regions, is to strengthen local authorities and their influence upon existing regional bodies.

Local authorities have substantial reservations about the Economic Planning Boards and Councils. They resent their seemingly easier access to government and they regard them as irresponsible since they are not elected. Local authorities have, however, established co-operative means of consultation with the planning councils, through standing conferences and study groups.

The economic machinery was, however, important to the consideration of reform because its advisory nature prevented the problem of a regional level of local government being tackled effectively. The Redcliffe-Maud Commission stopped short of elected regional assemblies, the government and the 1972 Act rejected a provincial authority altogether, and the Crowther consideration of constitutional devolution sank almost into oblivion.

The eight English provincial councils advocated by the Redcliffe-Maud Commission were made up of indirectly elected members, from the local authorities in the region, together with co-opted leading public figures. The provincial councils were to set the strategic planning framework within which the local authorities would work. Senior's memorandum of dissent was essentially that elected regional authorities should be based on large urban centres or city regions. They should absorb and replace the existing major authorities, not be imposed upon them as yet another tier of local government.

The Redcliffe-Maud proposals, given their limited terms of reference, were not concerned with the question of devolution of power and democratic control. This is a fundamental weakness. It is not the size of local units, but the location of power and control over those who make decisions, which is of interest. It is the invisibility of the decision-making process, not its scale or its location, which causes the increased feeling of distance between rulers and ruled. This, rather than technical questions, makes the issue of representative regional government a continuing issue.

Against this background the 1972 reforms contained, strikingly, no regional element at all, unless the two-tier metropolitan areas are viewed as 'regional' in the GLC sense. But the picture is not a static one. There are four broad developments. First, re-organisation of the water and health services continue the importance of *ad hoc* regional authorities outside local government. A second development has been the regional re-organisation of the Department of the Environment.

In 1972 the Department created the post of regional Director, of Under-Secretary status, with direct responsibility for planning, housing and transport functions. In each region the Director (who is the chairman of the regional Economic Planning Board), has a strong co-ordinating role in respect of other departments. He also has, most importantly, the power to transmit, in the Minister's name, planning appeal decisions. The Directors are thus a focus of consultation – what is acceptable to Ministry thinking and what influence can be brought to bear – in the eyes of local authorities.

The third development is along similar lines; in 1972, the Department of Trade and Industry appointed four regional Directors, with devolved authority for regional and industrial growth, in Wales, the North West, Northern region and Yorkshire and Humberside. These have their own separate advisory Industrial Development Boards. The fourth trend is rather different and arises directly from the fact that the reform of local government contains no regional level. As a result it is likely that both the metropolitan and other counties will need a regional arbitrator, especially for planning, transportation and roads, and urban development, redevelopment and overspill. This will almost inevitably be in the Ministry.

Regionalisation of services, outside local government, continued unabated. The re-organisation of the health service and of water supply have features which threaten to diminish democratic local control over services. The re-organisation of the National Health Service provided a system of eighteen non-elective Area Health Boards in England and Wales to which local authorities surrendered their personal health services. The fourteen new Regional Health Authorities, based on the existing hospital regions, have substantial financial and other powers over the area authorities. The Secretary of State nominates, after consultation, the Chairman and all members of the regional authority, and the Chairman of the Area Health Board. And the membership of the Area authority is greatly reduced in numbers and the local authority element is limited to four members. Following criticism from the local authority Associations, this was raised slightly for the largest areas. The lack of formal representation is mitigated, it is argued, by the provision for Community Health councils (half of whose members will be appointed by local district councils), in each of the 150 constituent districts within the area health authorities. But in fact their role is virtually that of consumer consultation.

The 1973 reform of water supply is a similar threat: local authorities' powers are eroded because there is no effective elected regional tier of government to which the powers can be given. Each of the nine English regional boards, however, has a clear majority of local authority members. The National Water Council is purely advisory and the British Waterways Board is left intact. Nevertheless, local authorities have lost their powers as water suppliers and sewerage authorities to the regional authorities though they retain certain powers as agents for sewerage. The legislation also compelled local authorities, unless they could sell out to private water companies in advance, to surrender their water undertakings to the regional water authorities without compensation.

Management needs have loomed large in the debate on health and water re-organisation. Similar concerns govern the administration of the national parks. Under the 1972 Local Government Act, there is a separate committee, under the parent county, for each national park. In the Peak and Lake Districts, exceptionally, the present boards remain. The result is that, although planning functions are in the formal hands of the counties they are largely delegated to the responsible national parks committee, which include one-third ministerial nominated members. Nevertheless there are fears that these will not be strong enough bodies to manage the parks effectively. A strong regional tier would have helped to solve this problem.

In health, water and parks the criteria are the need for management and resources, not the power and influence of democratic local government. And political considerations are very muted. Political regionalism is unlikely in this country since it would be opposed by local councillors, jealous of their traditional duties and by national politicians, fearing rival powers. There is another political argument against elected regional bodies. Elected members, whether MPs or councillors, represent groups of people, through the constituency or ward, rather than individuals. And electors are represented as a nation and as a community, both of which represent a genuine feeling of belonging. Regionalism can provide no such focus and so needs no such representation.[19]

All three political parties have, in modern times, argued for a variety of regional solutions to Britain's economic, social and political problems. The Liberal party has been an advocate of elected provincial assemblies (with parliaments for Scotland and Wales), while the Labour and Conservative parties have been more guarded in their approach. The background to the Crowther Commission was, however, more concerned with nationalism. The Labour government appointed the Commission on the Constitution (the Crowther Commission) in 1969 to examine 'the present functions of the central legislature and government in relation to the several countries, nations and regions of the United Kingdom.'

There are a possible range of regional forms available for the Commission's consideration. First, Parliament could include regional representation on the lines of the Scottish Grand Committee. Second, directly elected bodies could be evolved from the economic planning regions, with strategic powers and possibly devolved powers for hospitals, new towns and other services. Third, elected regional assemblies could be given certain legislative powers and control of their own legal system (on the lines of Liberal Party ideas). Finally, quasi-federal bodies with greatly increased powers could be given a fundamentally changed role in the tax system to reorientate financial control away from the centre for some services (along the lines advocated by John Mackintosh).[20]

The Crowther Commission finished taking evidence at the beginning of 1972 but its deliberations were affected by the death of the chairman at the end of that year and its report, under its new chairman Lord Kilbrandon, has yet to be digested. Forecasting in this situation is formidable. In addition to the limitations on the willingness of governments to devolve their powers to the regional level, three other questions remain. The first is Ulster. Future developments in Northern Ireland may re-activate demands for elected regional bodies for Wales and Scotland. Second, Britain's membership of the EEC may promote a different approach to regionalism. Finally, the Conservative party has been investigating the possibility of a Scottish Assembly with limited legislative powers (mainly the committee stages of Scottish Bills) and the government reaffirmed that this was still under investigation in the Spring of 1973. Even then, EEC membership and the reform of local government may have exhausted the will to change.

PROBLEMS FOR THE FUTURE

The 1972 reform was attacked because it ignored the major feature of modern English life – that it is predominantly urban or urban-influenced. The functional unity of large towns and the joint administration of planning and highways, it was said, was being destroyed. In the conurbations there would be two severe handicaps to good government. One was that the metropolitan boundaries were drawn too tightly round the built-up areas and good strategic planning would be difficult. The other was that the metropolitan county council, like the GLC, had too few real powers to enable it to plan successfully or play its rightful part in housing. This was particularly undesirable since these large urban areas suffered most from housing shortage and obsolescence and a lack of building land. London provides a good example, in fact, of the need to recognise that metropolitan areas require both an upper and lower tier. It is imperative to set some limit on the top tier and to provide an accessible district or borough system below it. In London, and in the new metropolitan counties, there may be insufficient effective power in the top tier. The county level has planning and strategic functions but its effectiveness depends on the political weight and leadership it is able to build up.

Another problem is, again, that of representation. The metropolitan counties are likely to attract younger, better educated, more middle-class members more interested in policy, 'management' and the long-term issues. Working-class representation at this level will be reduced. More traditional, service and constituent-oriented councillors will aim at district membership. Outside the metropolitan areas similar middle-class trends may be expected, due to the problems of travel, day-time meetings and committee time. The new attendance allowances for members are unlikely to affect this and the first elections for the county councils in 1973 showed a marked tendency towards the younger, better-educated councillor in white collar, professional and managerial occupations.

The general opinion is still that councillors should not be paid a full-time salary. To do so, it is argued, would alter the basis of public service. It encourages time-serving by those seeking personal reward at the ratepayers' expense, causes venality if not corruption, and is unnecessary if council work is properly organised. But better attendance allowances will be paid in future. The new code for attendance allowances allows members to claim a flat rate attendance allowance as of right. This is taxable, though subsistence payments are not. Local authorities decide the level of attendance allowance payable, within the maximum set by the Secretary of State.

The payment of councillors, and their social characteristics, were two worries. A third was the electoral system itself. At the same time as the Local Government Bill was published, two separate and permanent Boundary Commissions for England and Wales were designated to establish and maintain a regular review of county and district boundaries and their electoral arrangements.

The English Boundary Commission paid particular attention to the government's guideline that, wherever practicable, a new district should comprise the whole of one or more existing county boroughs or county districts. The final average population figure was

90,000. This represented a large increase in population size compared with the old system, where 80 per cent of the district authorities had less than 40,000 people. Parishes were a special problem. There were criticisms that successor council status would be sought merely on the grounds that the area had a previous separate existence. This would then work against the spirit of unity in a new district and fragment its work.

If parishes faced a secure future as the voice of truly local opinion, local government as a whole spoke with a more uncertain voice. Reform meant a change of the nature and direction of the local authority Associations. The Associations defended the views of their members, and were actively consulted by governments and civil servants. But, it was argued, this effort was dissipated between the different Associations whose influence and power would be increased if they were formed into one body with one voice.

With re-organisation, the Associations reconsidered the problem but, as ever, found agreement difficult. In the summer of 1973 it was announced that there would be an Association of the metropolitan county and district authorities (including the GLC and the London boroughs). There will also be an Association of non-metropolitan counties, and an Association of the non-metropolitan districts. A form of central federation would link the Associations. The parishes have also changed their style. In November 1972 they changed their association to the National Association of Local Councils, covering parishes, successor local councils and Welsh community councils.

The new local government system also continues to present problems because the need for a 'grass roots' voice has not been solved effectively. People now demand, at one and the same time, that government shall be responsive to the needs of their part of the country (a regional concern) and in their home area (a neighbourhood concern). It is now recognised that the relation between voting, interest in local affairs, and the individual's use of local services is a complex one. The individual cannot be forced to vote or take a general interest in 'local government'. Community life should, rather, enable the citizen to make his views felt and safeguard his interests as he sees them. It must facilitate access and democratic control rather than try to stimulate interest in its activities or raise the level of the poll as such. Greater local involvement will, it is argued, extend democratic control and tap mutual voluntary aid to enrich the social services. But, because defining community is a notoriously difficult exercise, the outcome has been ambiguous.

Community has both a geographical and a social dimension. It can refer to a particular area with definite administrative or other legal boundaries. Far more important, however, is the idea of community as social interaction: the common bonds of neighbour, friend, kin, which forms the actual pattern of behaviour and which people see as important in their lives.

The first definition – the geographical and legal area – may or may not provide some grass roots base for local democratic government. It is the second definition – community as neighbour interaction – which forms a natural base for encouraging greater citizen involvement. These attitudes may not relate to the local political system at all but reflect family, leisure and social networks which individuals do not necessarily translate into an interest in council affairs. Neighbourhood attachment is also influenced by class. Those with higher educational and social status have a wider concept of the community. More lower-class, less educated, elderly and long-established residents are attached to a much smaller area. 'Neighbourhood' may thus mean, in effect, the small self-contained area of the poor.

Local authorities, however, cannot be expected to set up or financially support local neighbourhood councils as a countervailing power. Their view of community involvement will necessarily be that of a forum of opinion or a kind of parish council pressure group. Parish councils have revived since 1945. The Redcliffe-Maud survey showed wide differences in activity, in financial and electoral terms, among parishes. Generally speaking, it was the bigger parishes that were most active, particularly in the suburban, as compared with the really rural, areas.

In 1971 the local authority Associations had welcomed the retention of rural parishes but reiterated their belief that urban community opinion was best voiced through voluntary, non-statutory bodies. The 1972 Act retained parish councils in rural areas, and small free-standing boroughs and urban districts which were to disappear into the new districts were allowed to have successor town councils, with parish powers.

It is still argued, however, that non-statutory neighbourhood councils are needed in order to enrich local representation. Gordon Rose, for example, suggests that local councils could change the relationships between authority and the citizen which would facilitate consultation and protest.[21] Other commentators also recognise that neighbourhood councils may challenge existing forms of representation. Some welcome this. They argue that, in local government, effective opposition may be lacking inside the council chamber and that the community council can and should be one of several forms of opposition. Others argue that this is too sanguine a view. Councillors and officers have legitimate power; they will resent opposition and protest and instead of using the community council as a sounding board of opinion they will ignore it, starve it of information and effectively block its activities.

It is not necessarily the case that councillors will be hostile to neighbourhood councils. The councillor may see them as having primarily a welfare role rather than challenging the council's right to make the decisions. If community councils also include representatives of local voluntary groups so that they appear akin to Councils of Social Service then they will again be more acceptable. It is where local councils seem to act as opposition, or claim to have a mandate for special groups, that councillors may react unfavourably.

The dilemma is a critical one since, however necessary it is for democratic societies to allow a multiplicity of opposing voices and channels of opinion the problem of responsibility and accountability cannot be ignored. If community councils are to have power – a real voice in making decisions or providing more than trivial services – then they must be accountable to their constituents. And this implies election. They must also be responsible and accountable to the wider community – or they degenerate into ghettos of sectional irresponsibility – and this appears to imply making them a formal part or tier of the local government structure.

Gordon Rose suggests that what the individual wants from this kind of body is a facility: making his voice heard, knowing it will represent his view, and espousing his cause.[22] If this is so then the parish council model is the appropriate one and it is vital that councillors are a part of the system. But, at the same time, such councils should not be instituted as a third tier uniform provision but allowed to emerge where the inhabitants themselves promote them. Of equal importance is the fact that, where a community of interests and values does arise in this way, it is a real expression of feelings of fraternity which actually exist and can be fruitfully put into practice.

THE TWO-TIER SYSTEM AND DEMOCRATIC LOCAL GOVERNMENT

The structure of local government is normally discussed in terms of more than one tier or kind of authority for both theoretical and practical reasons. Local government must both command sufficient staff and resources for overall planning and administration of the major services and allow for participation, effective personal community services and ease of access by ordinary people. Large, powerful authorities, it is said, can more easily avoid over-direction and control by central government. At the other end of the scale, small units should not be so minor as to degenerate into talking shops or gatherings of narrow vested interests.

Effective local services, efficient administration and citizen involvement immediately bring conflict. Local government is a political process, not just a matter of administrative convenience. It is more profitable, therefore, to focus on the problem of democratic control as a criteria and a measure of reform and its efficacy. The structure of reform – the number of tiers, the powers and functions – then has to be seen in direct relation to internal management developments, the pattern of electoral representation, and the gathering of opinion in modern society. Gradually, this is the kind of overall evaluation which is emerging, both inside and outside council offices. But the discussion is still segmented and specialised and the reforms which have been enacted may turn out to be too heavily concerned with structure at the expense of the democratic political process.

England is an urban and industrial society which should, perhaps, be thought of as inclining towards an 'urban' solution to its local government problems. The pressures of urban life, its significance in the economy as a whole, and the intractable problems of metropolitan areas, all seem to point in this direction. From this standpoint, the urban/rural dichotomy is a false one. The administrative division of towns from their surrounding suburbs and countryside is anachronistic and harmful. The rural resistance to the city is not, however, just the defence of an equally honourable tradition of two tier county government. It is practical politics also. The level of the rates, the problems of land use and overspill housing, and the extension of the suburbs are all prominent in the argument. So too are what are seen as the more intangible benefits of rural government: less formal and overt party politics, a vigorous tradition of parish discussion and pressure on higher levels, and a jealous defence of the virtues of village and small town life.

The 1972 reforms have now recast the political framework of community life. The metropolitan authorities retain the old style of city politics, since metropolitan counties and their districts are continuous urban areas in which Labour is the predominant party. In the non-metropolitan counties the two-tier system has finally ended the self-sufficient status of the county boroughs – although their 'city politics' style remains – who have emerged as districts or part of districts with severely reduced powers over their own areas. The new county authorities banish the old town/country dichotomy as far as the major services are concerned. They do, however, inevitably reduce the voice of any urban authority in the larger voice of the whole.

A further feature of recent years – the opposition of local and central party control at any given moment – may also be repeated in the new county system. In the last decade a situation has developed where there is an increasing tendency, as the life of a parliamentary session wears on, for one party to hold power in national government while the other main political party controls the majority of local authorities. This may also happen within the new counties. The party in power at county hall may face a set of district councils controlled by one or more opposing parties. This will be further enhanced by the easier possibility of Liberal intervention. The Liberals, who have concentrated on a 'community politics' strategy, may diversify the representative system at the district level.

Popular control in relation to area continues to give rise to disquiet. Reform reduced the number of elected local representatives from 40,000 to around 26,000 and charges of remoteness are still levelled against the new authorities. The counter-argument is that citizens will welcome reform because of improved services. Others suggest that the increase in size and functions of the new counties will increase party political activity which may help to maintain or improve democratic control.

There are a number of ways in which area and government may be adjusted to meet these demands. The areas can be changed, functions reallocated, or additional co-operative and collaborative machinery set up between a number of existing authorities. In practice all three devices are used. English reform has concentrated on the first two – adjustment of areas and functions – but it has changed areas far less dramatically than functions. The reforms of the 1970s do not completely recast the county map of England nor destroy in many cases those districts which were formerly county boroughs or boroughs. The third device, that of collaboration between existing authorities, has been used to a minor degree in the past (joint boards and committees for airports, water and sewerage services, crematoria etc.), but will decline in importance in the future.

An important element of future co-operation will be the county district agency arrangements. These are neither the old delegation arrangements of the past, nor do they have the formal constitutional pattern of the joint board. They may, however, still confuse the citizen. Horizontal (between adjoining authorities) and vertical (between county and districts) co-operative relations are sensible but there is always the danger that, if they are relied upon as an alternative to more radical reform of areas, then representative government may become a morass of *ad hoc* distribution of power away from popular control.

The reforms of recent years have recognised that changing the structure of local government is not enough. The basic issue is popular control. Democratic theory highlights the key elements: responsible and responsive elected members; access, information and redress of grievances for citizens; and a defined degree of local autonomy. The question of how much, and in what way, these aims are best served is the stuff of the political process. The argument is never finally decided and is usually thought of as 'a question of more or less'.

NOTES

1. Jane Moreton, *The Best Laid Schemes?* (Charles Knight, 1970), pp. 78-9.
2. J. A. Griffith, 'Second Thoughts on the Reform of England', *Justice of the Peace and Local Government Review*, Vol. 135, No. 25 (19 June 1971), p. 429.
3. 'Areas and Status of Local Authorities in England and Wales', *Cmd. 9831* (1955-6).
4. Owen A. Hartley, 'The Relations between Central and Local Authorities', *Public Administration*, Vol. 49 (Winter 1971), p. 439.
5. Owen A. Hartley, *op. cit.*, p. 450.
6. Peter G. Richards, *The New Local Government System*, 2nd edition (Allen & Unwin, 1970), p. 259.
7. Peter G. Richards, *op. cit.*, p. 259.
8. Elizabeth Layton, *Building by Local Authorities* (Allen & Unwin, 1961), p. 87.
9. 'Directly Employed Labour', *Circular 90/72*, Department of the Environment (1972).
10. J. A. G. Griffiths, 'Should Select Committees Probe Local Authorities?' *Municipal Review*, Vol. 40, No. 479 (November 1969), p. 538.
11. G. W. Jones, 'MPs – Eroding the Independence of Local Government?' *Municipal Review*, Vol. 41, No. 487 (July 1970), p. 280.
12. Ron Rhodes, 'Europe and the Town Hall: work in progress – 1', *Municipal Review*, Vol. 43, No. 511 (July 1972), p. 187.
13. K. J. Davey, 'Local Autonomy and Independent Revenues', *Public Administration*, Vol. 49 (Spring 1971), p. 45.
14. K. J. Davey, *op. cit.*, p. 50.
15. 'Councils Ponder "Freedom" ', *The Guardian* (24 November 1970).
16. Sir Harry Page, 'Public Expenditure – Central/Local Government Financial Relations', *Municipal Review Supplement* (May 1970), p. 115.
17. 'New Taxes for Local Government', *The Times* (15 March 1972).
18. L. J. Sharpe, 'British Politics and the Two Regionalisms' *in* W. D. C. Wright and D. H. Stewart (eds), *The Exploding City* (Edinburgh University Press, 1972), pp. 132-3.

19. William Thornhill, *The Case for Regional Reform* (Nelson, 1972), p. 5.
20. John Mackintosh, *The Devolution of Power* (Penguin, 1968).
21. Gordon Rose, 'Local Councils in Metropolitan Areas', *Fabian Research Series*, 296 (1971), p. 15.
22. Gordon Rose, *op. cit.*, p. 26.

Chapter IX

CONCLUSIONS – IDEALS AND REALITIES

DEMOCRATIC CITIZENSHIP

In a democratic society the ideals of liberty give individuals the right to expect to have their demands taken into account in a variety of ways. The right to vote is only the bare minimum of involvement. If people have problems, or want to make changes in their lives, then they must be able to get help quickly, relatively easily and in an informed way. The ordinary man does not take a deep interest in what government does but this does not mean that he is apathetic or incapable of action.

Democratic citizenship revolves around two problems. One is that of accountability and the related question of access to government and governors. Individuals must be able, in order to hold their representatives to account, to find out what they are doing. They must also be able to have their demands heard before final decisions are made. This in turn depends on the amount and kind of information that is available.

The second problem concerns the quality and extent of democratic citizenship. Although equality of consideration and equality of opportunity are vital in democratic society, individuals and groups vary enormously in their power and influence. It is argued that these disparities are now too large and that injustice results. It is also claimed that equality and fraternity are incompatible. Fraternity is best achieved in small communities among people with similar interests and values. Human beings are, however, very varied in the values which they place on different objectives: they discriminate between different aims (and people), have differing priorities, and will defend these against opposing views and groups. Equality is impossible, unless uniformity is imposed through the agency of national government. The opposite view stresses that, while recognising these difficulties, equality of consideration is still a prime factor in judging the democratic quality of local government, and in insisting that particular inequalities must be removed. Equality and fraternity may pull in differing directions but this is itself not a condemnation of democracy. Democratic society is complex and ambiguous, but both sets of ideas are vital to its well-being.

These are not the only difficulties. The overwhelming problem is that the majority of people are remote from government, from their representatives, and so face an implacable bureaucracy. Several undesirable results follow from this situation. First, people become less concerned with the community and retreat into sectional demands or into apathy. Second, because individuals have little say in what is decided, they have a declining regard for democratic politics. Finally, the fact that most people do not influence what is done may lead them into protest and a rejection of 'responsible' opposition.

One critic has argued that only the individual can decide whether the normal, fair, compromise procedures of democracy have broken down and when he has an overriding right to disobey. The same author also points out that democracy is imperfect, since governments and politicians reflect opinion statically and inaccurately. Access to power and authority is very unevenly distributed between different groups and classes, and individuals find it very hard to make the system respond to their needs.[1]

These are disquieting arguments. If the individual alone has the right to judge when to disobey, and power is distributed very unequally, then how are the false claims to be separated from the just claims? In practice, we rely on the – imperfect – operations of authority on the one hand and of various sanctions on the other. These problems are important at the local, as well as the national level, since confidence and disobedience are real questions which relate to immediate grievances. Prediction is difficult in this area. One possibility may be, however, that just as we were influenced by American ideas on 'participation' and the 'anti-poverty programmes' in the 1960s, we may equally be influenced by their current concerns with the question of authority and with problem-solving.

LOCAL AUTHORITIES AND LOCAL SELF-GOVERNMENT

The twin concerns of accountability of governments and of the nature of citizenship are central to the debate about the effectiveness of democratic society. One of the traditional justifications of local government is that it fulfils both of these needs. Individuals can influence what is done and can share in power. This orthodoxy still stands. English local government still has two features which are not found in every other advanced country. The first of these is the comprehensive nature of local services. Local councils are not the sole governing body in their communities but they do provide a significant range of services. Although this is often criticised as too burdensome – so that separate departments and committees behave like *ad hoc* bodies – the general view is that 'omnibus' authorities have many advantages.

The advantage of comprehensive local units is that authorities can plan services in an interelated way. And this co-ordination is done in an open and responsible manner. The elected members govern the community and are collectively answerable for all services. Omnibus authorities co-ordinate services where they are needed – at their point of delivery to the individual in his home setting. Since the reform of local government at the end of the last century this has been a central value.

The second feature of the system is that it is both *local* and *government*. However 'remote' the post-1974 authorities are in the eyes of some critics, the units of government are still defined in terms of patterns of settlement and in relation to the traditions of local administration. The basic units are also local in another sense. Those who rule the community are also local citizens, ratepayers and inhabitants and share in the common concern with the quality of services.

Local units are also local *government*. That is, there is no system of tutelage through centrally appointed Prefects, and local councils are responsible for their own budgets and rate levels. Although local authorities must perform many services as virtual agents of central government, they enjoy a constitutional right to govern. They control the elections to the council, they have the right to hire, deploy and fire staff, and they are empowered to make bylaws for the good order and government of their areas. All these powers are subject to legislative and other conditions but they are nevertheless real.

The local units are also governing bodies, not just local offices for different services, in another way. Local authorities are responsible, subject to national legislation and guidelines, for their own internal organisation. Within broad limits they determine how services shall be administered, how they shall be co-ordinated, and what priorities shall be set between them. Finally, local authorities are also governing bodies in the sense that, in common with central government, they are political. That is, to an important extent, they reflect party political electoral opinion and govern under the labels of the parties. There are regrets and fears at this situation; the point is, however, that governing means debate, discussion, compromise and conflict within known and visible divisions.

These factors, then, remain important contributors to democratic society. But precisely because it is a democracy, it is necessary to ask some searching questions. It is easy to attack government – for the last thirty years criticism has been as honourable a tradition as defence – but this does not mean that the questions can be dismissed.

A constructive approach is to concentrate on three areas. The first is the traditions and values of local government with which this book has been concerned. The second area of interest is the expectations which people have, both outside and inside the town hall, about local government. Finally, the quality of the services themselves is an integral part of what is meant by democratic local government. This is a controversial question. Democracy, it is argued, is about means, not ends. If procedures are fair, open, honest and conducted impartially and justly then government is democratic. The counter-argument agrees that while democratic procedures are vital, equality of opportunity is also important and this demands certain basic minimum standards of provision. Without these basic services democratic procedures, including equality of consideration, are mere shams.

LOCAL GOVERNMENT AND DEMOCRATIC SOCIETY

The first constructive approach is the values and traditions of local government. As this book has shown, these support the view that local government is an integral part of democracy. From John Stuart Mill onwards, the English tradition has claimed that democratic ideals were met in practice by national and local representative bodies based on liberty, equality and fraternity. Local people could take part in government, learn to respect the interests of other people, and hold leaders accountable.

In addition to this belief in representative government and in political education and self-realisation, there were several other – sometimes conflicting – values. Toulmin Smith and the virtues of localness and traditional leadership are at one end of the scale. At the other is a concern with administration of services in the modern state. What is then important is the size and resources of local units and their ability to carry out national policies in response to a general public opinion. At this end of the scale local government is the agent of the centre, not an autonomous partner.

'Partnership' versus 'agency' are not the only possibilities. No one now believes that the self-contained community can provide for all its wants unaided or that local self-sufficiency should be markedly at variance with the general public demand for territorial justice. Similarly, only a tiny minority of people would argue that local authorities should be merely the agents of the centre. Local knowledge, local influence and local variation are justified on grounds of flexibility and humanity. Government from the centre, through a national bureaucracy mitigated by local advisory panels, would be cumbersome and costly. Local government distributes the burden of decision-making and, most importantly, diversifies and enriches the channels of opinion, complaint, redress and demands. From this point of view alone central government must have local units where responsible power can be located. What is crucial is the nature and extent of local initiative in relation to the quality of democratic society as a whole and the changing expectations which people have.

Another important aspect of the debate over the last 150 years has been the question of participation – who took part, and on what terms – in local deliberations. Who should have the vote, how majorities should exercise their right to govern, and how minorities could be protected, were equally important. The exercise of power was the central issue in the closing years of the century. Once the principle of equal political rights was conceded then two problems immediately became apparent. Would the power of the numerical majority – the working class – mean class legislation? And would this exercise of power in turn reduce individual liberty and enhance state powers of intervention? By the end of the First World War the fears expressed in these questions had disappeared, at least in extreme terms. At the same time great social changes had indeed altered the role of government in the state and individual liberties were more circumscribed.

The decade following the First World War was a watershed of local government. The change was caused not just by the catalyst of war and its aftermath of rising expectations. Two other factors were crucial. One was the pace of change itself. The transport revolution and increasing government intervention transformed local communities. The second factor was the intellectual revolution. People's horizons widened and they acquired standards by which to judge their surroundings and their own place in community life.

The First World War was also a watershed in that councils faced an increasing 'bargaining' situation with political parties, pressure groups and with their own officers. But throughout all these changes local government remained remarkably stable. In spite of government intervention, increased mobility, and changing intellectual horizons, local authorities survived and adapted. This flexibility and

H

competence was to prove, however, dangerously complacent. The nineteen thirties, with their atmosphere of 'municipal economy' were deceptive. The demand for fresh thinking about social and economic problems was hidden, but it was there.

The Second World War shattered this quietism. As a result the Labour party, once the champion of municipal enterprise and initiative, found itself in a dilemma. Major reforms would clearly involve local authorities. But, at the same time, a completely recast system of local government seemed impossible. In the event the nationalised industries and the national health service were re-organised outside local government. New towns, under special development corporations, made brave fresh starts in tackling over-crowding and congestion in the cities. The attempt to reform local government, after the ill-fated Commission of inquiry, was abandoned.

As a result, the 1945 Labour government was forced to deal with the system as it existed. Two principles (or practical necessities) were used. On the one hand, major services were given to the county boroughs and county councils. On the other, since these services were so greatly expanded as to be virtually different in kind, then central standards, finance and supervision were imperative.

Chadwick seemed to have triumphed: 'inspectability' and standardisation underpinned the welfare state. This is a mistaken view. The changes which took place after 1945, far from under-mining a thriving local democracy, actually injected new life into the system. In many respects local authorities positively flourished under their new burdens. The professions expanded, new skills developed, and standards improved. Leading council members became import-ant men, ruling over services with large staffs and resources. Back-bench councillors, for their part, were increasingly called upon to deal with individual problems, exercise the voice of common sense in committee, and focus attention on the day-to-day problems as well as the big issues. Far from lessening democracy, these developments preserved it.

All this may seem a heresy in the face of the 'crisis criticism' which typified the debate of the last thirty years. It is important to under-stand what this disquiet was about. It was not, in any significant sense, merely a nostalgia for a past local democratic and self-contained society. The heart of the matter is a different, but very old, problem. Disquiet about local government, whether it is expressed as too much central control, the irrelevance of the division between town and country, the inadequate size, finance or internal administration of local authorities or whatever, stems from a common central issue. This is not nostalgia for what has been but, as it were, nostalgia for what could be. The new and expanded duties of the post-1945 period showed the capabilities of local authorities. Services of vital national importance could be given to them; how much more they could achieve if they were modernised and given greater local financial autonomy!

THE REFORM DEBATE SINCE 1945: THE NEED FOR LOCAL GOVERNMENT

From the 1940s onwards the arguments raged. Local authorities should be increased in size to cope with the technical and professional needs of modern services. Town and country should be administratively interdependent as they were socially and economically interdependent. The growth of regional economic planning, and central control, were inescapable proof of the weakened state of local government. Most critics were agreed on the truth of these points but bitterly divided on the correct solutions.

It is relatively easy to set all these arguments on their head. The need for increased size to ensure increased efficiency is by no means universally proven. Diseconomies of scale are now taken as seriously as the need to enlarge areas of operation were twenty years ago. Collaboration between authorities is potentially less disruptive than reorganisation. In any system, some staff and resource duplication is inevitable, but does not by itself warrant upheaval. In addition, those inside the town halls, both staff and members, were generally hostile to radical change while those outside were indifferent to it.

Does this mean that the arguments have been misplaced? Certainly, what is a sad omission is any suggestion that changes were needed solely on democratic grounds. This would be a perfectly rational approach. It is quite proper to argue that, regardless of technical questions, reform was needed to give people a democratic, open, responsive and comprehensible system of government, and for no other reason. The central cause for concern has been, and will continue to be, the need for local government to be responsible government, located in the hands of elected councils with genuine powers to provide important services over areas which are meaningful to those who live in them and without complete subservience to central government.

Democratic local government is that which is seen as important and relevant both to those who provide it and those who receive it.

In the wider sense, the questions are about the nature of responsiveness and accountability in society as a whole: the problem of democracy is the problem of democracy, no more and no less. It is not the problem of 'local government', just as it is not the problem of 'planning' or 'participation'. It is the question, rather, of the flexibility of society's responses to changing needs.

From this point of view, participation in local government is desirable to the extent that people are demanding a voice. People take part because they want to achieve something, either for themselves or for others, and it is in this sense that the effectiveness of participation must be judged. Effective participation is also a question of communication. People must have information if they need, or want, to hold government accountable.

Judged by this criterion, information must be full, reliable, up-to-date and balanced. In local government it is the last two factors that are still a problem. Topical, relevant information depends on the willingness of local authorities to release it and newspapers and local radio to report it. Attitudes are changing and, with the new authorities, has come a change in the law to open committees to the public and the press. Local authorities are still too reluctant, however, compared with Westminster and Whitehall, to publicise their efforts and monitor public opinion.

Diversity of information is also having an impact on attitudes and expectations. Local radio, community newspapers, local television experiments and, above all, the provincial press, all compete for news. But this competition is still not as great as it might be. Local newspaper editors claim, with justice, that they print more council news than the public demands. They must face the criticism, nevertheless, that they present too bland a picture. Community life could withstand more lively controversy.

This brings us to the question of balance. Balance has a specific meaning in national radio and television because of the BBC's original establishment as a public monopoly. There are thus rules on the amount of time which must be given, at election and other times, to party political broadcasts, ministerial pronouncements and opposition replies. Balance also has a more informal meaning. This is the general 'right of reply' in controversial issues and 'representation' of a broad spectrum of opinion in panel discussions and so on. In the national press, this does not work in the same way: balance operates through diversity and competition among newspapers and journals with specific viewpoints.

At local level, newspaper monopoly of news has created a curious situation as far as balance is concerned. As Morris Janowitz observed with regard to the local press in America, there is a tendency for a local newspaper to stress consensus, shared values, rather than to resolve values which conflict with each other.[2] In English community life, balance means blandness; not from a desire to conceal but from the need to 'live with' community leaders, councillors and business and commercial interests.

The demand for more 'open' government has been, both locally and nationally, a fear that specific large-scale developments will adversely affect people's lives, homes and communities. It is also, to a significant degree, a generalised hostility towards officials and 'their' plans. To some extent it is also a worry about corruption in public life. The problem was well put by Redlich and Hirst seventy years ago: 'Democracy and publicity together produce a sense of responsibility in the elected representatives of the town which makes them anxious to act, or at least appear to act, in all public matters solely in the interests of the town and of the ratepayers whom they represent.'[3]

ATTITUDES AND EXPECTATIONS

It was earlier suggested that there were three constructive approaches to modern local government. The first was the traditions, values and current justifications of local government. The second approach is to look at the expectations people have about local government.

Our knowledge in this area is far from complete. Several general themes are now, however, fairly well established. First, there are people's attitudes towards democracy as such. Most people cannot define what the word democracy means but strongly support a whole range of beliefs which are normally thought of as basic to democratic life: fairness, justice, allowing everyone to put their point of view, free elections and so on. In addition, ordinary people believe that, in national elections at least, they have a duty as well as a right to take part. Finally, English people have a general confidence that they can get their grievances heard, and influence what local councils do. This is a generalised belief, not necessarily a realistic evaluation of their actual influence.

This generalised goodwill is, however, not the same as people's attitudes towards particular services or to individual members or officers. In local government there are sensitive areas where people's beliefs are much more concrete. Planning is one such area. If the individual is directly affected by local plans then he is likely to judge democratic local government by very precise (if unspoken) criteria. Will he be told, in clear and unambiguous terms, what is to happen – and when? Will he be treated fairly and justly, and equally with fellow citizens in a similar position? Is there a right of appeal? If there is, how speedy, open and comprehensible is the appeal procedure?

In other services, democracy is also judged by its procedures and by its results. These views will vary according to the service and the circumstances of the individual. The individual who is directly affected by welfare provisions, for example, is not so interested in his – perhaps remote – potential influence over decisions but in the response he gets from officers. Is the service humane, speedy and flexible? Do people listen to what you have to say? Does the help that you receive offer you any kind of choice, or must you accept what the officer gives you or 'the law' lays down?

Not everyone has such a direct interest. Many people take a lively interest, of course, in the level of the rate but are otherwise content to regard local government with tolerant indifference. Two factors must be kept in mind in this respect. The 'tolerant indifference' of the majority must be seen in relation to what the minority does. There is a potential danger that the views of vocal middle-class minorities may, in certain circumstances, decide what is done. What is done is decided by the extent of likely opposition instead of by elected representatives coming to a decision after considering expert advice. 'Government by liberal veto' can only be countered by the quality of council decision-making. This in turn depends on the parties and their programmes, the quality of information which councillors have, the choices which officers give them, and the councillors' abilities to monitor and review what is done in their name. Only then can elected representatives govern, and explain and defend their plans to local people.

The other factor involved in 'tolerant indifference' flows from the first. Democracy is what councillors and officers do in their day-to-day work. The definition of democratic local government is their definition. From this point of view, as this book has tried to show, there is continuing cause for concern over the councillors' ability to control what is done and respond to the public's demands.

The local government reform debate has been concerned with the work of members and officers as well as with boundaries. Local authorities have responded with a fresh look at their internal organisation, at committee deliberations and at the work and qualifications of officers. There has also been a fresh appreciation of what councillors do. The fear for the 'calibre' of elected members has been countered by the argument that there can be no one criteria of quality since councillors vary widely both in their social characteristics and attitudes and in their roles.

Some councillors enjoy policy and power; many abjure policy for technicalities and detail. The majority find satisfaction in dealing with individual cases, feeling that they are really helping people and solving concrete problems. Detailed committee work is not, for them, a chore but an interesting and worthwhile attention to problems which they can comprehend. The committee system itself may have become a luxurious growth but in one sense at least it is eminently democratic. It involves members directly in the work and does so in a way which brings together the policy-maker and the ombudsman, the political leader and the defender of the ward or the cause.

Those who attack this system do so on two main grounds. One is in terms of time-wasting, detailed committee work, the ineffective setting of priorities and lack of comprehensive forward planning. Official inquiries, from Maud to Bains, as well as academic and professional analyses, have met these criticisms by reforms which emphasise comprehensive planning and an interdisciplinary approach. Committee administration, however, in which elected members are directly associated with decisions, will outlive criticisms that the system is cumbrous and outdated. It is right that it should do so. Democratic debate must take place between elected representatives of all shades of competence and interest and with all officers relevantly involved in services. It is round the committee table that local interests and demands should be reflected since that is what representative government is about.

The second criticism of council work is more serious. It is not based on an impatience with committees but on the fear that the amount and quality of internal information available to councillors is now a serious handicap to democratic government. In London and other large cities leading council members already find the work a demanding, almost full-time concern. The consequences of this do not make the impact that they should. We take pride in the fact that London and Birmingham control services and budgets which make them the equivalent of some independent nation states. We take similar pride in our major authorities which are again unique in the range of services that they command compared with cities and counties in other countries. But we do not recognise the full implication of this situation. The staff-work, including personal assistants and research and information facilities, for leading council members is clearly NOT that which they would enjoy if they were the statesmen of the independent states we believe to be their administrative comparison.

Gradually, this need is being recognised. In May 1973, following the Labour party's return to power in the Greater London Council, personal assistants were appointed to help the Leader of the Council and most of the committee chairmen. The Leader had two assistants, one of whom came from outside the Council, but the other appointees were from the local authority's professional staff. The GLC's Standing Orders, which prohibit officers from attending party group meetings, were suspended to allow the Leader's two assistants to attend such meetings. The main work of the committee chairmen's assistants is in sifting information, and in general briefing for the chairmen.[4]

But better internal communication and better facilities for members are still urgently needed for all authorities. Councillors need information that is clear and accessible. Officers must put alternatives to members. Interdisciplinary groups must cut across committee boundaries to show the interrelated consequences of actions. This is now being recognised. But there is more to it than this. Council work is a political process, in both main senses. That is, it is governed by party labels and it is 'political' in the (non-party) sense that it is public discussion, debate, argument and compromise.

This political variety, like the variety among councillors, has been largely ignored in criticisms of council work. The logical approach is to capitalise on these differences, not ignore them. If members enjoy their ombudsman role, helping constituents and individual cases, then the parties and the town hall should give them more help. This could be done by holding ward 'surgeries', by making a council room available, or by associating councillors with 'advice centre' work. Local authorities normally frown on allowing councillors a room in which to meet members of the public on the grounds that this should properly be the responsibility of the individual or his party. These attitudes are ripe for change.

Similarly, for councillors in leading positions, and those interested in policy, there is a great need for better facilities. The fear is, one supposes, that secretarial help, information and library facilities and personal staff assistants are either an unnecessary extravagance or dangerously professional. This is nonsense. Government by amateurs has much to commend it, not least the fact that it is accepted as proper whereas full-time local council politicians are not – or not yet. The amateurs, however, must not be put into a position which, in effect, treats them with contempt. They must be given better information and more administrative assistance, and quickly.

This is not to ignore human realities. Many, if not the majority of councillors will not wish to take up this professional help in the same way as chairmen and other leading members. Their concern is with constituents and with the routine problems. This is where the parties, and other groups, come in. Again, the need is for better facilities. One such help could be, for example, for Citizen Advice Bureaux, or Councils of Social Service, to offer facilities – a room, some secretarial help – to councillors who want to help constituents. No doubt this too may be dismissed as inappropriate, since bodies receiving public funds (grants from the council) should not appear to engage in anything which could be construed as party political.

This kind of attitude needs to be questioned. So too does the local parties' insistence that 'surgery' facilities are unnecessary, since people do not want to come to arranged meetings but prefer to take their problems to the town hall or contact councillors, informally. Of course. Why, then, not spend some time on a regular visit to where people do go – a room in the local library, the clinic, the town hall inquiry desk? The argument then tends to fall back on the defence of time: councillors are busy, dedicated people who already do as much as they can. Again, of course this is so. The suggestions are not that councillors should do more. The need is, rather, to help some councillors do some things some of the time – not that they should all be full-time universal ombudsmen. The point is that, for those councillors who are involved in such activities, helpful facilities are inexcusably, abysmally, absent. Amateurs need help, not replacement or dragooning into uniformity.

THE QUALITY OF SERVICES

The first two constructive approaches to modern local government were the traditions and values of the system, and the world of democracy as seen by those most directly involved. The third approach is to look at the quality of services, at what local government does and how well.

There are several factors at work in this area. One is the existence of variations between local authorities. This variation can be, and often is, due to the pioneer efforts of some local authorities. In recent years, however, two other kinds of attitude have been prominent. One is that, in some services, ordinary people see variations as inexcusable lapses rather than healthy variety. The second belief is more ambiguous

H*

and uncertain. This is the feeling that, regardless of the need for central standards and supervision, modern governments are imposing standardisation against the wishes of local people. The Housing Finance Act, for example, removed local authorities' traditional right to manage its housing, including rent levels, in the light of local conditions. In the education service, the issue of comprehensive secondary schooling, by contrast, is not being solved (as yet) by national legislation but by ministerial directives – which change as governments change. People are, as a result, confused about the nature and reliability of local services and how these can be influenced.

Democracy is always a question of 'more or less', of the quality of life as a whole, and how this changes as circumstances change. It is now well recognised that it is artificial to speak of national democracy and local democracy as separate entities. Democratic society is one in which there are many kinds of public and private bodies, central and local authorities. What is important to the individual is how these respond to his needs and listen to his demands. And it is this, at both national and local level, which causes disquiet.

The argument is ambiguous and uncertain because it varies from issue to issue and depends, as ever, on political controversy and individual preferences. What worries the – increasingly educated and vociferous – public is that in *neither* the central nor the local arena can they apparently influence what is done or make elected representatives respond to their wishes.

To a large extent, of course, this is the result of a more affluent society where expectations are rising rapidly. Again, it is also due to the diversity of local groups and the seeming weakness of governors to speak strongly enough for 'the community' or 'the public good'. But a great deal of the concern is sheer frustration. Local people feel that they can neither campaign effectively for or against an issue – education for example – at either local or central level. No one asks their opinion or seeks to enlist their support.

The ambiguity and uncertainty about what freedoms local authorities should have, and what the scope of functions should be, has another worrying aspect. In place of eliciting and mobilising opinion about large public issues there is a dangerous tendency to narrow the problem down to the group involved. To state the case bluntly, we are evolving ghetto programmes for ghetto problems. English pragmatism and flexibility is a commendable approach to the immediate stresses of inner city areas. Instead of congratulating ourselves on special government financial aid to community action and urban programmes, however, we should be severely self-critical. If local government and its constituent units cannot govern without problems being tackled by special additional methods then there must be severe defects in the system itself. And this is why the regional, and neighbourhood arguments, deserve more attention than they currently receive.

LOCAL GOVERNMENT, DEMOCRACY AND 'ETERNAL VIGILANCE'

Local government is judged in terms of justice and fairness: due performance of known laws affecting all citizens equally. Honesty, probity and accountability are equally essential. But it is also judged by its provisions: social justice and equality as well as equality of consideration.

The original justification for local government – that councillors were close to those they served in the ward or division – is not destroyed by the new local government system. What counts is the effectiveness of services, their democratic control and the citizens' access. The virtues of small size, and the need for continuous individual participation and interest, have always been myths. What is essential is to see the system as a political process which, in the 1970s, has aimed at reforms to make it 'more democratic' in certain ways: more open, more effective, and by its increased attractiveness, more representative (by drawing in younger people and by reducing the number of uncontested elections).

It is on this last point that many fear that it may not live up to the aims of reform. Representation may become narrower rather than bring in new people. A longer-term difficulty is the unresolved one of regionalism. Constitutionally, economically and politically this remains the 'missing dimension' of local government. As long as this is the case local government will remain uneasy about the regional structures which surround it and which undermine its claim to give the democratic dimension to all the services which citizens receive in their localities.

A critical appreciation is still essential. In the hundred or so years since J. S. Mill urged that local government was vital as a politically educative and self-realising force in individual's lives, the whole fabric of society has changed. But these values have remained important, as has the idea of the locality and the ideal of the self-governing community. But in judging the relation of democratic theory and local government we no longer see 'democracy' as being about means rather than ends. Perhaps the majority of people would now agree with L. J. Sharpe that local government is justified as the effective provider of services rather than the means of liberty, participation or democracy. Or, with Brian C. Smith, that local government is 'to some extent a unique opportunity for the measurement of consumer satisfaction'.[5]

William Thornhill states that democracy is basically the ability of ordinary people, through their representatives, to influence what public authorities do.[6] But democratic control over representatives is only meaningful if they in turn control what the executive – the officials – do. We can conclude that territorial justice – the quality and extent of local services locally administered – is justified if these conditions are met. To be the effective provider of services local authorities must be more than efficient. They must still be judged by that justice, fairness, equality and openness by which democratic society as a whole is judged.

NOTES

1. Peter Singer, *Democracy and Disobedience* (Oxford University Press, 1973), p. 68 and pp. 130-1.
2. Morris Janowitz, *The Community Press in an Urban Setting* (The Free Press, 1952), pp. 20-1.
3. Josef Redlich and Francis W. Hirst, *Local Government in England*, Vol. I (Macmillan, 1903), p. 227.
4. 'Conservatives Raise Political Issue over New Appointment of Labour Aide to GLC Leader', *The Times* (4 May 1973). I am also indebted to officers of the Greater London Council for information on this point.
5. Brian C. Smith, 'The Justification of Local Government' *in* Lionel D. Feldman and Michael D. Goldrick, *Politics and Government of Urban Canada* (Toronto, Methuen, 1969), p. 346.
6. William Thornhill, *The Case For Regional Reform* (Nelson, 1972), p. 230.

INDEX